Critical Essays on

E. L. DOCTOROW

CRITICAL ESSAYS
ON
AMERICAN LITERATURE

James Nagel, General Editor
University of Georgia, Athens

Critical Essays on
E. L. DOCTOROW

edited by

BEN SIEGEL

G. K. Hall & Co.
New York

G. K. Hall & Co.
1633 Broadway
New York, NY 10019

Library of Congress Cataloging-in-Publication Data
Critical essays on E. L. Doctorow / edited by Ben Siegel.
    p. cm. — (Critical essays on American literature)
  Includes bibliographical references and index.
    ISBN 0-7838-0046-0 (alk. paper)
    1. Doctorow, E. L., 1931– —Criticism and interpretation.
  2. Historical fiction, American—History and criticism.
  I. Siegel, Ben, 1925–   II. Series.
  PS3554.O3 Z6 2000
  813'.54—dc21   00-025705

This paper meets the requirements of ANSI/NISO Z3948-1992 (Permanence of Paper).

10 9 8 7 6 5 4 3 2 1

Printed in the United States of America

For Melvin J. Friedman

Contents

◆

General Editor's Note

♦

This series seeks to anthologize the most important criticism on a wide variety of topics and writers in American literature. Our readers will find in various volumes not only a generous selection of reprinted articles and reviews but original essays, bibliographies, manuscript selections, and other materials brought to public attention for the first time. This volume, *Critical Essays on E. L. Doctorow,* is the most comprehensive gathering of essays ever published on one of the most important modern writers in the United States. It contains both a sizable gathering of early reviews and a broad selection of more modern scholarship. Among the authors of the articles and reviews offering fresh insights are Gwendolyn Brooks, John T. Osborne, Anthony Burgess, Marilyn Arnold, Eugénie L. Hamner, Angela Hague, Mark Busby, John Clayton, Susan Brienza, Minako Baba, and Andrew Delbanco. In addition, a substantial introduction by Ben Siegel presents an important overview of Doctorow's career and the critical response to it. We are confident that this book will make a permanent and significant contribution to the study of American literature.

JAMES NAGEL
University of Georgia

Publisher's Note

◆

Producing a volume that contains both newly commissioned and reprinted material presents the publisher with the challenge of balancing the desire to achieve stylistic consistency with the need to preserve the integrity of works first published elsewhere. In the Critical Essays series, essays commissioned especially for a particular volume are edited to be consistent with G. K. Hall's house style; reprinted essays appear in the style in which they were first published, with only typographical errors corrected. Consequently, shifts in style from one essay to another are the result of our efforts to be faithful to each text as it was originally published.

Introduction

BEN SIEGEL

I

Edgar Lawrence Doctorow is one of America's most respected contemporary novelists. His intellectual and verbal brilliance; comic gifts; imaginative craftsmanship; and fluid, flexible style have earned him both critical esteem and commercial success. He was born on January 6, 1931, in New York City, the son of David Richard Doctorow and Rose Levine Doctorow (later Rose Doctorow Buck). Both parents were children of Russian-Jewish immigrants. Doctorow traces his love of books to an early childhood experience. When he was 8 he developed appendicitis; his problem was misdiagnosed and his appendix burst. "I nearly died," he reports. "I was in the hospital several weeks and at home convalescing for weeks after that. I read a lot. That was 1940 and the beginning of paperbacks. My father began buying me Pocket Books. I read *Bambi, Bring Them Back Alive* by Frank Buck, *Wuthering Heights, Lost Horizon,* and on and on. I remember one whole summer reading *Les Misérables* on the subway going for my allergy shots. It was very important to me to understand Jean Valjean had a tougher life than I did."[1]

Doctorow decided early that writing would be his vocation, but he was uncertain as to what form it would take. Growing up in the Bronx, he attended the Bronx High School of Science and then moved on to Ohio's Kenyon College to study with John Crowe Ransom. "As much as I learned from him—I studied prosody with him for instance—somehow I was inclined to a different kind of mental life." He found his focus had shifted: "I had a mind for philosophy and although I kept taking English courses, it was never with the same excitement I felt for my philosophy work." The man to whom he most responded was not Ransom but Philip Blair Rice, "a brilliant philosopher and also the associate editor of the *Kenyon Review*—Ransom being the editor. I studied metaphysics and aesthetics with Rice and ethics and logic with his colleague, Virgil Aldridge. I loved it." During his four years at

Kenyon, Doctorow "did relatively little writing and had little interest in the established English Department requirements." Instead, he was bitten by the acting bug, so he hung around the campus theater and tried out for plays. "I had no plan," he recalls. "I just did what interested me."[2]

Doctorow took his B. A. degree in 1952 and for the next year did graduate work at Columbia University in English drama and in playwriting, acting, and directing. This was during the Korean War, and in 1953 he was drafted. He served two years with the Army Signal Corps, primarily in Germany. During this period, he again decided to devote himself to writing. He married Helen Esther Setzer on August 20, 1954, and they have three children: Jenny, Caroline, and Richard. To support his growing family, Doctorow took on a series of jobs for which he had little taste, such as reservations clerk for American Airlines. Friends were free with advice. "People told me to look for physical labor," Doctorow recalls, "and under no circumstances to get involved with the book business in Manhattan."[3] Not surprisingly, he ignored them, and in the late 1950s he became a script reader for Columbia Pictures Industries in New York City. There he suffered through what he terms "one lousy Western after another." He finally decided he could "lie in a much more interesting way" than the writers of the scripts he was evaluating, so he would write a short story of the Old West. "I don't imagine I would have written *Welcome to Hard Times*," he explains, "if I'd not been working at that film company and reading lousy screenplays week after week." Undaunted by the fact that he knew almost nothing of the West, he went to the library and checked out Walter Prescott Webb's *The Great Plains*. "Webb said what I wanted to hear: no trees out there. Jesus. That was beautiful. I could spin the whole book out of the one image. And I did."[4] The story itself evolved into the opening chapter of *Welcome to Hard Times*.[5] His announced intent was to "take a disreputable genre, cheap materials of a nonliterary kind and . . . fuse them in some way that was valid."[6]

He also formulated here the theme basic to all his subsequent writings: the difficulty of separating fact from fancy, of distinguishing history from fiction—that is, of grasping and conveying reality or the truth in imaginative terms. This is especially hard when dealing with this nation's past. America may be a remarkable country, he points out, but it has often been hostile to the poor and vulnerable, a sad fact often ignored or distorted by politicians and historians. Therefore, notes Sabine Sauter, beginning with his first novel, Doctorow has repeatedly rewritten earlier periods and altered their "crucial events" and characters or personalities of their famous public figures. "Doctorow's elaborate, sophisticated, and astonishing trick," Sauter adds, is to make it appear by "his verbal performance as though there is no substantial difference between fact and fiction."[7]

II

These elements are evident in *Welcome to Hard Times*. The novel's narrator is Blue, the self-anointed mayor of the struggling Dakota community of Hard Times, which consists of little more than a straggling line of tents and wooden shacks. This motley assemblage serves a small silver-mining operation in the nearby hills while struggling with its inhabitants' internal strife and malicious behavior. Into town rides a killer aptly named Clay Turner. Known as "the Bad Man from Bodie," Turner quickly and effortlessly kills, rapes, and totally intimidates the residents, then casually rides off. Thanks to Blue, the town is rebuilt, but Turner returns, and he and the now-destitute miners destroy the town once more. This time Blue fatally wounds Turner and carts the dying man back to his own shack to be finished off by Molly, the prostitute with whom he has been living.

Blue not only records his town's history in three ledgers, but he also articulates Doctorow's recognition of the difficulties involved in relying on memory to separate fact from fiction. Starting his third ledger, Blue complains that he has "been trying to write what happened but it is hard, wishful work. Time is beginning to run out on me, and the form remembrance puts on things is making its own time and guiding my pen in ways I don't trust" (*WHT,* 147). Later he confesses his growing sense of frustration and defeat. He notes that "the closer I've come in time the less clear I am in my mind." To make matters worse, "I have the cold feeling everything I've written doesn't tell how it was, no matter how careful I've been to get it all down it still escapes me" (199). In his brief final chapter, Blue lies dying. Summoning his strength, he makes his last ledger entries: "And now I've put down what happened, everything that happened from one end to the other. And it scares me more than death scares me that it may show the truth. But how can it if I've written as if I knew as I lived them which moments were important and which not; and spoken as if I knew the exact words everyone spoke? Does the truth come out in such scrawls, so bound by my limits?" (210). One "truth" that does emerge clearly from Blue's ledgers is the rejection of the formula Western's comfortable division of good and evil, of "good guys" and "bad guys." Human evil is not to be isolated in a few individuals, Doctorow suggests. It is to be accepted as endemic, given the right conditions, to the worst in all men.

This first novel stirred little initial attention, garnering but four reviews. Of these, two were little more than notices. Briefly summarizing the plot in the *Library Journal,* John T. Osborne described the book as "a well-written, above-average adult western novel" and recommended it "for all public libraries." This recommendation jarred the journal's editor into adding a warning note. "Because of Mr. Osborne's broad recommendation," stated this unsigned worthy, "we think some libraries should know that for sheer brutality graphically portrayed this novel is close to those of [Mickey] Spillane."[8] Several weeks later the *Springfield (Mass.) Republican* offered two brief paragraphs signed with the initials S. E. B. Sounding much like John Osborne, this reviewer concluded that "Despite the familiar setting, the author puts aside the shopworn sentiment and melodrama of the usual western novel and uses the conventional framework for the creation of a serious literary structure."[9]

A week after this notice was published, the first review of substance appeared. Only slightly longer than the previous two, it was written by novelist Wirt Williams for the *New York Times Book Review.* Attempting to place Doctorow's novel in context, Williams declared, "It is time to acknowledge that the 'serious Western' has established itself firmly [as] a sub-genre of fiction." In short, *Welcome to Hard Times* proves "an exfoliation on a quite sturdy branch." The novel's primary theme, he stated, "is that evil can only be resisted psychically: when the rational controls that order man's existence slacken, destruction comes. Conrad said it best in *Heart of Darkness,* but Mr. Doctorow has said it impressively. His book is taut and dramatic, exciting and successfully symbolic."[10] A somewhat similar note was sounded by Oscar Lewis in the *New York Herald Tribune Lively Arts* section. Expressing his approval of the novel, Lewis added a slight qualification: "While it is unlikely that habitual readers—and viewers—of Westerns will find *Welcome to Hard Times* altogether to their taste," he observed, "the novel nonetheless serves a worthwhile and long overdue purpose." In effect, it shows "the other side of the shield; namely, that in the West as elsewhere virtue is not invariably triumphant." Doctorow's novel "is a Western with a difference"; it "should prove a wholesome corrective to those too long exposed to the brand of Wild West fiction purveyed in the magazines and radio and on the TV screen."[11]

Despite having published his first novel, Doctorow was hardly able to give up his day jobs. From 1959 to 1964, he was an associate editor and then a senior editor under Victor Weybright at the New American Library in New York City.[12] "It was a great life, publishing good books in big printings—and, in those days—selling them for pocket change. You could feel good about the way you made your living—reprinting a first novel that nobody knew about, working on everything from Ian Fleming to Shakespeare to books on astronomy and every other damned thing, and seeing those books go out with price tags of fifty or seventy-five cents. I felt very good." In 1964 the Times Mirror Corporation of Los Angeles bought up the New American Library; they "brought in their business consultants and personnel people," states Doctorow, ". . . and the soul went out of the place."[13] So he moved over to Dial Press as editor in chief and during the next five years became that publishing house's vice president and then publisher. At Dial he worked with such writers as Norman Mailer and James Baldwin, but he quickly rejects the notion that he used a heavy editing pencil on the writings of these luminaries. "Writers like Mailer and Baldwin I didn't sit down and correct, but sometimes we'd talk about something that worked or didn't work. But even if something didn't work, it usually stood as it was done."[14]

III

As always, Doctorow continued his own writing. In 1966, he brought out his most unusual novel, *Big as Life*.[15] This second effort garnered only three reviews. Two were brief notices and the other was a plot summary by Gwendolyn Brooks in *Book Week*. The basic details are that a gigantic nude man and woman materialize one day in New York Harbor. Each is 2,000 feet high— "They lean against the horizon," noted Brooks. "They are beautiful, burnished, odorous." The newcomers "have a powerful effect" on the city's inhabitants, who tumble over themselves "to huddle, to pray." Consternation spreads as abashed national and city leaders resort frantically to "consultation, defense command, intellectual research, jetliner, helicopter, and practical philosophy." The president and his cabinet, as well as the governors of New York, New Jersey, Connecticut, and Pennsylvania, offer suggestions. But the general panic is intensified rather than diminished by an inept military command and a science establishment interested primarily in accumulating data. Luckily, the giants are able to move only inches a week. Doctorow's point is that modern society is so bogged down in bureaucratic inefficiency and self-interest that it is unable to resolve the problem. As the social order disintegrates into hysteria, three huddled figures emerge: Wallace Creighton, a Columbia University history professor; Red Bloom, a jazz bassist; and Red's love, Sugarbush. These individuals move through the violence, death, confusion, and personal uncertainties to emerge with new attitudes of acceptance of the creatures. Brooks observed that what Doctorow is suggesting is the necessity of "making the best of things." She considered it "a good recommendation," so much so that she suggested readers mitigate their "regret that his characters and style are servants to his message."[16]

Early readers appear to have been somewhat baffled by Doctorow's strange novel. The unidentified reviewer in *Choice* saw it as the work of "a kind of space-age Evelyn Waugh." This reviewer then added: "Doctorow's dead-pan manner in this second novel turns from satire to tenderness and human concern." It is "a performance closer to James Purdy than to Orwell and Huxley, but in a minor key."[17] Malcolm M. Ferguson, in the *Library Journal,* was far less kind. "This fantasy novel," he declared, can claim "neither memorable details nor turn of plot to warrant comparison with *Brave New World* or *1984*." Ferguson was reminded "of the Orson Welles' radiocast of an H. G. Wells story, back in 1938 when the voices of the announcers alone caused panic." He also detected "hints of *Dr. Strangelove,*" but these hints lack that movie's "humor" or "situation resolution."[18] Doctorow would appear to agree. Looking back on this early effort, he does not mince words: "Unquestionably, it's the worst I've done. I think about going back and re-doing it some day, but the whole experience was so unhappy, both the writing and the publishing of it, that maybe I never will. It's my *Mardi*—you know, Melville's *Mardi*? *Big As Life* is mine."[19]

IV

Doctorow had now published two novels, but neither had made a strong impression on the reading public or literary circles. But he now thinks those initial efforts helped him find himself as a writer. "What happens is that you do something and only then do you figure out what it is," he reasons. "You write to find out what you're writing. It was only after I had written those first two books, for example, that I developed a rationale for the approaches I had taken." He realized he "liked the idea of using disreputable genre materials and doing something serious with them. I liked invention. I liked myth."[20] For a time he continued as an executive at Dial Press. But in 1969 he accepted a one-year appointment as writer in residence at the University of California at Irvine. Apparently he liked teaching, for in 1971 he officially left publishing to join the Sarah Lawrence College faculty, and the following year he received a Guggenheim Fellowship to continue his writing. Also in 1971 he brought out his first major novel, *The Book of Daniel,*[21] and was hailed by critics as a new literary star. "This is less a review than a celebration," declared the usually acerbic Stanley Kauffmann in the *New Republic.* "E. L. Doctorow has written the political novel of our age, the best American work of its kind that I know since Lionel Trilling's *The Middle of the Journey.*" Kauffmann added that, although the two writers differ sharply "in style and temper," Doctorow here catches "the quintessence of the '60s, as Trilling, in 1947, fixed the political '30s."[22]

The novel's primary action is set in 1967, between Memorial Day and Christmas. The central figure is Daniel Lewin, a 27-year-old graduate student at Columbia; this narrative is ostensibly what he is writing instead of his dissertation. He and his younger sister, Susan, are the children of Communist parents, Bronx Jews named Isaacson, who were executed at Sing Sing in the early 1950s for conspiring to steal atomic secrets for Russia. After the Isaacsons' execution, their two children, then 14 and 9, were adopted by a Boston law professor named Robert Lewin and his wife, Lise. The story evolves from Daniel's efforts to discover "the truth about his parents, about himself in relation to them, and on his relations with his sister in her attempts to regain sanity." For Stanley Kauffmann, this novel "is an artwork about the *idea* of the Rosenbergs and people like them, how they came into being in this country, why their trial was needed, what their legacy is, and the intertexture of that legacy with the social-political climate today." Kauffmann finds little to criticize here. For him, *The Book of Daniel* "is beautiful and harrowing, rhapsodic and exact. Like all good artists dealing with such subjects, Doctorow does not give answers." He also is not content merely "to pose questions. At one point Daniel says of his father: 'He wrestled society for my soul.' " Kauffmann believes these words could serve as "a motto for this fine book."[23]

Peter Prescott was equally impressed. He described Doctorow's novel as "a purgative book, angry and more deeply felt than all but a few contemporary American novels." It is, he added, "a novel about defeat, impotent rage, the passing of the burden of suffering through generations and 'the progress of madness inherited through the heart.' "[24] No less enthusiastic was Aaron Fessler, who, in a brief summary in the *Library Journal,* declared, "The bitterness perceptible in every word flavors the whole novel with a Biblical eloquence and fervor rare in today's fiction." He found Doctorow's third novel "a magnificent achievement not only as a work of fiction fecund in word and image, but [also] as a stirring and provocative presentation of the feeling of dissent rampant in this country today. Everyone who reads it will be touched."[25] Less impressed was novelist Jerome Charyn, whose reactions were mixed. "Doctorow, like his persona Daniel," observed Charyn in the *New York Times Book Review,* "is a 'small criminal of perception,' whose psyche connects intimately with the '40s and '50s, but who cannot quite give himself over to the shocks and ambiguities of Kennedy, Johnson and Nixon's America." The result, Charyn concludes, is that despite the length of his beard, Daniel remains "a child of the Cold War." Yet perhaps even this limitation offers value. For ultimately *The Book of Daniel* "does take hold of us and force us to squint at ourselves because of its ability to energize the wreckage of our own past."[26]

Bernard Hrico, in *Best Sellers,* also offered a caveat, as he found the narrator's shifts from first- to third-person narrative "a bit bothersome." Still, he saw the novel as the "accomplishment of a writer who knows what he wants to say." For example, Doctorow's description of the electrocution of Daniel's parents "sends the charge right through the reader's body."[27] The reviewer in *Harper's* (identified only by the initials R. S.) thought the novel catches "more truly than any fiction I have ever read the quality of the Stalinist mind, voice, and life-style, without sacrificing our human sympathy for the elder Isaacsons." The work may be, above all, "a political novel," R. S. conceded, but he did not consider it to be "the work of a politicalized writer." Rather, Doctorow appears to be "trying desperately to catch hold of at least a fragment of the truth of our time and succeeding in getting hold of more than most have lately managed to capture." In short, Doctorow "has the right kind of integrity and is worth reading and remembering."[28]

Doctorow himself speaks of this novel in terms of its characters. Earlier, with *Welcome to Hard Times,* he had been creatively charged primarily by the bleak Dakota landscape. With *Daniel* he states, "It was the characters and their complexity that moved me." More precisely, it was "the historical intersection of social and personal agony, history moving in Daniel, shaping his own pathology." All these things, Doctorow explains, "had an enormous meaning and interest for me." So did Daniel's "relationship to his sister and the parents' relationship to each other, and Daniel's relationship to himself as he sits in that library and does these historical essays and descriptions of himself in the third person, breaking down his own voice and transforming his own being to produce this work. Daniel breaks himself down constantly to reconcile himself to what is happening and what has happened to him. This kind of act that the book is—Daniel's book—is the central force that I felt in the writing of it."[29]

Yet Doctorow was influenced also by his love of film, of the "cinematic" way of telling a story. "I don't know how anyone can write today," he says, "without accommodating eighty or ninety years of film technology. Films and the perception of films and of television are enormously important factors in the way people read today." His own experience offers example. Starting with *The Book of Daniel,* he "gave up trying to write with the concern for transition characteristic of the nineteenth-century novel. Other writers may be able to, but I can't accept the conventions of realism any more. It doesn't interest me as I write." Instead he is convinced that "the rhythms of perception in me, as in most people who read today, have been transformed immensely by films and television." He does not even "know what non-visual writing is. I think all writing puts pictures in people's heads—pictures of different things, but always pictures of the moral state of the characters being written about. Good fiction is interested in the moral fate of its people. Who they are or how they look or what they do or how they live—these are judgments of character, finally." He recalls that *Laugh-In* was a big television hit while he was writing *Daniel:* "I told people when *Daniel* was published that it was constructed like *Laugh-In.* They thought I was not serious. But the idea of discontinuity and black-outs and running changes in voice and character—it was that kind of nerve energy I was looking for. *Loon Lake,* too, is powered by discontinuity, switches in scene, tense, voice, the mystery of who's talking. Will people be able to understand it? I think they will. Anyone who's ever watched a news broadcast on television knows all about discontinuity."[30]

V

In 1974 Doctorow was appointed a creative writing fellow at the Yale School of Drama, and the following year he moved on to the University of Utah as a visiting professor. Also in 1975, Doctorow published his fourth novel, *Ragtime.*[31] This "cinematic" work brought him not only more critical accolades but also his first popular success. Yet the novel itself did not come easily, at least not at first. After speaking with Doctorow, one interviewer described the novelist's state of mind when trying to begin his new work. Having expended great "emotional energy" on *The Book of Daniel,* Doctorow "sank into a creative stupor" and would stare for hours at his study walls. From time to time he would "peck at his typewriter with pitiful results." He began to fear that whatever he wrote would prove "an exercise in futility." This fear stemmed from his growing conviction "that the potential audience for novels had been turned off by the modern novelist's preoccupation with static stories, with minutely detailed but frustratingly remote pieces of literary sculpture." Doctorow explains: "In my reading I found myself responding to work done before the onset of the modern novel, and somewhere along the line I got the idea of doing a relentless narrative of a pseudo-historical kind, a story with ongoing energy and a real sense of motion."[32]

The real challenge lay in getting started, but finally inspiration came. "After about a year of not knowing what to do," Doctorow recalls, "I found myself writing about the wall I was staring at." He wrote, "'I live in a house that was built in 1906,' and that led to certain images. Teddy Roosevelt. People wearing white in summer." He realized quickly that "writing *Ragtime* was a matter of discovering the logic of those images and following them where they took me."[33] Where they took him was back to his usual writing schedule. "Ever since I began to write for my living I've always gotten up and gone to work. If I miss one day it takes me two days to catch up. Writing generates writing. The more you do it, the more you are able to do it. I work very inefficiently, going along for a good clip for a long while and then going back and painstakingly revising. Or, sometime, I stay on one page obsessively. In *Ragtime,* there are not many pages that were not written five or six times."[34]

In essence, Doctorow in *Ragtime* goes back in time to delineate some of the people and events that shaped the American society that would later generate the political malaise of the 1950s and 1960s. Most critics missed this cultural connection, but Stanley Kauffmann saw it clearly: "Quintessentially *The Book of Daniel* depicted the ideological climate of mid-century: showing how political radicalism had been brought to this country from Central and Eastern Europe, how it had flourished under the economic pressures of the Thirties, and how the predominantly Anglo-Saxon, gently meliorist qualities of this country had been irrevocably changed." In *Ragtime* Doctorow returns to the years between this century's start and World War I. He goes back "to the beginnings of that change, and he extends the scope from politics to a wide spectrum of an era, a fateful era."[35] Those years saw the creation of the auto assembly line and the Model T Ford, moving pictures and ragtime music—most notably in Scott Joplin's rags. They witnessed also the growth of professional baseball and the constant arrivals of "rag ships" laden with immigrants.

Expanding on the varied uses of historical figures by fiction writers as different as William Thackeray in *Henry Esmond* and John Dos Passos in

U.S.A., Doctorow intermingles in *Ragtime* a cluster of that era's significant individuals with three fictional families. He draws on pop histories and biographies of such colorful individuals as J. P. Morgan and Henry Ford, Emma Goldman and Evelyn Nesbit, Harry K. Thaw and Stanford White, Harry Houdini and Archduke Franz Ferdinand, Sigmund Freud and Carl Jung, Theodore Dreiser and Arctic explorer Robert E. Peary. He then rearranges events in their lives to interweave them with those of his fictional characters. Thus Doctorow blends fact and fiction to create what some critics have termed "faction." Such a "method gives equal vitality to all," stated Stanley Kauffmann. "The actual people are breathed into rounded life; the invented people take on historical weight." Kauffmann, who had praised *The Book of Daniel* profusely, was again unstinting in his praise. "*Ragtime* is a unique and beautiful work of art about American destiny," he wrote in *Saturday Review.* The novel is "built of fact and logical fantasy, governed by music heard and sensed, responsive to cinema both as method and historical datum, shaken by a continental pulse."[36]

All Doctorow's figures may take on form and substance, but they do so in different ways. For example, his invented white people are given not names but merely generic labels to suggest their emblematic or "silhouette" qualities. However, his black people require individuality; hence they are given names to indicate how atypical they are for their time. Doctorow's central metaphor is the American "family," and he quickly intermingles the lives of three very different family groups. The first is that of a stolid, respectable, upper-middle-class WASP flag and fireworks manufacturer. Comfortably ensconced in their New Rochelle hilltop house are Father; Mother; Grandfather; Mother's lonely, withdrawn Younger Brother; and the Little Boy in the sailor blouse, who ultimately proves the novel's narrator. One hot Sunday afternoon, a 45-horsepower Pope-Toledo automobile swerves into a telephone pole in front of the house, and out steps the celebrated escape artist Harry Houdini, who has been house hunting in the neighborhood.

Soon Houdini is more impressed with Father's adventures than his own. Father is a formidable figure: Spanish-American War veteran, president of the New York Explorers Club, and soon a member of Admiral Peary's third expedition to the North Pole. Most critics have given Father short shrift, dismissing him as embodying everything the novel is satirizing. They are mistaken. Father is essentially decent and conscientious, but his patrician Victorian standards make it difficult for him to cope with either the new century or an America he no longer recognizes. Immigrants and Negroes seem to be everywhere, and women—his beautiful, demure blonde wife included—are increasingly restive and assertive. When Mother finds a brown baby nearly buried in her garden, she insists on taking him and his unmarried young mother, Sarah, into her home. Thus does the one family become two.

One day the baby's father shows up at Father's door. He is Coalhouse Walker Jr., a gifted jazz pianist and a member of Harlem's Jim Europe Clef

Club Orchestra. Dignified, polite, articulate, Coalhouse appears every Sunday for over a year in his shiny Model T Ford. He enthralls the family—Younger Brother in particular—by his musicianship, especially when he offers them "the clusters of syncopating chords and the thumping octaves" of Scott Joplin's *Maple Leaf Rag.* Tragedy strikes when some rowdy Irish volunteer firemen demand Coalhouse pay them a toll for passing on their street. When he refuses, they vandalize his car. Despite his—and Father's—best efforts, Coalhouse is unable to get legal redress. He turns then to terrorism, and a literal bloodbath ensues. (Doctorow is indicating his admiration for the nineteenth-century German writer Heinrich von Kleist. Coalhouse is clearly named after the violent hero of Kleist's, *Michael Kohlhaas.* The German novelist had also blended fact and fiction, having likely derived his plot from reading Peter Hafftiz's sixteenth-century chronicle of the historical Kohlhaas.[37]) Younger Brother, when his brief romance with Evelyn Nesbit ends, joins Coalhouse's group as its explosives expert. Coalhouse is ultimately shot to death and Younger Brother drives the restored car to Mexico, joining the revolutionary army of Emiliano Zapata and eventually dying there.

Quickly coming into focus is the very different household of a desperately poor Jewish immigrant family. Tateh (Yiddish for father), Mameh, and their beautiful Little Girl in the pinafore all live in one room. Tateh is a peddler who soon becomes a street-corner silhouette artist. Mameh and the Little Girl sew knee pants and earn 70 cents a dozen. With two weeks' rent due, Mameh lets her boss have his way on a cutting table. Tateh drives her from the house and mourns her as if she were dead. Politically active, Tateh is president of the Socialist Artists' Alliance of the Lower East Side. When he stands before the display cart of his framed silhouette portraits, he keeps one end of a clothesline tied around his waist and the other around the wrist of his Little Girl, fearing the white slavers who abound in the surrounding tenements. While driving through the Lower East Side to escape pursuing reporters, Evelyn Nesbit is attracted to the forlorn child's beauty and briefly becomes a part of the little family.

Tateh is not without talent. For 15 cents he will cut a bystander's image on a piece of white paper and mount it on a black background. After police break up an Emma Goldman lecture, Tateh leaves with his daughter for Lawrence, Massachusetts, where he becomes a millworker caught up in a violent textile strike. He soon moves on to a more peaceful Philadelphia. There, to entertain his daughter, he puts 120 silhouettes on tiny pages and binds them with string. When the Little Girl flips the pages with her thumb, she sees herself skating away and returning, gliding into a figure eight, pirouetting, and finishing with a polite bow. The movies are in their infancy and Tateh, by means of his flip book, has just entered their world. When he meets Mother and Father some time later in Atlantic City, he is the Baron Ashkenazy, a noted movie mogul. Mother and Father have grown estranged, and Father dies when the *Lusitania* explodes, thanks in large part to munitions devices aboard that Younger Brother had designed and Father was taking to the Allies in Europe. Mother and Tateh marry. When the latter observes their children playing, he gets the idea for the "Our Gang" comedies. Doctorow is then ready to conclude: "And by that time the era of Ragtime had run out, with the heavy breath of the machine, as if history were no more than a tune on a player piano" (*R,* 270).

George Stade, in the *New York Times Book Review,* setting the tone for most of the early reviewers, was fulsome in his praise. "[I]n this excellent novel," he stated, "silhouettes and rags not only make fiction out of history but also reveal the fictions out of which history is made. It incorporates the fiction and realities of the era of ragtime while it rags our fictions about it." Doctorow has written "an anti-nostalgic novel that incorporates our nostalgia about its subject. It is cool, hard, controlled, utterly unsentimental, an art of sharp outlines and clipped phrases. Yet it implies all we could ask for in the way of texture, mood, character and despair."[38]

R. Z. Sheppard, in *Time,* was equally impressed: "Literal descriptions and interpretations make many novels sound better than they are. With *Ragtime,* just the opposite is true," he stated. "Its lyric tone, fluid structure and vigorous rhythms give it a musical quality that explanation mutes." Doctorow has here "managed to seize the strands of actuality and transform them into fabulous tale."[39] For Walter Clemons, in *Newsweek,* the novel proves "as exhilarating as a deep breath of pure oxygen" and reminiscent of past classic narratives. "E. L. Doctorow boldly aspires to the power the novel once had to convince us its story was real," Clemons explained. "Not 'realistic,' you understand—lifelike, possibly even based on actual events—but real in the way Defoe's first readers believed *A Journal of the Plague Year* and *Robinson Crusoe* to be true histories." In essence, "the illusion that the novel has a mysterious life of its own is strong in *Ragtime.*"[40] The *New Yorker*'s anonymous reviewer was even more enthusiastic and succinct. He or she found *Ragtime* to be "an extraordinarily deft, lyrical, rich novel that catches the spirit of this country in the era between the turn of the century and the First World War in a fluid, musical way that is as original as it is satisfying."[41]

The first discordant note was struck by Jeffrey Hart in, not surprisingly, the politically conservative *National Review.* Hart acknowledged Doctorow's narrative skills: "Almost magically, Doctorow recreates the atmosphere of pre-WWI America. His sense of the telling detail is superb, and even if that were his only triumph—it is not—this novel would still be something to treasure." But whereas the novel's "powerful narrative thrust" is part of the "Good News," Doctorow's obvious political bias and faulty "moral vision" are for Hart strictly "Bad News." In short, "one mode of moral judgment is applied to the middle- and upper-class WASPs throughout; another mode of moral judgment is reserved for Jews, blacks, and turn-of-the-century radicals." The result is that "where rebellious minority characters are concerned, we have mostly what can be called left-wing pastoral."[42] Alfred P. Klauser, in

Christian Century, was less judgmental. He read the novel as "something of an ironic bicentennial gift to a nation seemingly intent on glorifying its past achievements." Doctorow here offers a caveat by depicting "an era when . . . the Protestant ethic reigned supreme but somehow failed to bring lasting happiness."[43]

Most other early reviewers also expressed measured or qualified praise. Joseph Moses, in *The Nation,* found Doctorow to be "a remarkable novelist precisely because he confronts the mockery of time directly and attempts to master it with footwork fancier and more playful." Exhibiting "showmanship and comic control . . . Doctorow, the silhouette artist, the Houdini escapologist, the Scott Joplin-composer of ragtime-Ragtime is seated at the piano controls domesticating time, outdoing time at its own game." His goal "is to impose a phrasing of history, to syncopate its rhythm—to rag time."[44] In *Commonweal,* Leonard Kriegel also balanced praise and criticism. "*Ragtime* is not a 'masterpiece' but it is a brilliantly written novel," he stated, "one that manages to be thoroughly enjoyable and thoroughly serious." Kriegel thought Doctorow's melding of fiction and history "even more intriguing" than that of Dos Passos in *U.S.A.,* for Doctorow stitches together "the lives of the common and the uncommon." Yet ironically, if this stitching is the book's "great success," it proves also its "chief weakness." The narrative "is dominated by its surface. It lacks depth, in much the same way as the music from which it derives its title lacks depth." Yes, declared Kriegel, there is "suffering made history and there is joy made history." However, he felt that neither the suffering nor the joy was "individualized." Most of the characters fail to arouse reader sympathy. They simply "live and die as part of the history that embodies them. But they do not live in the fiction." Still, in certain instances, "most notably with Houdini and Emma Goldman, what emerges is more human, more fundamental, than what a biographer could capture." *Ragtime* then "may point toward a new direction for the American novel," in particular for those readers "who have come to feel that contemporary American fiction has created a strait jacket out of individuality." For them, "*Ragtime* is bound to be exciting reading."[45]

Roger Sale liked the novel but also harbored reservations. In the *New York Review* he explained that he "didn't like the first half of *Ragtime* as much as the first half of *The Book of Daniel*" but, he concedes, "unquestionably it is very good. The characters are figures rather than people, the result is all surface, but the surface shimmers and shines." Despite these limitations, the fact remains that "no one has written a book quite like *Ragtime* just as no one had written one quite like *The Book of Daniel.*" *Ragtime* then "may not be an entirely successful book," Sale concluded, "but the writer who can do this, and as well as Doctorow has, need set no limits on what he can do next."[46] But if discerning critics like Kriegel and Sale were willing to give Doctorow his due, others chose to follow Jeffrey Hart's lead by chastising Doctorow for what they considered an ultra-liberal political bias. In *Commentary,* Hilton

Kramer complained, "To have had a hand in shaping American life in the 20th century to any appreciable degree is, in *Ragtime,* a crime not easily forgiven." By adroit use of style and tone, Doctorow here consigns "bourgeois America . . . to eternal damnation" and elevates "its antagonists . . . to political sainthood." But if the novelist's major crime is hypocrisy, his readers are not without guilt. Their crime is being obtuse and smug and securing Doctorow "in the knowledge that he can have it both ways." Kramer refers to the sad fact that there is nothing Doctorow's "middle-class readers so much relish nowadays as an assault on their integrity suitably embellished with signs of their superior taste."[47]

Martin Green echoed these charges in the *American Scholar.* But Green also offered a detailed analysis of what he termed "a new genre, or sub-genre" of historical fiction. *Ragtime* was for him a prime example of this new genre, mixing as it did historical figures and events in highly imaginative and personal terms. But, like Kramer, he was annoyed by what he perceived to be Doctorow's romanticism and leftist leanings. "What is wrong with the book seems to be locatable in two large elements," Green stated, "its nostalgia for the period and its revolutionary politics, and the relation between them." But what Green found "still more disagreeable is the conjunction of this candy-sucking comfortableness of nostalgia with a radical severity of judgment on the characters." In short, middle-class whites are always villainous, whereas women and minorities (except the Irish) are presented as without sin. "In itself the radicalism is, therefore, unsatisfactory. But in conjunction with the nostalgia, it surely means that we are being invited to put ourselves on the side of revolutionaries, to give ourselves the airs of revolutionaries, in purely fantasy and wish-fulfillment conditions—as part of a voluptuous dream."[48]

Richard Todd, in the *Atlantic,* was even more hostile to the novel's political ideas. "The politics of *Ragtime* are boringly tractlike, a caricature of the past as the liberal imagination conceives it. You may agree with Doctorow's outline of history—you can hardly disagree—and yet resist its simplicity, and bridle at the pleasure the author seems to take in introducing to us the iniquity of capitalism, the suffering of the oppressed, and the fatuity of the middle class." Such one-sidedness takes its toll. "Despite the mannered prose, the sensibility behind this book seems to me," declared Todd, "anti-literary, uninterested in subtle emotions and in life lived outside of categories. *Ragtime* gets my vote as The Most Overrated Book of the Year."[49] Novelist Maureen Howard, in the *Yale Review,* was a bit more temperate but still essentially negative. "Doctorow's whimsy of intermingling *real* historical figures with his fictional characters cuts Emma Goldman, J. P. Morgan, Freud, Stanford White down into quickly researched personalities who hold our attention about as long as last week's celebrities in *People* magazine." But the novel's major flaw is that it "patronizes its readers as true popular art never does." For Howard, then, "the very fantasy on which this novel depends is opportunistic and [its] history is a *shtick.*" She hoped Doctorow had "done well enough with *Ragtime* to write as he once did in *The Book of Daniel,* that fully imagined story based on the Rosenberg case."[50]

Across the Atlantic some reviewers also appeared angered by the novel's critical and popular reception. Following the lead of the negative American reviewers, the English quickly turned those narrative elements most praised into literary shortcomings. For example, Philip French, in the *New Statesman,* dismissed Doctorow's novel as a frightening portent of a mind-narrowing Disneyland world to come. French thought Doctorow employed techniques reminiscent of the movie cameras to "construct . . . an extraordinary kaleidoscopic picture of an energetic, cruel, deeply divided society running dangerously out of control. His method resembles a documentary movie combining old newsreels, feature films and still photographs, or an adult, nightmare version of Disneyland."[51] Russell Davies, in the *Times Literary Supplement,* was even more caustic. What Doctorow has created, Davies charged, is "a simple-minded, whimsical, socio-historical pageant that comes nearer to qualifying as a comic-book than any unillustrated volume I have ever seen."[52] A different reaction was that of the unidentified reviewer in the *Economist.* Like Davies, he admitted he had been put off by the praise heaped on the novel by American reviewers, especially those "rave extracts on the jacket back." Thus he had approached the novel "with the suspicion proper to the mechanised literary cuisine of America." But once he started to read, he was, to his amazement, "at once transported, compelled to a kind of greedy, gourmandizing engulfment, for it is a splendid novel." He considered it "bitter, often funny, admirably and economically graceful, intelligent, passionate and sad." In all, he now felt *Ragtime* to be "one of the best American novels for years."[53]

But Jonathan Raban, in *Encounter,* was not to be placated. He was especially angered by Doctorow's overreliance on journalism and his abuse of history or historical figures. "Doctorow is a jackdaw writer," charged Raban. "He has feathered his nest with bits and pieces drawn from all sorts of disparate sources, some of them classy and some of them not. The main question that *Ragtime* raises is whether it succeeds in fusing its disparate components . . . into a single new object. I think that, despite its evident ambitiousness, its considerable finesse and its cool wit, it does not." He then added, "It is written to be read fast: too much attention on the reader's part kills it stonedead." What most bothers Raban is that "a very large number of people who know little, and care less, about either the novel or history" will view *Ragtime* "as the most dazzlingly sophisticated exploration of both the novel and history that they have ever read."[54] Yet Raban fails to cite any such claim by even the most enthusiastic of American reviewers.

Doctorow has not accepted such negative comments silently. In interview and essay, he has spoken to most of the charges leveled by critics. Asked repeatedly about the repercussions of his blending fact and fiction or of using historical figures in his fiction, especially in *Ragtime,* Doctorow is sanguine. "You mean you think the book might be libelous?" he responded to one interviewer: "Well, no one has tried to get in touch with me, no relatives or lawyers. I suppose what you're really asking is did I have the right to use real-life people in a novel. My answer is that, first, imagination has the right, and second, that history exists in people's minds as images. This book is a set of historical images, images of the way people lived, the houses they lived in, the dress they wore and images of domestic life. The more remote the time is, the fewer the images by which we know it." He is hardly alone. He thinks "every novelist works with the presumption that the facts he offers, however fictive they may be, are a broader, straighter avenue toward the truth. *Ragtime* exists somewhere between fiction and history, and what defines it is a certain distancing from the characters and a narrative presumption that's carried in small function words like 'The next day . . .' or 'At the same time. . . .'" His novel "proposes that the distinction between fact and fiction is not as clear-cut as Americans imagine it."[55]

Doctorow returned to this distinction between reality and art on another occasion. Here he stated that "if you do this kind of work, you can't finally accept the distinction between reality and books. In fact, no fiction writer has ever stood still for that distinction and that's why Defoe pretended that Robinson Crusoe was really written by Crusoe. I don't want to understand that distinction between art and everything else, so I don't. This is not merely an aesthetic position, you understand, I get impatient with people who are moralistic about this issue." What Doctorow believes has happened is that people used to know what fiction was and now they've forgotten. It comes as a surprise when they're reading a novel and they find Harry Houdini saying things and carrying on. It could be that there's been such a total disintegration into specialist thinking on the part of all of us in our trades and jargons that no one remembers what the whole life is. What is imagined and what is experienced? The imagination obviously imposes itself on the world, composes a world that, in turn, affects what is imagined.[56]

That this give-and-take applies even in science is for Doctorow "indisputable." He explains, "Books create constituencies that have their own effect on history, and that's been proven time and again." So he does not see the vaunted "distinction between facts and art." He suggests, "If you read a good social scientist, an anthropologist, a sociologist, you'll find they do everything we fiction writers do. These people who write sociology create composite characters. Anyone who represents a class or a kind of ethnic or economic group is dealing in characterization. That's what I do." In other words, suggests Doctorow, "All history is composed. A professional historian won't make the claims for the objectivity of his discipline that the lay person grants him. He knows how creative he is." Doctorow offers an example of what he means. "It turned out," he states, "that American historians had written, for the most part, as an establishment. They had written out of existence the history of black people and women and Indians and Chinese people in this country. What could be more apparent than the creativity of that? That's part of what I meant when I said of the little boy in *Ragtime* that "it was evident to him that the world composed and re-composed itself constantly in an endless process of dissatisfaction."[57]

When asked about his "liberal" political views, Doctorow answers in literary as well as political terms. "As a writer I don't have ideas so much as I have feelings. I'm trying to write about whatever suggests itself to me." He explains: "I think basically I write to find out what it is I'm writing. The primary condition for a writer is openness, a state of alert readiness for whatever happens, to be mercurial, volatile and erratic." The irony here is that "all the things that in a love are so immoral are in a writer a source of power. A book can start as an image, a voice in your ear, a sense of rhythm. For me, the voice of a rather complicated imagination precedes the intent. The language precedes the intent. That's not to say you don't have ideas, convictions, social and political attitudes. You have to trust the work itself to include all of this. Writing is something you give yourself to."[58]

Doctorow has no qualms about describing himself as a political liberal, but he dislikes making predictions or pronouncements. "I hate to make pronouncements," he declares. "Whatever thinking of value I do, I do in the act of writing a book. The fact is, we all have the same capacity of insights and judgments. It's idiotic for me to sit here and pretend to know more about the state of the country than anyone else in the world. There is, of course, a paradox in an artist who seems to be without hope, no matter how critical he may be, no matter how despairing." In other words, merely by writing, he indicates he has not quite given up on the political process. As for himself, says Doctorow, "I am Left, but I've been a registered Democrat all my voting life. I call myself a social democrat, or maybe a wishful anarchist."[59]

So despite his personal views, he feels his "political" characters are complex enough to merit a careful separate reading. Therefore, "when people claim that I have this sentimental, simplistic approach to the characters on the left, they're not reading carefully," he argues. "As compassionate as we feel for Tateh and as much as we love him, here's a man who has betrayed his principles and sympathies and gotten ahead that way. After all, he has gotten to enjoy his life by abandoning his commitment to the working class. So that's hardly an uncomplicated, simplistic view of one of the book's leftists. I think I also portray Emma Goldman as a person who stomps all over people's feelings, who just wreaks havoc with people's personal lives wherever she goes. This sort of thing is true of the radical idealist personality, though it's hardly a simplistic portrayal of her."[60] Doctorow may again have given fresh thought to the trials of conscience of people like Tateh and Emma Goldman when the *Ragtime* paperback rights alone brought him a then-record $1.85 million and freed him of the need of a nine-to-five job.

VI

In 1979, Doctorow tried his hand at a play he called *Drinks Before Dinner*.[61] The few reviewers who bothered to acknowledge its existence agreed the work was not a success. "In his first play," noted Lee F. Kornblum in the *Library Journal*, Doctorow rejects "psychological drama of character and action in favor of 'a theatre of language . . . a theatre of ideas.'" As a result, his characters, "who are deliberately lacking in individuality, discuss philosophical ideas in long monologues." Not surprisingly, the resulting play "is a very static and fairly tedious" one. The plot is flatly structured. At a Manhattan cocktail party preceding dinner, a guest named Edgar offers a suggestion: "Let's not have the evening we all expect to have" because, he explains, "I won't survive it" (*DBD*, 3). Perhaps to ensure an audience for his rhetorical musings, Edgar then reveals a gun and directs the others to discuss life's sterility and the imminence of its end. At one point Edgar even ties the guest of honor to a chair. These acts literally exhaust the action, and the rest of the play consists of the dialogue, at times a monologue, between Edgar and the other guests. Dismissing many of Doctorow's ideas as "clichés," Kornblum does concede that "the rhetoric with which they are presented is interesting, and the play probably makes better reading than viewing."[62]

Doctorow appears to have agreed with this conclusion. He provided the grist for Kornblum and the other reviewers by explaining in his introduction his rejection of the drama of character and action in favor of a play of language and ideas. "The idea of character as we normally celebrate it on the American stage is what this play seems to question," he states. "I must here confess to a disposition for a theatre of language, in which the contemplation of this man's fate or that woman's is illuminated by poetry or philosophical paradox or rhetoric or wit. A theatre of ideas is what has always interested me, plays in which the holding of ideas or the arguing of ideas is a matter of life or death, and characters take the ideas they hold as serious as survival." He realizes that "all of this is, dramatically speaking, un-American" (*DBD*, xi). Doctorow also feels compelled to "warn future directors and actors of the play that with a language frankly rhetorical and sometimes incantatory, with a playwright who prefers a hundred words to one gesture, with a text that neglects the ordinary benefits of characterization and the interaction of ordinarily characterized persons, in which the spectacle is static and the words tumultuous and relentless," that they are dealing with a play that "does not solicit conventional theatrical sentiment from its audience" (*DBD*, xvii).

Predictably, reviewers eagerly followed Doctorow's lead. Martin McNamee, in *Best Sellers*, was quick to cite Doctorow's admission that his play "does not solicit conventional theatrical sentiment." To this, McNamee added: "Unfortunately his willingness to state this does not change the fact that he is correct." If "Edgar is assured of a captive audience," the playwright is unfortunate in that he "does not have the same trick at his disposal. He could use it." His play is more "an experiment with language" than a drama; "the language preceded the intention." McNamee warns that, as a result, "those seeking such experimentation will be satisfied. Those seeking more will be disappointed."[63]

An even more negative response was that of the anonymous reviewer in *Choice.* "Pretentious, ponderous, and dull are words that well describe E. L. Doctorow's *Drinks Before Dinner,*" declared that critic. "In his introduction (which is far more provocative and dramatic than the play it strives to illuminate) the author announces his intention to abandon the theater of psychology and biography in order to align himself with the theater of language and ideas. As it is, having read the play, one senses that in making the shift he has simply abandoned the theater itself." The basic problem is that "Doctorow has failed to recognize that any play, even a play of ideas, must be more than a text in dialogue form. The 'language of the theater' consists of nonverbal as well as verbal codes. By ignoring the fact that stage imagery and visual metaphor are every bit as important as verbal imagery, Doctorow has created a heavily rhetorical monologue disguised as a play." In other words, *Drinks Before Dinner* also "lacks the commitment and passion requisite for bringing its ideas to full theatrical life." The reviewer, perhaps feeling he or she had been too heavy-handed, tried to end on a positive note: "[T]he drama should still be of considerable interest as the first published play of a distinguished American author."[64]

VII

Returning to his novels, Doctorow undoubtedly took little solace in that final observation. In 1980, he launched the new decade by taking up residence at Princeton University as a visiting senior fellow and by publishing *Loon Lake.*[65] As with his previous novels, he claimed this one too sprang from an "accident" or unexpected image or scene. "I was driving through the Adirondacks a couple of years ago," he recalled. "I found myself incredibly responsive to everything I saw and heard and smelled. The Adirondacks are very beautiful—but more than that, [they are] a palpably mysterious wilderness, a place full of dark secrets, history rotting in the forests. At least that was my sense of things." He spotted a road sign: Loon Lake. "Everything I felt came to a point in those words. I liked their sound. I imagined a private railroad train going through the forest. The train was taking a party of gangsters to the mountain retreat of a powerful man of great wealth. So there it was: a feeling for a place, an image or two, and I was off in pursuit of my book." Asked to explain this new work, Doctorow compared it primarily with *The Book of Daniel.* "It is more like *Daniel* in being a discontinuous narrative, with deferred resolutions, and in the throwing of multiple voices that turn out to be the work of one narrator. So there are similarities with *Daniel* but the subject is far different and the tone is also different. It takes place in the Depression, a sort of Depression *Bildungsroman.* But not with that form's characteristic accumulation of data. I have a lot of broken-line stuff in it—weighted lines, that's new for me. In *Loon Lake* the sound the words make is important—the sound in the words and their rhythm. I think a good many parts of it are better read aloud."[66]

More specifically, the novel is essentially a dual narrative that follows two working-class youths striving for their own conceptions of the American Dream and whose paths cross on the estate of a powerful capitalist. Narrative time is 1936—the heart of the Depression. The unidentified primary narrator finally reveals his name, on page 71, as Joe of Paterson. To that point he tells his story in both the first and third persons as if he chooses at times to play dispassionate observer of his own actions. To one English reviewer Joe is "a self-centered tough . . . a Huck without conscience," whom life has taught to look out primarily for "number one."[67] Joe's experiences are somewhat confusingly blended with the first- and third-person narrating of a down-at-the-heels poet named Warren Penfield. At 18, Joe abandons Paterson, New Jersey (here a much more grim and nasty locale than in William Carlos Williams's long poem), and his inept, impoverished parents. A latter-day picaro, Joe works at odd jobs, sleeps with older women, lives in hobo camps, and becomes a carnival roustabout. Tragedy strikes when he fails to prevent his slow-witted friend, the carnival fat lady, from being raped to death. Joe runs off once more, this time to the Adirondacks forest. There, gazing up at the night stars he sees, in the richly furnished back car of a passing private train, a naked young woman holding a dress before her.

Intrigued by the girl's beauty, Joe follows the track to an isolated 50,000-acre mountain estate overlooking a lake. This retreat, known as Loon Lake, is owned by F. W. Bennett, a mysterious robber baron industrialist with gangster connections. Chief among the latter is Tommy Crapo, a flashy, strike-breaking thug who heads up Crapo Industrial Services. Crapo has come to Loon Lake with an entourage that includes Clara Lukacs, his tough young girlfriend. To seal his business deal with his host, Crapo generously makes Bennett a present of his brassy blonde moll, and the tycoon passes her along for safekeeping to the alcoholic, overweight, failed poet Warren Penfield, another son of crushed labor-class parents. Joe inadvertently also becomes a guest of the estate. Attacked by a pack of starving wild dogs, he is rescued and permitted to recuperate in the staff house. There, Joe learns that Bennett is one of the country's most powerful men and that he hosts at Loon Lake not only gangsters but also some of the world's most celebrated figures. Becoming an estate worker, Joe discovers people are as manipulated and exploited there as at the circus, though in a more subtle and elegant fashion. Still, he is befriended by Bennett, who is capable on occasion of being both likable and sensitive. The tycoon advises the young man to live with the consequences of one's actions. Later, Joe befriends Warren Penfield, the son of evicted miners, who years earlier had come to Loon Lake to kill the mine-owning industrialist out of revenge for his exploited parents. He too had been attacked by the hungry dogs and had stayed on to become the resident poet. Thus do the powerful co-opt enemies or aspiring assassins.

Also in residence is Lucinda Bennett, the land baron's elegant and aloof wife. She is a renowned pilot whose accomplishments are meant to echo those of Amelia Earhart. Lucinda is an "ironical, frigid" woman whose seaplane landings and takeoffs reinforce the narrative's "central image." This is, observes George Stade, "that of a loon diving into the cold, dark, obliterating water, and then struggling up and out, fish in beak, emitting loony cries."[68] Escape becomes an important theme. For like the loon, the central figures wish to fly free of Bennett's domain. With Penfield's help, Joe heads for California with Clara in a Mercedes-Benz. Penfield takes to the air with Lucinda in her seaplane but, like Amelia Earhart's, their plane disappears. Clearly Warren Penfield lacked the strength, talent, or good luck to withstand the reach of the Bennetts and to attain his version of the American Dream.

At this point, Doctorow moves from romanticism to realism, which quickly shades into melodrama as Joe, hoping to avoid possible pursuers, opts to lose himself in ordinary life. He ends up in a cold, bleak Indiana town working on the assembly line in one of Bennett's auto-body factories. There he is made painfully aware that Loon Lake's good life derives from Jacksontown's pain and grind. He becomes friends with a union activist named Lyle Red James, a Southern redneck who lives next door with his young wife, Sandy, and infant daughter. Joe the hustler is temporarily transformed by his work in the factory and in its underground union and by his relentless fear that he and Clara are being pursued by Crapo's thugs. But Joe's idealism is short-lived; Red James, he discovers, is also working for Tommy Crapo's union-busting agency. When his double-dealing is exposed, Red becomes expendable and is killed by Crapo's goons. Joe is badly beaten, and then he is questioned by the town police, who also work with Crapo. Clara returns to the gangster. Joe is released only after he urges the police to call a secret emergency telephone number Bennett had given him. Joe strikes out once more for California, this time with Sandy and her child, but he soon abandons them. By this point, as George Stade points out, "Joe has come through many variations of the stock scenes and characters of road and Depression fiction. There are bindle stiffs and meaty cops, faded wives and brutalized husbands, itinerant Marxists, coal-mine cave-ins, comradely strikers and goons with bad consciences, lecherous matrons, snooty servants, overloaded tin lizzies heading west, murderous rubes." All these elements are played out amid "the violence that is as pervasive as the harsh and haunted American landscape." Stade then adds: "Doctorow's treatment of these scenes and characters is at once traditional, odd and dissonantly beautiful, like a chorus of the blues played by Dizzy Gillespie."[69]

Fate deals both protagonists an ironic hand. Penfield escaped his troubled life in a plane crash. Joe, having lost everything, returns—like Penfield before him—to Loon Lake to exact revenge on Bennett, whom he blames for all his misfortunes. But his "revenge" takes a peculiar turn, for the powerful industrialist, wasted by guilt and grief over his wife's death, is no longer the man he was. So Joe of Paterson (father/son—his name now becomes meaningful) decides to save his "father" from total deterioration. He will find the older man's humanity, make the tycoon love him, and become his adopted "son."

Doctorow closes his narrative with a Dos Passos–like capsule profile of his hero's remaining years. His final page outlines quickly Joseph Paterson Bennett's later life and career. Joe has gone on to prove himself as a soldier, as a—the ironies never cease—deputy assistant director of the Central Intelligence Agency, as a board chairman and trustee of numerous corporations, and, in the novel's ringing conclusion, "Master of Loon Lake," Joe has not only replaced but has also become his "father." Several reviewers have pointed up Doctorow's use of familiar American literary myths of ambition and power, success and failure, guilt and loneliness as shaped by Thomas Wolfe, Scott Fitzgerald, and in particular here John Dos Passos. But in this variation on the familiar American rags-to-riches theme, or at least on its Horatio Alger pattern, Doctorow has again drawn as well on European literary sources. For Joe's true family name is belatedly revealed to be Korzeniowski, and readers of modern literature will recognize it as the original surname of the redoubtable Joseph Conrad. Doctorow is once more acknowledging his sources. Here, as George Stade has pointed out, Doctorow is paying his respects to that looming modern literary presence. "Like Conrad's major fictions," Stade noted, "*Loon Lake* is narrated discontinuously, through various styles and voices, and in a shuffled chronology. But in Conrad's major novels—*Lord Jim, Nostromo, The Secret Agent* and *Victory*—and in a number of his minor ones, the real or adoptive father undoes his son. . . . Conrad's point roughly is that the past destroys the present." But in America matters are reversed: "In America, to generalize further," concluded Stade, "the sons win; they destroy the past only to preserve the worst of it in themselves, and thereby destroy the future. Such is Doctorow's variation on the conventional American success story."[70]

The critical and commercial success of *Ragtime* made Doctorow a major literary figure whose novels merited extensive coverage. But reviewers were now inclined to greet his next novel with a show of skepticism. Not surprisingly, then, most early reviewers offered mixed reactions. However, Paul Gray, *Time*'s reviewer, liked *Loon Lake* and tried to warn readers not to expect the "spare, metronomic prose" of *Ragtime*. For the new novel's "written surface," he noted, "is ruffled and choppy. Swatches of poetry are jumbled together with passages of computerese and snippets of mysteriously disembodied conversation. Narration switches suddenly from first to third person, or vice versa, and it is not always clear just who is telling what." Yet despite acknowledging the novel's shortcomings, Gray was determined to conclude on a positive note: "But the author's skill at historical reconstruction, so evident in *Ragtime,* remains impressive here; the novel's fragments and edgy, nervous rhythms call up an age of clashing anxiety. *Loon Lake* tantalizes long after it is ended."[71]

Peter Prescott was equally conflicted, seeing *Loon Lake* as both "an irritating book and an engrossing one." He, too, thought it "difficult to keep Joe's story separate from Penfield's," and he found it "alarming to see how easily the author slips from really elegant writing into pretentious, even purple prose." Yet Prescott, too, felt the need to end on an upbeat note. "Still, Doctorow *is* a storyteller, a myth-maker," he stated. "The scenes he develops have hooks that catch and hold."[72] Robert Towers had a similar reaction, but he found more to praise than to blame. The novel was for him "so rich in its disorder" that he could "regret only to a point the lack of a final coherence. The experience of reading *Loon Lake*—even its pages of bad poetry—was exhilarating. It is a book I want to discuss and argue about with my friends; I hope they will quickly get around to reading it."[73]

The novel's more scathing reviews were still to come. For example, novelist Mark Harris, in the *New Republic,* dismissed *Loon Lake* as the "failed work of a serious man." One reason that Doctorow has not developed his narrative more effectively is because "he has told it before," and he "cannot go forward by clinging wholly to his past." Hence the novel proves "an unfinished, unresolved" effort "in search of synthesis," declared Harris. "Does it, perhaps, embody "a system . . . a figure in the carpet" that time will reveal? Does it hold, hidden, "a myth or legend which scholarship will illuminate?" Harris did not think so. Nor did he expect the book to "snap open surprisingly to the exertion of our minds," or that "it will receive the corroboration of time."[74] Pearl K. Bell's review was as negative as Harris's but for a different reason. Writing in the politically conservative *Commentary,* she targeted Doctorow primarily for his outdated liberalism. After a retrospective attack on *The Book of Daniel* and *Ragtime,* Bell conceded that Doctorow's new novel was "remarkably unlike anything he has published before." Yet it was not "a remarkable novel," as its "mannered incoherence and stylistic confusion are in sharp contrast to the sleek, bright assurance of *Ragtime.*" To make matters worse, young Joe Paterson's adventures "are repeatedly interrupted by mysterious computer printouts supplying biographical data on the various characters or offering elaborate rationales for the sins of capitalism." This "ubiquitous computer that knows all and tells all is Doctorow's symbol for the dehumanized technology of a military-industrial world, the tyrannical machine that overwhelms its operators and reduces the entire culture to unfeeling statistics." In addition, Doctorow "strews the narrative with elaborate verbal tricks, puns, pseudo-poetic doodling, and signals leading nowhere." Obviously the "unacknowledged ghost of John Dos Passos—the brilliantly innovative Dos Passos of *U.S.A.*—haunts just about every page of *Loon Lake*." Both Joe and Penfield, Bell argued, have numerous counterparts in the Depression figures of Dos Passos's *U.S.A.* "The impressionistic commentaries of the 'Camera Eye' in *U.S.A.*—the voice of Dos Passos—are also paralleled in Doctorow's ironic and bitter soliloquies." He uses these commentaries to indict "the industrial Western democracies" for fashioning "legislation to serve the interests of the ruling business oligarchy." Seemingly, Doctorow angered Bell by appearing "determined to resist any counterrevolutionary suggestion that anything has changed for the better over the course of the last half-century. But since he fails to enrich his judgment with anything like the immediacy Dos Passos achieved with his technical experiments, *Loon Lake* conveys little more than the author's hortatory ineptitude." To Bell, Doctorow clearly had "nothing new to add to his old radical litany. Trapped in the simpleminded futility of his political dogmas, he is doomed to sing these same old songs over and over again."[75]

Also coming down hard on Doctorow for his political ideology was Diane Johnson, who did, however, find some merit in his willingness to take literary risks. "Like any other idealistic and perceptive person, Doctorow has a complaint about history, that it contained brutality and villainy." But here his anger and political views intrude into his fiction so that "in *Loon Lake* as in *Ragtime,* punishments and rewards are appointed not by considerations of realism and not by fictional conventions of retributive justice but by Doctorow's personal scheme." Still, this biased approach, she conceded, also has its upside. For "Doctorow's faith in his version of American history, and his willingness to run the large artistic risks involved in asserting it, make him one of the bravest and most interesting of modern American novelists." In short, Doctorow is "reviving the discredited function of artist as judge" and striving to find the proper literary forms by which to render "judgment."[76]

Saul Maloff, in *Commonweal,* divided his review into two parts. First he focused on Doctorow's mockery of "the primary American fantasy" of poor boy running away from home and making good in a very big way. He then dwelt on the novelist's "governing aesthetic principles" or narrative "strategies of discontinuity, splintering, fragmentation, and innovations." Maloff did not find the novel a total success, but he still felt *Loon Lake* to be "a work of marvelous fragments and noble intentions. In effect, it proves the kind of superb failure" that reveals "the hollowness and glitter of most literary success."[77] Another who had mixed reactions to Doctorow's narrative strategies was Douglas C. Runnels. In a relatively brief review in *Christian Century,* Runnels quickly summarized the plot and then declared the novel to be "not so much a sequence of events in the lives or even minds of its characters as it is a concerted effort to render nonlinear thinking in linear language." Runnels insisted that, in essence, Doctorow's novel holds in adroit "suspension all the elements of a Marxist critique of capitalist America, a Freudian study of postadolescence, and even a Wordsworthian lament for the lost perceptions of childhood." But, sadly enough, none of these elements ever distills out. "Instead, the book is filled with mirrors, disguises, transfigurations, and unlikely but satisfying parallels between events and perceptions in the main characters' lives." However, despite the author's overly playful and experimental devices, stated Runnels, "the reader willing to surrender" to the world of *Loon Lake* "will appreciate the integrity of Doctorow's regard . . . [and] obvious love for his creatures"—not to mention his "language of amazing flexibility and precision."[78]

Richard H. King, in the *Virginia Quarterly Review,* offered an essay review of both *Loon Lake* and Walker Percy's *The Second Coming.* After pointing out a few "superficial" biographical similarities, he conceded that Percy and Doctorow had "little in common." Focusing first on *Loon Lake,* King suggested that it "can be read on two different, though related levels." It can be viewed first as "a romantic quest for the ideal woman, the golden girl." Both Warren Penfield and Joe of Paterson "are in pursuit of a vision of femininity to which each was exposed as a young boy." Yet their "story is not simply a 20th-century version of the quest for the ideal object," said King; "it is also a quest for legitimacy, for authorization of one's self as counting in the social order." It is one that inevitably becomes a "quest for status, power, and class." Hence *Loon Lake* can also be seen as being in that novel tradition "tracing back to Stendhal's *The Red and the Black* and represented most clearly in American Fiction by *The Great Gatsby,* not to mention the Horatio Alger stories." But Doctorow puts his own societal twist on things. Hence his Joe of Paterson "is not without a rudimentary sense of injustice and a sympathy with the downtrodden. But his taste for what money can do leads him to cast his lot with the powerful, not the proletariat." Nor is his F. W. Bennett merely "a coarse capitalist of degraded sensibilities"; instead, he proves "a shrewd judge of people, patient in his desires and his designs, and capable of genuine grief." In addition, Doctorow's "prose is always seductive and extremely readable," and he knows how to keep events moving. So if this novel lacks the "compelling power" of *The Book of Daniel,* King reasoned, it does have "its moments and its rewards." But if "formally impressive," *Loon Lake* still "fails ultimately to engage our minds or emotions to a sufficient degree."[79]

Another "thumbs-down" was extended by Ronald Curran in *World Literature Today.* Doctorow's tale of these three pathetically "dispossessed seekers," Curran noted, "tells the tale, once again, of the failure of the American Dream." The novelist's "bitter irony illuminates the insidious attraction of money and power" to society's outcasts, as his three main figures "abandon their search for authenticity and settle for an enervating and lonely security." Admittedly, Doctorow's varied narrative strategies do at times suggest "effects that Faulkner achieved in his best work, yet they fail to reach the same level of integration in this novel." Indeed, it is "the complete interconnection of these techniques," Curran thought, "that causes the confusion about point of view and intention." So *Loon Lake* remains an interesting and ambitious fiction that doesn't put its themes and characters very smoothly together."[80] Amid such negative or at best lukewarm reviews, Doctorow must have been heartened by Thomas Lavoie's strong endorsement in the *Library Journal*. "Richly imbued with symbolism and mythical implications," beamed Lavoie, "*Loon Lake* is an exquisitely woven literary tapestry wherein history, language, philosophy join to create a marvelous and distinctively American 'text.'" Simply put, *Loon Lake* proves Doctorow's "most complex and challenging novel."[81]

Across the Atlantic, the reviews also tended to be mixed, with the negative ones outnumbering the positive. British novelist Anthony Burgess, who generally found it difficult to compliment American writers, seems to have made an unsuccessful attempt to do just that. He conceded that "*Loon Lake* exhibits a new formal direction" but then added that "it is a difficult book and I don't think it is a successful one." At the same time, "it is a very honorable attempt at expanding the resources of the genre." That the novel "breaks new technical ground and yet possesses so many of the traditional virtues of fiction," he concluded, "must be accounted its peculiar distinction."[82] Nicholas Shrimpton, in the *New Statesman,* also tried to pinpoint the strengths and weaknesses of both writer and novel. "The trouble with Doctorow is that he's twice the man you expect him to be." He is both "an aesthete, concerned to have fun with form," said Shrimpton, and "a dourly political novelist who writes serious books about American economic and social history." But he does not always meld effectively his experimental "exploration[s] of the interior life" with his political fiction's "plain, precise and pellucid" prose. This awkwardness is evident in *Loon Lake,* with its quixotic "time sequence[s]" and repeated "shifts of narrative viewpoint." Still, despite its stylistic shortcomings, *Loon Lake* remains for Shrimpton "a strong but simple book. The feverish haste of *Ragtime* has been cured. But Doctorow's narrative sophistication and political engagement still await a corresponding subtlety of thought."[83]

John Lucas, in the *Times Literary Supplement,* also felt the novel's varied elements fail to meld. "The prime difficulty," he thought, was not the book's fussy "narrative method, but its sense of having been written to a thesis." Lucas faulted the novel's central argument, which "takes for granted a whole number of films, novels and poems" that insist on the painful failure of the American Dream. Hence, despite "its cleverness and occasional brilliantly imagined scene, *Loon Lake* is finally too insistent, too hectoring, too much in love with its own diagnosis of cultural chaos. In a word, it is too adjectival." At bottom, then, Lucas finds "too much thesis about *Loon Lake* and too little life."[84] Alan Brownjohn, in *Encounter,* struck a different note. Aware also of its shortcomings, Brownjohn was still favorably inclined toward the novel. Recalling the generally positive critical reaction to *Ragtime,* he argued that *Loon Lake* merited, for at least two significant reasons, an even "more level-headed and more generally favourable reception." The first is that *Loon Lake* "comes to grips with the era (the 1930s) in an altogether more subtle and purposeful way" than does *Ragtime* with its time and setting. The second is that "it is a better story." Admittedly, Doctorow has not adequately developed the fates of his dual heroes. Still, his literary skills enable him to make the "allegorical wanderings of Warren and Joe part of so vivid a past world that its implied links with the present leave the reader incredulous."[85]

Back on this side of the Atlantic, Douglas Hill, in *Books in Canada,* focused on the novel's structure and composition rather than its political messages. "The story unfolds in richly textured patterns," Hill noted. "There are wonderful surprises, twists and turns of plot, revelations of identity, recurring images." What Hill finds most "striking is Doctorow's concern with composition." He "has 'composed' his story; he's put the parts of it together with an eye to rhythm, balance, and proportion." Indeed, "a principle of composition informs the novel's vision." All in all, "*Loon Lake* is better than *Ragtime,* as good as *The Book of Daniel,*" concluded Hill. "'The cry of loons once heard,' one bit of a Penfield poem ends, 'is not forgotten.' Moments in Loon Lake are like that."[86]

VIII

In 1982, Doctorow settled into a steady teaching position at New York University, as the Glucksman Professor of English and American Letters, a position he holds to this day. In 1984, he published *Lives of the Poets,*[87] a book somewhat different from his previous ones, consisting as it did of six short stories and a novella. It was his sixth published book and garnered reviews even more mixed or contrasting than did his previous ones.

Many reviewers agreed the short stories in themselves were rather slight efforts. Most also agreed the strongest of these was the first story, "The Writer in the Family." Here a teenaged boy named Jonathan, pressured by his aunt, agrees to write letters to his failing old grandmother in his dead father's name. (The story is a foreshadowing of his later, autobiographical novel, *World's Fair.*) It is followed by "The Water Works," a brief but grimly dark tale of a child drowned in a reservoir that points ahead to his later, similarly titled novel. In "Willi," Doctorow offers his elderly narrator's Freudian account of a traumatic experience in Galicia in 1910. Shocked at finding his mother and his tutor making love, the teenaged Willi betrays them to his father, only to be appalled at the resulting violence. The third story, "The Hunter," evokes memories of Sherwood Anderson's "Winesburg, Ohio" tales, revealing as it does the loneliness of a sensitive young grade-school teacher, a single woman in a factory town, edging close to a nervous breakdown. Then, in "The Foreign Legation," a deserted husband strives to fill his time with routine tasks and hard physical exercise, until he becomes the accidental victim of a terrorist atrocity. The last of the short stories is "The Leather Man," and it is a curious series of parodies of an FBI or other government surveillance team offering up reports and observations on the nonconformists in our midst. These loners include a peculiar tramp who roamed southern New England in the nineteenth century wearing leather armor of his own devising. Other lost figures depicted are derelicts and street people, Woodstock festival participants, a man arrested for voyeurism at his own house with his own wife (an apparent variation of a Hawthorne tale in which the character bears the same name of Wakefield), and a former astronaut gone bad. In their isolation and idiosyncrasies, these characters can all be viewed, Doctorow seems to suggest, as variations of the artist in America today.

Some critics felt these brief sketches were connected and strengthened by the novella that follows them. Others disagreed. Peter Prescott, in *Newsweek,* was among the favorably impressed. Doctorow's new book "works in a way I've never seen attempted before," he wrote. "It can be read as a collection of short stories, or as a novel, or as both at once." Holding these stories together, said Prescott, was a painfully familiar literary theme: "the peculiar vulnerability of a writer transmuting fragments of his own experience into fiction." Yes, the reader may find it difficult to imagine how Doctorow could fashion anything new from such tired material. "Yet Doctorow brings it off triumphantly," stated Prescott, "in part because he never shows us his writer writing and because he says nothing directly about the process of writing fiction. Instead, he shows how a writer's mind works." For example, Doctorow never allows his novella's narrator, Jonathan, to comment on his own work. But "the reader is able to recognize certain phrases, images and turns of thought that Jonathan has already altered to serve the six preceding stories. In creating the fictional Jonathan, said Prescott, Doctorow created the fiction that he has made art of his life; the truth is, he has created a life to account for the fiction."[88]

C. G. Storms in *Choice* offered a few more specific details. "As the stories' characters move from childhood to maturity and learn about the realities of death, sexuality, and loneliness, Doctorow portrays, as he has in earlier works, the ways in which these characters impose a fictive order upon experience." In his novella, Doctorow has his "imaginary author of the stories" explain that "he has left his wife in order to live and write in a Manhattan apartment. As he describes his own life and the lives of his friends, the images and themes of the earlier stories emerge, revealing how the material for the artist's fiction is gathered in his experience and transformed in his imagination." For Storms, then, *Lives of the Poets* proves "a bold formal experiment" that offers "sharply focused satire on failed marriages, middle-aged crises of confidence, and the social life of New York literary society."[89]

By now English reviewers were very familiar with Doctorow's work. Andrianne Blue, in the *New Statesman,* found *Lives of the Poets* "an able, agile, touching collection." So impressed was she that she declared Doctorow "a better writer (more percipient) than either Philip Roth or Norman Mailer, the other major exponents of American Jewish exurban fiction." She felt this way because, in Doctorow's stories, "menopausal male intellectual types not only face the paucity of life and their disappointment with women, they also face disappointment in themselves."[90] Aside from the likelihood that Mailer would be taken aback to find himself described as a "major exponent of American Jewish exurban fiction," Blue's observations seem reasonably valid. However, Adam Mars-Jones, in the *Times Literary Supplement,* disliked the entire book, especially the novella. He found its "reflexiveness"—that is, the fleeting allusions to the short stories that establish Jonathan as their author— to be "tired and not carried through." Mars-Jones also disliked the narrator. Jonathan is not only unpleasant to his "quick-witted and attractive wife," but he also never considers a writer's career in terms of "a body of work, only as an aggregate of grants, fellowships and propositions." Even so, the novella might prove enjoyable if its hero were "an aggressively brilliant critic of the world, but his rage is too small-minded to be impressive." To make matters worse, Jonathan, reacting against his own self-absorption and misanthropy, unexpectedly fills his studio "with needy illegal immigrants. Not since the 1960s has a writer so crudely used a social problem to shore up his solipsism."[91] The reader can only assume Mars-Jones meant to apply "writer" to both Jonathan and Doctorow.

Some American reviewers were also less than pleased with *Lives of the Poets.* John Skow, *Time*'s reviewer, opted for a tone of mild reproach. He observed that Doctorow, to his credit, includes here "no commencement speeches, letters to the *Times,* book reviews or similar lint balls in this between-books collection." Instead, he "offers six short stories, impeccably done, rather academic, mostly forgettable, and one 65-page mishmash called, for want of an accurate tag, a novella." The book's "odd arrangement" suggests to Skow that Doctorow himself "is not altogether happy with the stories." Still, the novella, this "mishmash, surprisingly enough, is a delight, largely because it knits up all that has gone before." It may be "totally shapeless," declared Skow, "but it is also funny and full of juice."[92] Richard Beards, in *World Literature Today,* did not agree that the novella unified and illuminated all that had gone before. "The novella ('Lives of the Poets') that ends the collection," he stated, "gives us the writer at midlife, suburban family abandoned for a tiny space in the city where he can write, think and act out his needs unhampered. Something about his intensely solipsistic life echoes the dreary popular accounts of midlife crisis so that the novella, far from pulling together the shorter works which precede it, vitiates their impact."[93]

Conversely, Benjamin DeMott thought Doctorow's new book his "subtlest work of fiction," one distinguished by its "gradual, patiently deliberated, austerely self-effacing unfolding of a moral core." The novella, "Lives of the Poets," that closes the volume "strikingly fuses" the six stories that precede it. "As we penetrate the writer's consciousness, touching the stories' common root, feelings that earlier were enigmatic are re-experienced as pointedly intense."[94] James Wolcott, in the *New Republic,* offered a sharply different reaction: "In *Lives of the Poets* E. L. Doctorow is squeaking open the cupboard doors of his imagination and saying, 'Welcome to my clutter,'" for "this collection is a showcase of personal debris, a shelf display of memories and mouse-hairs and glum, musing asides. Despite its classical title . . . *Lives of the Poets* is a slight, jittery book, a bulletin from the silk-stocking districts of the *Zeitgeist,* where the rents are high, the morale low."[95] Robert Towers, who had very favorable things to say about most of Doctorow's previous books, found the writing here to be "clumsy at times, with lots of strung-together clauses, as if Doctorow were deliberately roughing up his prose for the sake of a spurious authenticity." On the other hand, "there are also passages of driving power and eloquence." Indeed, if *Lives of the Poets* "is hardly comparable to Doctorow's best work," Towers added, it does offer the reader "a grimacing, arresting portrait of an artist who, in midlife, finds himself consumed by that which he was nourished by."[96]

In an interview with Herbert Mitgang in the *New York Times Book Review,* Doctorow offered his own thoughts on his latest book: "I write to find out what I'm writing," he explained. "In *The Book of Daniel,* I had to find the voice before I could tell the story. In *Lives of the Poets,* I was lucky. The voice came to me." He considered the book's short stories and novella to be unified. "I found myself writing them in sequence as they appear in the book. As I read the stories over, I discovered a connection, like a mind looking for its own geography. I found that I was creating the character of the person creating them. So I wrote the novella to give him a voice. I saw the possibility of presenting a writer's mind in both formal stories and then in a confessional mode. The novella is the story of the stories."[97]

IX

The next year Doctorow published his most directly autobiographical work, *World's Fair* (1985),[98] characterized by David Leavitt in the *New York Times Book Review* as "a peculiar hybrid of novel and memoir."[99] It is a nostalgic view of life in New York during the Depression, as experienced by a young boy who recounts his first nine years and ends his account with his 1939 visit to the World's Fair in Flushing Meadow. The boy's first name is Edgar (as is Doctorow's), and he grows up in the Bronx in the 1930s. His parents, like those of Doctorow, are named Rose and Dave. His brother's name—like that of the author's brother—is Donald. But here the family's last name is Altschuler. (Readers familiar with Doctorow's earlier story "The Writer in the Family" have already learned that Edgar's father died young. Indeed, that first story in *Lives of the Poets,* as Whitney Balliett suggests, "can be read as an epilogue to it. It's as if the idea for *World's Fair* had grown backward out of the story."[100]) Edgar's narration is interrupted from time to time by chapters related by his mother, older brother, and aunt. Their more realistic adult observations underscore Edgar's innocence regarding World War II, his father's bankruptcy, the deterioration of his parents' marriage, and his grandmother's descent into a raging senility. While acutely aware of these events, young Edgar focuses on the family living room, radio and movie serials, the schoolyard and neighborhood park, and the nearby street corner where a pushcart vendor serves up deliciously hot sweet potatoes. He wins honorable mention in an essay contest on the theme of the typical American boy, which Edgar, as his father reminds him, is not. Indeed, Edgar's carefully calculated one-paragraph essay drips irony. His prize is a family pass to the World's Fair, and the Altschulers' visit to that great exhibition ends the novel.

But that is Edgar's second trip there. On his first visit to the Fair, Edgar had been fascinated by corporate America's vision of the future. Their nation, the various exhibits made clear, would harbor only serene, secure, and prosperous cities; rapid and cheap transportation; and countless modern inventions to make daily life easier. On his second visit, however, Edgar realizes the exhibits are constructed of gypsum, marred by peeling paint, and the impressive displays are merely toys. Edgar is growing up, but what he cannot know is that World War II will soon follow. In much of the novel Doctorow, in the voice of "the older Edgar," said Leavitt, "describes that world in language that is both hypnotic and wonderfully precise, skillfully articulating the inarticulate passions of childhood." But there are other passages where the prose is "characterized by stunted or run-on sentences, narrative slackness and a blurring rather than a crystallization of detail," stated Leavitt. The reader suspects, according to Leavitt, that the author "is trying to recreate here the rhythms of speech, the sound of oral history, but instead has lapsed into prose that seems merely lazy." Still, what Doctorow essentially does here is flaunt "the artificial line dividing the true from the imagined." In doing so, he not only suggests "that the process of remembering is by definition a process of invention," but he also rejects "altogether the notion that imagination and memory are ever pure of each other." Doctorow's intention in *World's Fair* then appears, Leavitt concluded, "to be to create a work that succeeds as oral history, memoir and novel all at once. Unfortunately, these disparate genres don't always make the best of bedfellows, and until its breathtaking final 100 pages, when it becomes most fully novelistic, Mr. Doctorow's new novel seems as peculiar a mix of brilliant vision and clumsy self-indulgences as the fair it so artfully describes."[101]

Walter Clemons, in *Newsweek,* also expressed his appreciation of Doctorow's "exquisitely rendered details of a lost way of life in New York 50 years ago." But, like Leavitt, he was otherwise generally disappointed. What Doctorow had produced, complained Clemons, was "an entirely convincing facsimile of a loving, discursive, rather tedious memoir by a long-winded middle-aged author." In doing so, "Doctorow has successfully suppressed any detectable evidence of novelistic invention, plot complication or fictional surprise. Was this worth doing?" Literally rubbing salt in Doctorow's wounds, Clemons concluded by comparing him unfavorably with his "exact contemporary, Philip Roth." In his *Zuckerman Bound*, Roth had "recently completed a stinging, comic quasi-autobiography," Clemons noted, that "Doctorow's ruminations don't even approach in shrewdness, seriousness and sheer fun." The sad fact is that this novel remains "a work of austere majesty, slow, pretty and dull."[102] R. Z. Sheppard, in *Time,* voiced similar complaints: "*World's Fair* is not a happy book," he declared. "The dreariness of the '30s and the strains of family life appear to have had a bad effect on Edgar's style. He is either too terse or verbosely academic, as if the boy grew up to be a literary critic rather than a novelist." Admittedly, Doctorow tries to fashion "a myth to link a nation on the edge of war and a boy approaching adolescence, but he is too cautious with his material."[103]

Whitney Balliett also expressed irritation at Doctorow's blending of autobiography and fiction. "You never know what kind of hat E. L. Doctorow will be wearing when he writes a new book," said Balliett in his *New Yorker* review. He is a novelist who "likes to play games with his readers." In one interview Doctorow described his novel as offering "the illusion of a memoir." In another he referred to it as "really a story about memory," or in one sense "a time capsule." This last comment, Balliett observed, "is accurate, if incomplete." The book is basically "fragments of a novel embedded in a kind of catalogue of the everyday detritus of the thirties." Doctorow literally surrounds the boy "with his accurately researched lists of the artifacts of the thirties." The sad result is that not until "two-thirds of the way through the book [does] the novel hidden within it [begin] to be visible."[104]

Not all reviewers were negative. Edmund White, in the *Nation,* admired the same caution that had irritated Sheppard. "The very modesty of E. L. Doctorow's new novel," wrote White, "is its most daring aspect, but it's a dare that pays off." Here the city's "brick buildings and the summer light are as intense, as substantial and as present as in a Hopper painting." As for Doctorow's prose, "the sentences are short, the presentation straightforward, the chronology strict," with family members and other characters as sharply delineated "as if they had been etched out of wood with fire." Doctorow has plumbed human emotions "that are deep in the settings of a more innocent past. His past purrs and hisses and is capable of scratching deep enough to draw blood."[105] The reviewer in the *School Library Journal* was another who liked Doctorow's use of recent history. At first glance, *World's Fair* may appear "a seemingly simplistic view of life," this reviewer conceded. But more careful reading will reveal "a rich narrative of history, political and personal values and points for discussion." All in all, the reviewer thought it "a remarkable book for perceptive readers."[106]

Robert Towers, too, admired Doctorow's evocation of the past, although he thought the novel otherwise not overly impressive. Doctorow's "material is familiar from a dozen novels," said Towers, "from books on the Depression era, and from memoirs of growing up Jewish in New York." But Doctorow has added "so much observed period detail that a reader who has lived through the Thirties will experience repeated tremors, if not shocks, of recognition," as the narrative "is authoritatively documented and evocative." However, the characters do not fare as well. They may be "convincingly reproduced and analyzed," he concedes, but they are not truly "memorable, and the book as a whole lacks the movement and suspense of good fiction."[107] The normally generous Phoebe-Lou Adams, veteran reviewer of the *Atlantic,* expressed similar disappointment. While conceding that Doctorow's "material details . . . are plausible, as are the family tensions over status and money," she found young Edgar's "emotions and reflections" to be "implausibly adult and the characters in general arouse little interest." The sad result is that "the novel induces a weary sense of déjà vu, which is the last thing a reader expects from the work of this normally stimulating and original author."[108] But Mary C. Erler, in the Catholic magazine *America,* came to Doctorow's defense. "The book is notable both for its rich evocation of place and period," she wrote, as well as "for its effort to transform these into the stuff of universal experience." She did find Doctorow's prose somewhat mixed, as his "words can sometimes strain" and his "similes stretch too hard." Still, Doctorow remains "a commanding myth-maker" and very strong "on the war between the sexes."[109]

Another reviewer who liked the novel despite its obvious shortcomings was Keith Mano. "Well, *World's Fair* is sure a sweet mnemonic device," he wrote in the *National Review,* a publication generally hostile to Doctorow because of his liberal views. "I was enfolded by it." It was the first time, Mano explained, that he "felt nostalgia for someone else's life." He attributed Doctorow's success, at least in part, to the fact that "he writes for our last live reading generation. The rest is MTV and topless radio." Doctorow's imagery generally recalls "some trite object, some event forgotten now and not well perceived even then." But this focused trivia that comprises so much of the familiar "urban Jewish *Bildungsroman*" works to some degree against him. Major incidents like his young hero's appendix removal, the *Hindenburg* crash, and even the 1939 World's Fair itself appear "unspecific and cursory" amid the story's "elegant minutiae." But having registered his quibbles, Mano considered Doctorow's novel to be a deposit matching the 1939 time capsule. Indeed, "a time capsule can have its own instructive and delicious purpose," he stated, "beyond the quibble of literary criticism."[110]

X

Four years after *World's Fair,* Doctorow published *Billy Bathgate,*[111] described by novelist Anne Tyler as "a richly detailed report of a 15-year-old boy's journey from childhood to adulthood, with plenty of cliff-hanging adventure along the way." Young Billy has replaced his family name with that of the street on which he lives. He "is a rough, tough high school dropout living by his wits in the Bronx. His father has long ago disappeared, his mother is an impoverished laundry worker given to periods of distraction (some might say insanity) and Billy himself possesses only one distinguishing feature: he knows how to juggle."[112]

With this his eighth novel, Doctorow received what he very likely had been desperately wanting—an almost unqualified critical success. The few reviewers who did not like the book were, as usual, vehement in their dislike, but many reviewers who had been halting in their praise of his previous work now hailed the new novel. Of course, he also had his familiar champions. "Let's not sit on the good news," declared Peter S. Prescott in *Newsweek,* setting the tone for the favorable reviews to follow. "It's been a long, dry time since we've had a novel as fine as this. To put it another way, *Billy Bathgate* is by a considerable length E. L. Doctorow's best book." He here meets the challenge, said Prescott, of embracing "sex and violence, those staples of best-selling fiction" that many critics claim "cannot be treated explicitly in literary works." But Doctorow succeeds because of "his concentration on detail, the sharpness of his metaphors, from humor that glints unexpectedly even from the most grisly events." Prescott did not think anyone "should call a novel great in the month of its publication; greatness requires a resonance that only time confers." But this novel, he declared, "carries the credentials," as Doctorow weaves "a nice sense of moral ambiguity and creates characters who develop or deteriorate at an appropriate pace. His fecund run-on sentences are a pleasure to read. It all adds up to that rarity: a formal literary work that's also hugely entertaining."[113] Equally positive was Barbara Hoffert. "Though at times 15-year-old Billy seems far too precocious, even for a streetwise punk," she wrote in the *Library Journal,* "ultimately we are made to feel his apprehension" of a looming, "'empty resounding adulthood booming with terror.'" Doctorow has fashioned "an engrossing tale that successfully re-creates a world gone by in loving and meticulous detail."[114]

Anne Tyler shared the general enthusiasm, declaring the new novel "Mr. Doctorow's shapeliest piece of work." But what is to be found here, she warned, "is something considerably darker than Huck and Jim floating down a river together. The fact is that Dutch Schultz is a scary man. His position in Billy's life is much like that of a powerful but capricious parent." Interjecting her one caveat, Tyler said, "but if Billy is dextrous and clever, he is also astonishingly articulate . . . [for] a nearly uneducated street urchin." As a result, the reader cannot help but notice "the author himself lurking behind the backdrop." There is, however, "a trade-off," declared Tyler, as what the narrative "loses in authenticity, it gains in eloquence," especially in the voice and figure of Billy Bathgate. He is "Huck Finn and Tom Sawyer with more poetry, Holden Caulfield with more zest and spirit—a wonderful new addition to the ranks of American boy heroes."[115]

Doctorow, explaining to an interviewer the novel's origins, emphasized one specific image: men in tuxedos on a tugboat. "I don't know where the image came from, whether it was self-generated or something I saw 30 years ago in a magazine," he informed Michael Freitag of the *New York Times Book Review*. "I just kept thinking about what it meant and what it could possibly mean, and that's how the book got started." That image moved him to consider "the culture of gangsterism." He was interested primarily in "the mythic dimension in which we place gangsters and the meaning of them generally for us." Hence Doctorow centered the story less on the gangster, Dutch Schultz, than on "the fascination that the boy, Billy, feels for him—the attraction to the disreputable." He wanted to point up the fact that "there is some synchronous pulse we have with the atavism of gangster life," Doctorow explained. "Those guys are very tribal, and they live off at the edge of civilization, just where it abuts death. And the extremity of that life to those of us in the safe center is what pulls us." Doctorow claimed he wrote Billy Bathgate's story more by listening to his hero's voice than by remembering what it was like for Edgar Doctorow to grow up in New York City in the 1930s. Billy Bathgate "was born in that first sentence, in the rhythm of it, in the syntax," said Doctorow. "You could even hear his breath just by reading that sentence out loud to yourself."[116]

Doctorow repeated and expanded these comments in a *Time* magazine interview with Paul Gray: "I have never been an aficionado of crime, organized or disorganized," he stated. "Unlike Billy Bathgate, I don't follow the papers, trying to keep up with the heroes in this line of work." Nevertheless, he was fully aware of a thread of interest in his fiction in individuals functioning outside the law. "Dedicated criminals live on the extreme edge of civilization," he explained, "where manners and morals unravel and the underlying impetus of our tribal, primordial origins breaks through. My background, which was safe and conventional, may have made me attentive to the mysteries of life beyond the pale." Doctorow was also keenly aware of the gap between his own lifestyle and that of his characters. He owned, he admitted, comfortable New Rochelle and Long Island homes as well as a Manhattan studio apartment, and he held an endowed chair at New York University. "And then," he noted wryly, "I write a gangster novel. My life is bad for my image. I should be able to say that I spend my time hanging out in lowlife saloons."[117]

In an adjoining piece, Paul Gray summed up his personal reactions to Doctorow's new novel. Readers familiar with Doctorow's fiction, Gray observed, will find that in *Billy Bathgate* Doctorow again "mingles fictional characters with historical ones." But rather than merely repeating himself, Doctorow "is mixing elements from his other novels in a manner that proves combustible and incandescent." Billy's language offers example: "Breathy, breakneck, massing phrases into great cumulus sentences that rumble with coming rough weather," the style "is totally unlike the short, syncopated rhythms of *Ragtime*." Admittedly, Doctorow accounts late "for Billy's erudition, but by that time, no explanation is really required. Billy's voice has long since justified both itself and the unique power of the written word: it is convincing, mesmerizing and finally unforgettable."[118]

For Gary Wills, as for Anne Tyler, Doctorow's young hero was strongly reminiscent of Huck Finn. "Doctorow, like Twain, like Dickens," stated Wills in the *New York Review of Books,* "sees adult possibilities in 'the boy's book.'" Like Huck, Billy too finds himself "outside accepted moral systems" and has to "create his own code of responsibility." The narrative's varied components fuse smoothly for Wills. "This is Doctorow's first superbly constructed novel," he insisted. Even the tone proves "consistent, convincing despite a lingering tendency to the precious." So does the language, being "itself charged with the three-dimensionality of danger.'" This is also true of the characters, especially the young hero. "Billy is always the juggler inside and outside his own action, making it look easy." His juggling skills help define not only him but also his time and place. For "in a nation that thinks of itself as having a special destiny, he can only stay true to his own sense of balance by refusing to be absorbed in the communal myths of destiny—that of the gang as well as that of 'one's country.'" Young Billy "remains the only one who can appreciate his own performance." He alone "can be the juggler and juggled, the judge and the judged."[119]

Alfred Kazin, in the *New Republic,* found *Billy Bathgate* "a deliciously irreverent and quite wonderful novel about the life and death of [Dutch] Schultz." Kazin was another who saw its young hero as a latter-day Huck Finn, more precisely, "as the Bronx's own Huck Finn. Like Huck, he is encased in a violence not his own. Like Huck, he is so sentient, self-dependent, and in a sense self-'educated' that he brings a special style of his own to the book." Doctorow's portrait "is quite lyrical at times and amusingly overdrawn in a style that rises at times to Joyce and descends to the darling vernacular of Damon Runyon. . . . With his usual irony about the moneyed goings-on in the upper levels of American society, [Doctorow] has Billy conclude that the gangster world is not untypical of, at least, corporate America." Kazin realized some readers would "bridle at the destined conclusion of the fable." They were likely to be unhappy also with "the all too assured tone in which the grown and successful Billy identifies the slipperiness he has survived with the corporate America in which he now rules." But whether these readers "bridle at the conclusion or not, it is all less serious in the end than what has come before," said Kazin. "And if the conclusion is shocking, it is no less shocking because it is so amusing."[120]

One who not only bridled at the novel but also remained unamused by it was the *New Yorker*'s Terrence Rafferty. Declaring *Billy Bathgate* "a maddeningly peculiar book," he thought it "a novel that explains itself compulsively yet doesn't seem to know itself very well." Doctorow's books are for Rafferty "the work of a sane, civilized, intelligent man who feels driven to look for some trace of himself in the most brutal moments of his country's history. And, in novel after novel, he can't quite find it." This latest effort "is essentially the work of a brilliant student, one who has nearly convinced himself that 'all we are made of is words'—that language is the substance of the world." But in Rafferty's opinion, Doctorow is at his best "when he forgets his craft and gives himself over to his terrors, as in *The Book of Daniel* (which is both his richest and his worst-constructed novel), or when he detaches himself entirely and indulges his talent for lofty, arrogant literary play, as in the first half of *Ragtime*." But Doctorow now "straddles the two modes in *Billy Bathgate*, and leaves the novel in the middle of nowhere"; the sad result is that "it reads like a translation." This is because Doctorow "clings—self-defeatingly—to the notion that the only true culture is that of the Old World. The over-refined prose of *Billy Bathgate* is defensive, a gesture of refusal. It tells us that E. L. Doctorow won't assimilate, won't identify with the worst of America even as he's struggling to interpret it—that juggling and sleight of hand and elegant subterfuge will have to do."[121]

Terence Rafferty may not have cared much for the novel, but Paul Stuewe liked it even less. In a *Quill Quire* review as brief as it is mean-spirited, Stuewe charged that "*Billy Bathgate* reads as if it had been churned out on a word-processing system that didn't support editing. This extraordinarily tedious novel about a New York boy's fascination with Depression-era gangsters has just about everything wrong with it, beginning with a clotted literary style that makes Gertrude Stein seem a model of concision, and plodding on toward an equally presumptuous set of intellectual conceits. Doctorow appears to be under the impression that he is writing a sort of Tom Sawyer meets The Untouchables opus, but what he has produced is a pallid set of variations on the undeniably refreshing melodies of *Ragtime*."[122] Offering an equally negative but much longer critique was Chilton Williamson Jr., in the *National Review*, a magazine whose editors have long had little use for Doctorow's liberal political views. "It is a long time since I have looked at a novel so shamelessly commercial in general intent and so tediously pretentious in execution," he declared. As if giving voice to some personal animus, Williamson insisted he found the book "so ineffably vulgar and so insufferably boring" that he quickly reached "the point where turning over the page becomes . . . a daunting, indeed almost impossible, chore." Williamson accused Doctorow of "writing almost entirely out of control," a lack seen most clearly in Billy Bathgate himself. For this youthful "protagonist's first-person voice remains from start to finish a ludicrously discordant mélange of disparate levels of tone and language." These shortcomings are best seen in the "appalling rhetoric, run-on sentences, false poetry, and fake gusto." Williamson conceded that the novel's second half is "perceptibly better than the first," and that there are "a few good moments . . . and even a few good lines." But the conclusion is "absurd" and, overall, Doctorow should have "abided by an ancient piece of wisdom: If you don't have it, don't flaunt it."[123]

Despite such negative reviews, *Billy Bathgate* had more defenders than attackers. John Leonard was one adamant champion. Just how much he admired the novel Leonard made clear with a review in the *Nation* that was more rhapsodic than analytic. "To the radical politics of *The Book of Daniel,* the revisionist history of *Ragtime* and the collective, elegiac American dream worlds of *Loon Lake* and *World's Fair,*" he declared, "E. L. Doctorow has added some amazing grace and made a masterwork." He deals here with matters as varied as "mobsters and orphans, the East Bronx and the Great Depression, the politics of sex and the psychology of class," Leonard added, but the reader should "think of it . . . as a fairy tale about capitalism. And color it wonderful."[124]

Leonard was also taken with Doctorow's morally persuasive language, but Melvin J. Friedman, in the *Progressive,* was struck primarily by his flair for negotiating "the thin line separating fact from fiction." This is a skill Doctorow sustains, Friedman thought, "more successfully than any of his contemporaries." Here Doctorow again deftly blends history and myth in chronicling his young hero's "changing, disruptive views" of Dutch Schultz's final months. The result, said Friedman, is "a compelling story, elegantly told."[125] Michael Wood, too, was impressed with Doctorow's melding of fact and fiction. In this "picaresque, stylized, smooth-running novel," wrote Wood in the *Times Literary Supplement,* Doctorow "expertly evokes the Depression and the colourful legends that dark time threw up." Most real "is the strength and reach of the gangsters, the allure of their refusal of ordinariness, and the horror" of their vengeful acts. Doctorow catches "both the charm and the horror of the Schultz myth." A more discerning reader than most of the novel's detractors, Wood observed that Doctorow's lush rhetoric is meant to be read as satire. "There is spoof on spoof here," he warned, "a fine travesty of fine writing." For example, there may be "blood everywhere, but it touches no one, fades in the soft focus, leaves no serious trace: an American romance." What readers get, then, concluded Wood, is "an elegant, light-hearted tale of modern butchery, a stylish new relative for *The Godfather,* an offer we could hardly refuse."[126]

English reviewer Boyd Tonkin echoed Wood's emphasis on "legend and romance," but he added a "chivalric" twist. "What chivalry did for the medieval epic, organised crime does for the American imagination," Tonkin wrote in *New Statesman & Society.* This latest effort is Doctorow's "Arthurian novel, hatched to the perennial American tale of a boy's growing-up into the 'realm of high audacity' inhabited by men who start as demigods and end as beasts." His imaginative approach enables Doctorow to a fair degree of literary license. "No one ever spoke like Billy. But this bardic high style whisks the reader breathless through his story." Still, Billy has a long literary "ancestry on his side," Tonkin noted. "The novel was debauched in its cot with legend and rumour. From the days of Fielding's *Life of Jonathan Wild the Great* it battened on to first-division rogues whose exploits mocked and mirrored the deeds of monarchs or heroes. Doctorow's Dutch Schultz belongs in their company. He will also rank high in American fiction's legion of false fathers, those giants of childhood who shrink to midgets in the eye of memory."[127]

Quickly acknowledging Doctorow's use of myth, John Sutherland, in the *London Review of Books,* like so many of the earlier reviewers, emphasized the novel's language and style, which he found both entertaining and troubling. "*Billy Bathgate* is half-fairy-tale, half-Puzo-style shoot-em-up thriller," Sutherland stated. While he found the novel "wonderfully easy to read and in its last pages gripping," Doctorow's language here is marked by its "immensely extended syntax," and its "looping intricately-linked clauses [bear] witness to Billy's skill as a verbal juggler." Yet the end result, as Sutherland saw it, is overkill. For the young hero's "constant overreaching for the ten-dollar word and turn of phrase belies the grand CV which he presents to us. Baloney. Billy Bathgate is another Billy Liar."[128]

A more positive, even enthusiastic, response was that of Marvin LaHood in *World Literature Today.* Doctorow's "brilliant re-creation" of America's violent gangster world "makes the past seem even more vital than the present," he declared. His "game is an ability to re-create the past as if it were still here, part is a style polished enough to do everything he desires, and part is a love of New York that gives his descriptions of it a feel and a texture almost never matched by others." In *Billy Bathgate* all of Doctorow's "extraordinary powers coalesce to produce a profoundly moving, haunting novel."[129] Donald Pease, in the Catholic magazine *America,* also focused on Doctorow's ability to reclaim the past through language, his own and his hero's. "Like his talent for juggling, Billy's gift for fluency takes hold of events otherwise falling out of the time of his life." His true gift is to retain always his mental distance from his own actions and the acts of those around him. The result is that "instead of quite belonging to the Schultz gang, Billy articulates for it the only order capable of preserving it from oblivion." By thus composing *Billy Bathgate* out of his young hero's "divided loyalties," Doctorow has accomplished two things: He has not only recovered the Depression era's "cultural legacy," but he has also produced a novel "that promises to remain as permanent an addition" to this nation's culture "as *The Adventures of Huckleberry Finn,* its cultural predecessor."[130]

XI

Doctorow must have been buoyed by such positive reviews. Still, he waited four years to publish *Jack London, Hemingway, and the Constitution: Selected Essays, 1977–1992.*[131] As the title suggests, this was not another novel but a collection of 14 pieces on historical, political, and literary matters. Not surprisingly, reviews were sparse, as most major publications pay little heed to essay collections. The few reviews that did appear were generally favorable, with one expected negative reaction. Janice Braun, in the *Library Journal*, set the general positive tone by declaring the essays to be "without exception, well crafted, thoughtprovoking, and entertaining." She singled out "False Documents," describing it as "an extraordinary essay on the subjectivity of fact as opposed to the visionary nature of fiction." She liked also Doctorow's "deconstruction of the Constitution," as well as a 1989 speech "that deals damningly with issues of the Reagan/Bush era." She predicted, correctly as it turned out, that this "eloquent articulation" of that Republican administration's legacy "may anger some whose political beliefs are not in accord with those of the author."[132] Alice Joyce, in *Booklist,* struck much the same note, but she focused her brief review primarily on the literary pieces. Doctorow, she noted, "approaches the American literary tradition from various angles, looking at the men behind the classics. Dreiser's *Sister Carrie,* London's *Call of the Wild,* and the posthumous work of Hemingway all provide material for Doctorow's incisive and provocative views." But Joyce also found "trenchant" his comments on Reagan and his presidential successors. "Whether Doctorow is reflecting on the Constitution's sacred status or looking back on James Wright at Kenyon College," she concluded, "the mind of a great humanist is apparent on every page."[133]

Braun's prediction that political conservatives would dislike Doctorow's opinions was borne out by Donald Lyons in the *National Review.* "This exiguous assembly of prefaces and assignments is unstartling," he declared. In fact, "in this salad bar of limp banalities, there is not a fresh thought, a crisp phrase, or a morsel of original research." Lest any reader not grasp fully his disdain for his subject, Lyons finished up with a painfully familiar smear. "The dreariest thing about this book," he literally snarled, "is its inability ever to rise above generic comsympsprach."[134] A calmer, more balanced reading was that of English reviewer Stephen Fender, who divided his *Times Literary Supplement* discussion between Doctorow's essays and his new novel, *The Waterworks.* For Fender, Doctorow's most significant essay is "False Documents," with its insightful distinctions between history and fiction. In fact, Fender was impressed with the entire collection. "Trenchant and illuminating as they are on topics ranging from Dreiser and Jack London to popular songs and the American Constitution," he stated, "these essays provide a key to the author's own work in a way that no other criticism by a contemporary novelist does." Doctorow's direct aim in his fiction, said Fender, has been "to deconstruct crucial episodes in American political history and to rebuild them out of the hidden, or suppressed, or forgotten 'false documents' of his own speculative imagination." But Doctorow does have to meet the challenge of apparent authenticity. "If Doctorow's false documents were just false," Fender explained, "they would stand no chance against the official facts they confront. It is their documentary nature—or the appearance of it—that makes them authentic."[135]

XII

Fender then moved on to discuss briefly Doctorow's ninth novel, *The Waterworks*,[136] which was then making its Spring 1994 appearance in both America and England. The new work, he stated, "is a Poe-like novel of detection." But it is also "a story in which the mystery, as befits Doctorow's project, involves civic, as well as familial and individual issues." What made the novel "worth reading," he thought, were "the inventive details" of its "improbable but believable chain of events." For, as do "all good novels of detection," *The Waterworks* "resolves its mystery through the patient investigations of freelancers and renegades: reporters and policemen out of favour with their bosses. And that's what Doctorow is too." He may not lack readers, sales, and literary prizes, said Fender, but Doctorow does remain "something of a renegade in his pursuit of the American historical imagination."[137]

The novel is narrated in retrospective old age by McIlvaine (no first name given), a quick-witted but lapsed Presbyterian and former city editor of the *New York Evening Telegraph*. The action year is 1871, when the corruptions of the Grant administration are known to all, and Boss Tweed runs the city's political machine. Graft, greed, and grime prevail, and Horatio Alger's would-be heroes are nowhere to be seen. Children are the city's primary victims, with grimy young girls selling flowers or themselves in alleys and newsboys brawling viciously for street corners. Action truly begins with the disappearance of Martin Pemberton, the editor's favorite freelance book reviewer. Moody and uncompromising, young Martin could have been rich since his profiteering father, the notorious Augustus Pemberton, had amassed vast sums by slave trading and war profiteering. Objecting instead to his father's venality and immorality, Martin has been disowned. His handsome young stepmother has voiced no complaints, but when old Pemberton dies she is left destitute: the family fortune is nowhere to be found.

Just before Martin vanishes, he tells friends he has seen his allegedly dead father riding around in a white horse-drawn coach with five other ghostly looking old men in black coats and top hats. (Black and white prove the novel's basic colors.) McIlvaine turns to the one official he trusts, Captain Edmund Donne of the Municipal Police, that redoubtable "organization of licensed thieves." (Doctorow may have been reading Ambrose Bierce.) Donne proves an upright man of uncommon height and shrewdness. As the pair pursue their investigation, a surprisingly ghoulish tale unfolds. Readers will detect echoes not only of Sherlock Holmes and Dr. Watson but also of the familiar pop-culture escapades of mad scientists and vampires, the night openings of graves and coffins, police informers, the finding and decoding of documents, a child-buying ring, and the pursuit by wealthy tycoons (like *Ragtime*'s J. P. Morgan) of eternal life. New York City itself, seething as it does with frenetic street hustlers, urchins, thugs, and corrupt officials, becomes the novel's central character.

Donne and McIlvaine soon find that Pemberton's ailing father, Augustus, is involved in an elaborate medical experiment. It is conducted by a brilliant but cold-blooded German émigré, Dr. Wrede Sartorius (an obvious echo of Thomas Carlyle's savage satire of English society, *Sartor Resartus*). Having proved himself a brilliant Civil War surgeon, Sartorius now prolongs the lives of old millionaires by draining into them the blood, bone marrow, and glandular matter of unwanted street children. In the process he extracts their fortunes. With ironic humor, Doctorow attributes to his madly amoral scientist surgical methods that are now common medical procedures. The obsessed doctor's "scientific orphanage" (his Home for Little Wanderers) is hidden in the Croton Holding Reservoir—that is, the municipal "waterworks" on 42nd Street. Doctorow wants his readers to see the reservoir as his central symbol of urban corruption. To underscore this point, he has McIlvaine recall the reservoir's dedication day and his feeling then that, as "the wheels are turned, the sluice gates are opened and the water thunders in . . . [it is] as if it were not a reservoir at all, but a baptismal font for the gigantic absolution we require as a people" (*TW*, 61).

Led by Edmund Donne and McIlvaine, the police finally raid the waterworks and discover the doctor's "research institute," with its half-dozen zombielike patients, their deaf-and-dumb female caretakers, and in a basement cell the now-catatonic Martin Pemberton. The doctor is arrested, young Martin is reunited with his faithful Emily, and the good police captain wins the hand of the beautiful young widow. Despite this seemingly happy Dickensian conclusion, the novel closes with the narrator, still battling his memory, recalling a frozen, deserted metropolis. It was, states McIlvaine, a Sunday, and everything appeared "still, unmoving, stricken, as if the entire city of New York would be forever encased and frozen, aglitter and God-stunned. And let me leave you with that illusion . . . though in reality we would soon be driving ourselves up Broadway in the new Year of Our Lord, 1872" (*TW*, 253).

In a brief interview with Laurel Graeber of the *New York Times Book Review,* Doctorow offered a few thoughts on his new novel. The book, he felt, might well be the one he was most destined to write. "I was named for Edgar Allan Poe," he noted. "My father, particularly, was an admirer of Poe's work. This book, in many senses a 19th-century tale—I love that word—may . . . [signify] my finally coming around to do Poe honor," despite his having been "a drug-addicted, alcohol-abusing narcissist." Indeed, *The Waterworks* had its genesis in the short sketch of the same title in Doctorow's *Lives of The Poets.* In that sketch a bearded stranger spots an abandoned toy boat floating in a reservoir. Entering the nearby waterworks building, he comes upon the body of a drowned child. Pulling the boy from the water, the man wraps him in his coat and rushes out of the building and into a waiting carriage. The somber vignette ends without explanation. Unable to get those images out of his mind, Doctorow began to expand them. (For example, his novel's narrator, the former newspaperman McIlvaine, is haunted by his recollection of seeing a drowned child in the reservoir, with the boy's toy boat drifting helplessly against the tank walls.) Doctorow quickly realized his story now "had to be a 19th-century piece because of the waterworks." He knew that the huge Croton Holding Reservoir had occupied the site at 42nd Street and Fifth Avenue, "where the New York Public Library now stands, so I had my city."[138]

But he had not planned anything else. His book, he explained, gave him "gifts" as he wrote it. The major gift was the narrator, McIlvaine, whose journalistic profession supplied Doctorow with his strongest image. This was, in Graeber's paraphrase, "the 19th-century newspaper page, printed in seven uniform columns with no banner headlines." Doctorow explained that he "saw how that image could describe the different things McIlvaine has to accommodate as he uncovers this story." For the columns are "apparently unrelated parallel descents, as he calls them." Another happy surprise for Doctorow was the degree to which the city and its "amoral spirit" pervaded his narrative and enabled him to realize he "was writing about everyone Edith Wharton had left out." In effect, said Doctorow, "this was the rest of us, as it were."[139]

Donna Seaman, in *Booklist,* agreed that the "suspenseful" new work was "an entirely different creature than its predecessors." The setting is New York City during the Civil War's "frenzied and cynical aftermath," Seaman observed. "Doctorow revels in dramatic descriptions of the rapidly mutating cityscape while he dramatizes life's brutal pragmatism and our capacity for sinister acts. Gothic and penetrating, rooted in Poe and Melville, and crisply written, this [novel] is a rare treat."[140] Barbara Hoffert, in the *Library Journal,* was a shade less impressed. "Doctorow wants us to think about issues of mortality and morality," she noted, "and indeed this piece works better as a philosophical treatise than a novel. The points are neatly made, the characters well etched, and the plot hums along nicely, but it doesn't quite come alive."[141] Walter Goodman, in the *New Leader,* expressed similar disappointment. "Now, if the reader is expected to get into the spirit of such an adventure, to take it seriously on its own terms, the author is obliged to provide a fascinating character or two, plot surprises, dramatic confrontations and so forth. *The Waterworks* is short on all these ingredients." Goodman compares Doctorow to a skilled and "veteran captain who keeps his ship moving along more or less steadily despite dire thumping in the hold." The trouble is that "the voyage is not much fun, and when the ship is finally unloaded the payoff is slight."[142]

Ted Solotaroff expressed a very different opinion. In a lengthy essay-review in the *Nation,* Solotaroff argued that *The Waterworks* embodies elements not only of Edgar Allan Poe and "the dark meditative tales and romances" of the last century's early years but also of such post–Civil War realists as James, Twain, Howells, and Crane. Equally evident throughout is Herman Melville's brooding presence; his looming shadow has caused Doctorow to weave his darkly negative allegory into "a distinctively American" update of "the era of the New England oversoul and whaling industry." Yet *The Waterworks* is also "controlled by a direct, reportorial realism that looks forward to the urban, industrial-age fiction of Crane, Upton Sinclair and Dreiser." This rich two-layered context moves Solotaroff to declare Doctorow "a remarkable writer" who repeatedly "casts his imagination into a patch of American history" and offers up an accurately "rendered, resonating 'repository of myth.'" Collectively, then, Doctorow's novels "form a highly composed vision of American history."[143]

Historian Simon Schama, in the *New York Times Book Review,* was reminded of a "wicked" sketch ("One Summer Night") by Ambrose Bierce, which, although only two pages long, is "a coffin-side view of an exhumation." Schama pointed out that an exhumation plays an important role in Doctorow's "startling and spellbinding new novel." But he thought that "what Mr. Doctorow has truly exhumed are the remains of the 19th-century genre of the science-detection mystery, originated by Poe and richly developed by Bierce and Wilkie Collins." Yet Doctorow has designed his book not as a ghost story but as "a heavyweight novel of ideas, an allegory of vitality, mortality and the manipulation of nature." More precisely, most of Doctorow's "novels have been, to some degree, documents of New York history." But here that city "is no longer a setting for the action: it *is* the action, the principal character, the presiding genius and the trap of history." Doctorow has captured "this vision of a gaslight necropolis, where distinctions between the living and the dead are blurred by the presence of so many species of dead-and-alive souls, with forensic precision."[144]

Paul Gray, of *Time,* was less taken by the novel than was Schama, but he still found much to admire in its "story." Even his "longtime readers," Gray stated, "are likely to find *The Waterworks* Doctorow's strangest and most problematic invention so far." For example, even the shocking, Poe-like tale at the center of the novel does not achieve the emblematic significance that Doctorow wishes it to have. It is simply too bizarre to stand for—or comment on—anything outside itself, particularly the entire City of New York." In fact, the narrative "is at its best when Doctorow stops McIlvaine's huffing and puffing about social significance and lets him get on with the business of telling an entertaining and sometimes truly haunting story."[145]

Luc Sante, in the *New York Review of Books,* traced those earlier writers whose works provided Doctorow with literary prototypes for his novel. *The Waterworks,* Sante noted, "owes its form to a mode slightly later than the period of its setting, the 'scientific romance.' Such is its flavor—cartoonish and cryptic, flatfooted and lyrical, slight and profound at once." Its two dogged heroes "uncover a hidden world presided over by the mysterious Doctor Sartorius. In this realm unimaginably sinister depths are sounded, justified by the claims of pure disinterested science. This is a familiar state of affairs for the genre, and Dr. Sartorius is a familiar figure." He evokes "Wells's Dr. Moreau, Verne's Dr. Ox, Gustave Le Rouge's Dr. Cornelius, and a long line of twisted medicos down to Dr. Mabuse and Dr. Phibes, all of them descended from Dr. Frankenstein." Doctorow does not quite meld these outsized figures and their outlandish actions, Sante insisted. "In the end, the novel's contradictions are not resolved. But then contradictions are at the heart of the plot. For Doctorow seems to be saying 'that progress is a slippery matter, that change does not move in a straight line, and that orders of succession are not to be trusted. Fathers can succeed sons . . . and the present has little to teach the past.'" The only true constant for Doctorow is "change . . . as New York, of all cities, proves by its history."[146] In his much shorter *Newsweek* review, Malcolm Jones Jr. also charged Doctorow with "heisting" his latest characters, plot, and setting from familiar folk history and its legends. "[Y]ou're likely to have the feeling," he warned the reader, "that you've heard this tale—or better yet, seen it—somewhere before." It is essentially "a sci-fi-horror movie masquerading as a novel, with every wisp of fog, every plot twist in place. It's a terrific piece of literary larceny." In Doctorow's "artful hands, Manhattan becomes the book's most memorable character, its flawed hero. The gutter vitality of the grimy old city seeps through every page, malign but also magical. . . . Doctorow is not a first-rate thinker. What he has to say about the evils of power and unchecked ambition has been better said elsewhere. But he knows the art of storytelling inside and out, and in *The Waterworks* he weaves a spell of genuine creepiness."[147]

XIII

Many reviewers and critics would dispute Jones's claim that "Doctorow is not a first-rate thinker," whatever that may mean. Here there is no room to debate that contention or to summarize the countless critical essays written about Doctorow's novels. But, as can be seen from the essays included in this volume, while they broaden, deepen, and enrich the critical profile that emerges from the reviews, they do not alter it in any substantial way. What is incontestable is that Doctorow has published eight novels, one drama, a volume of short stories, screenplays for two of his own novels, the text for a book of American photographs, and a collection of essays. His work has been translated into more than 20 languages, and three of his novels, *Welcome to Hard Times, Ragtime,* and *Billy Bathgate,* have been made into films. And as the world is well aware, the musical version of *Ragtime* has been a smashing success on Broadway and around the country.

In addition, the numerous honors and awards he has garnered for his work establish Doctorow as one of the most respected as well as most popular writers in recent American letters. His *Book of Daniel* was nominated for a National Book Award in 1972. The next year Doctorow was appointed a Guggenheim Fellow and a Creative Artists Service Fellow (1973–1974). In 1976, *Ragtime* won him his first National Book Critics Circle Award. In 1978, his play *Drinks Before Dinner* was produced by the New York Shakespeare Festival and published the following year. Also in 1979, Hobart & William Smith Colleges awarded him a Litt.D. The next year *Loon Lake* received a National Book Award nomination, and in 1986 *World's Fair* won the National Book Award. In 1989 *Billy Bathgate* was nominated for a National Book Award, and in 1990 it won the PEN/Faulkner Award for Fiction, the National Book Critics Circle Award (Doctorow's second), and the William Dean Howells Medal of the American Academy of Arts and Letters. Doctorow's latest novel, *The Waterworks,* was a national best-seller. A concerned member of the American Academy and Institute of Arts and Letters, Doctorow is a director of the Authors Guild, a director of PEN, and an active participant in the Writers Guild of America. All in all, E. L. Doctorow is a formidable presence in contemporary American literature and the arts.

Notes

1.   Wayne Warga, "No Retreating by E. L. Doctorow," *Los Angeles Times,* October 3, 1980, sec. 5, p. 2.

2.   Larry McCaffery, "A Spirit of Transgression," in *E. L. Doctorow: Essays and Conversations,* ed. Richard Trenner (Princeton, N.J.: Ontario Review Press, 1983), 35. Also published in *Anything Can Happen: Interviews with Contemporary American Novelists,* ed. Tom LeClair and Larry McCaffery (Urbana: University of Illinois Press, 1983), 91–105. All page references here are to the Trenner volume.

3.   Paul Gray, "Attentive to the Mysteries," *Time,* February 27, 1989, 76.

4.   McCaffery, "A Spirit of Transgression," 33, 39.

5.   E. L. Doctorow, *Welcome to Hard Times* (New York: Random House, 1960; New York: Penguin, 1988). Hereafter all page references are to the Penguin edition and cited in text as *WHT.*

6.   Daniel L. Zins, "E. L. Doctorow: The Novelist as Historian," *Hollins Critic* 36, no. 5 (December 1976): 4.

7.   Sabine Sauter, "E. L. Doctorow," in *Contemporary Jewish-American Novelists: A Bio-Critical Sourcebook,* ed. Joel Shatsky and Michael Taub (Westport, Conn.: Greenwood Press, 1997), 56.

8.   John T. Osborne, a review of *Welcome to Hard Times,* by E. L. Doctorow, *Library Journal,* September 1, 1960, 2956.

9.   S. E. B., "Novel of Old West by E. L. Doctorow," a review of *Welcome to Hard Times,* by E. L. Doctorow, *Springfield (Mass.) Republican,* September 18, 1960, sec. D, p. 5.

10.   Wirt Williams, "Bad Man from Bodie," a review of *Welcome to Hard Times,* by E. L. Doctorow, *New York Times Book Review,* September 25, 1960, 15.

11.   Oscar Lewis, "A Realistic Western," a review of *Welcome to Hard Times,* by E. L. Doctorow, *New York Herald Tribune Lively Arts,* January 22, 1960, 40.

12. In fact, Mr. Doctorow was the house editor of my first book, Joseph Gaer and Ben Siegel, *The Puritan Heritage: America's Roots in the Bible* (New York: New American Library, 1964).

13. McCaffery, "A Spirit of Transgression," 32–33.

14. Guy Flatly, "Author as Actor? Sweet Success Played in *Ragtime*," *Los Angeles Times Calendar,* October 12, 1975, 75.

15. E. L. Doctorow, *Big as Life* (New York: Simon and Schuster, 1966).

16. Gwendolyn Brooks, "The Menace," a review of *Big as Life,* by E. L. Doctorow, *Book Week,* July 10, 1966, 17.

17. A review of *Big as Life,* by E. L Doctorow, *Choice,* November 1966, 769.

18. Malcolm M. Ferguson, a review of *Big as Life,* by E. L. Doctorow, *Library Journal,* April 15, 1966, 2086.

19. McCaffery, "A Spirit of Transgression," 37.

20. Ibid., 36.

21. E. L. Doctorow, *The Book of Daniel* (New York: Random House, 1971).

22. Stanley Kauffmann, "Wrestling Society for a Soul," a review of *The Book of Daniel,* by E. L. Doctorow, *New Republic,* June 15, 1971, 25.

23. Ibid., 25–27.

24. Peter S. Prescott, "Lion's Den," a review of *The Book of Daniel,* by E. L. Doctorow, *Newsweek,* June 7, 1971, 114.

25. Aaron L. Fessler, a review of *The Book of Daniel,* by E. L. Doctorow, *Library Journal,* June 15, 1971, 2.

26. Jerome Charyn, "Deprived of the Right to Be Dangerous," a review of *The Book of Daniel,* by E. L. Doctorow, *New York Times Book Review,* July 4, 1971, 6.

27. Bernard Hrico, a review of *The Book of Daniel,* by E. L. Doctorow, *Best Sellers,* August 15, 1971, 218-19.

28. R. S., a review of *The Book of Daniel,* by E. L. Doctorow, *Harper's* 243 (August 1971): 94.

29. McCaffery, "A Spirit of Transgression," 39.

30. Ibid., 40–41.

31. E. L. Doctorow, *Ragtime* (New York: Random House, 1975; New York: Penguin, 1996). Hereafter all page references are to the Penguin edition and cited in text as *R.*

32. Flatly, "Author as Actor?," 75.

33. Zins, "The Novelist as Historian," 9.

34. Flatly, "Author as Actor?," 75.

35. Stanley Kauffmann, "A Central Vision," a review of *Ragtime,* by E. L. Doctorow, *Saturday Review,* July 26, 1975, 20.

36. Ibid., 20–21.

37. See Robert E. Helbling, *Heinrich von Kleist: The Major Works* (New York: New Directions, 1975). See also Kenneth L. Donelson, *Teaching Guide to E. L. Doctorow's Ragtime* (New York: Bantam Books, 1976), 46.

38. George Stade, "A Fiction Made of History, Which in Turn Was Made of Fictions," a review of *Ragtime,* by E. L. Doctorow, *New York Times Book Review,* July 6, 1975, 2.

39. R. Z. Sheppard, "The Music of Time," a review of *Ragtime,* by E. L. Doctorow, *Time,* July 14, 1975, 64.

40. Walter Clemons, "Houdini, Meet Ferdinand," a review of *Ragtime,* by E. L. Doctorow, *Newsweek,* July 14, 1975, 73, 76.

41. "Briefly Noted," a review of *Ragtime,* by E. L. Doctorow, *New Yorker,* July 28, 1975, 79.

42. Jeffrey Hart, "Doctorow Time," a review of *Ragtime,* by E. L. Doctorow, *National Review,* August 15, 1975, 893.

43. Alfred P. Klausler, "Portrait of an Era," a review of *Ragtime,* by E. L. Doctorow, *Christian Century,* September 3–10, 1975, 77.

44. Joseph Moses, "To Impose a Phrasing on History," a review of *Ragtime,* by E. L. Doctorow, *Nation,* October 4, 1975, 310, 312.

45. Leonard Kriegel, "The Stuff of Fictional History," a review of *Ragtime,* by E. L. Doctorow, *Commonweal,* December 19, 1975, 631–32.

46. Roger Sale, "From Ragtime to Riches," a review of *Ragtime,* by E. L. Doctorow, *New York Review of Books,* August 7, 1975, 21–22.

47. Hilton Kramer, "Political Romance," a review of *Ragtime,* by E. L. Doctorow, *Commentary* 60 (October 1975): 79.

48. Martin Green, "Nostalgia Politics," a review of *Ragtime,* by E. L. Doctorow, *American Scholar* 45 (Winter 1975–1976): 842–43.

49. Richard Todd, "The Most-Overrated-Book-of-the-Year Award, and Other Literary Prizes," a review of *Ragtime,* by E. L. Doctorow, *Atlantic* 237 (January 1976): 95–96.

50. Maureen Howard, "Recent Novels: A Backward Glance," a review of *Ragtime,* by E. L. Doctorow, *Yale Review* 65 (Spring 1976): 406–7.

51. Philip French, "In Darkest Disneyland," a review of *Ragtime,* by E. L. Doctorow, *New Statesman,* January 23, 1976, 103.

52. Russell Davies, "Mingle with the Mighty," a review of *Ragtime,* by E. L. Doctorow, *Times Literary Supplement,* January 23, 1976, 77.

53. "Birth of the Blues," a review of *Ragtime,* by E. L. Doctorow, *Economist,* January 24, 1976, 108.

54. Jonathan Raban, "Easy Virtue: On Doctorow's *Ragtime,*" a review of *Ragtime,* by E. L. Doctorow, *Encounter* 46 (February 1976): 72, 74.

55. Flatly, "Author as Actor?," 75.

56. McCaffery, "A Spirit of Transgression," 43.

57. Ibid., 43.

58. Warga, "No Retreating," 16, 2.

59. Flatly, Author as Actor?," 1, 75–76.

60. McCaffery, "A Spirit of Transgression," 45.

61. E. L. Doctorow, *Drinks Before Dinner: A Play* (New York: Random House, 1979; New York: Theatre Communications Group, 1996). Hereafter all page references in the text are to the later edition and cited as *DBD.*

62. Lee F. Kornblum, a review of *Drinks Before Dinner: A Play,* by E. L. Doctorow, *Library Journal,* January 15, 1979, 1353.

63. Martin McNamee, a review of *Drinks Before Dinner: A Play,* by E. L. Doctorow, *Best Sellers* 39 (October 1979): 262.

64. A review of *Drinks Before Dinner: A Play,* by E. L. Doctorow, *Choice,* November 16, 1979, 1170.

65. E. L. Doctorow, *Loon Lake* (New York: Random House, 1980).

66. McCaffery, "A Spirit of Transgression," 39–40.

67. John Lucas, "Dust Behind the Dream," a review of *Loon Lake,* by E. L. Doctorow, *Times Literary Supplement,* November 7, 1980, 1250.

68. George Stade, "Types Defamiliarized," a review of *Loon Lake,* by E. L. Doctorow, *Nation,* September 27, 1980, 285.

69. Ibid., 285.

70. Ibid., 286.

71. Paul Gray, "The Nightmare and the Dream," a review of *Loon Lake,* by E. L. Doctorow, *Time,* September 22, 1980, 81.

72. Peter S. Prescott, "Doctorow's Daring Epic," a review of *Loon Lake,* by E. L. Doctorow, *Newsweek,* September 15, 1980, 88–89.

73. Robert Towers, "A Brilliant World of Mirrors," a review of *Loon Lake,* by E. L. Doctorow, *New York Times Book Review,* September 28, 1980, 47.

74. Mark Harris, a review of *Loon Lake*, by E. L. Doctorow, *New Republic*, September 20, 1980, 31–34.

75. Pearl K. Bell, "Singing the Same Old Songs," a review of *Loon Lake*, by E. L. Doctorow, *Commentary*, October 1980, 70–72.

76. Diane Johnson, "Waiting for Righty," a review of *Loon Lake*, by E. L. Doctorow, *New York Review of Books*, November 6, 1980, 19–20.

77. Saul Maloff, "The American Dream in Fragments," a review of *Loon Lake*, by E. L. Doctorow, *Commonweal*, November 7, 1980, 628–30.

78. Douglas C. Runnels, "Restless Roads," a review of *Loon Lake*, by E. L. Doctorow, *Christian Century*, January 7–14, 1981, 20–21.

79. Richard H. King, "Two Lights That Failed," a review of *Loon Lake*, by E. L. Doctorow, *Virginia Quarterly Review* 57 (Spring 1981): 342–46, 350.

80. Donald Curran, "Fiction," a review of *Loon Lake*, by E. L. Doctorow, *World Literature Today* 55 (Summer 1981): 472.

81. Thomas Lavoie, a review of *Loon Lake*, by E. L. Doctorow, *Library Journal*, October 1, 1980, 2105.

82. Anthony Burgess, "Doctorow's Hit Is a Miss," a review of *Loon Lake*, by E. L. Doctorow, *Saturday Review* 7 (September 1980): 66–67.

83. Nicholas Shrimpton, "New Jersey Joe," a review of *Loon Lake*, by E. L. Doctorow, *New Statesman*, October 31, 1980, 27.

84. Lucas, "Dust Behind the Dream," 1250.

85. Alan Brownjohn, "Breaking the Rules," a review of *Loon Lake*, by E. L. Doctorow, *Encounter* 56 (May 1981): 86.

86. Douglas Hill, "From Ragtime to Mood Indigo," a review of *Loon Lake*, by E. L. Doctorow, *Books in Canada* 10 (February 1981): 21.

87. E. L. Doctorow, *Lives of the Poets: Six Stories and a Novella* (New York: Random House, 1984).

88. Peter S. Prescott, "The Creative Muse," a review of *Lives of the Poets: Six Stories and a Novella*, by E. L. Doctorow, *Newsweek*, November 19, 1984, 107.

89. C. G. Storms, a review of *Lives of the Poets: Six Stories and a Novella*, by E. L. Doctorow, *Choice*, March 1985, 987.

90. Andrianne Blue, a review of *Lives of the Poets: Six Stories and a Novella*, by E. L. Doctorow, *New Statesman*, April 5, 1985, 32.

91. Adam Mars-Jones, "Boosting the Status of the Text," a review of *Lives of the Poets: Six Stories and a Novella*, by E. L. Doctorow, *Times Literary Supplement*, April 5, 1985, 367.

92. John Skow, "Between Books," a review of *Lives of the Poets: Six Stories and a Novella*, by E. L. Doctorow, *Time*, December 24, 1984, 69–70.

93. Richard D. Beards, "Fiction," a review of *Lives of the Poets: Six Stories and a Novella*, by E. L. Doctorow, *World Literature Today* (Summer 1985): 427.

94. Benjamin DeMott, "Pilgrim Among the Culturati," a review of *Lives of the Poets: Six Stories and a Novella*, by E. L. Doctorow, *New York Times Book Review*, November 11, 1984, 1.

95. James Wolcott, "Rag Time," a review of *Lives of the Poets: Six Stories and a Novella*, by E. L. Doctorow, *New Republic*, December 3, 1984, 31.

96. Robert Towers, "Light and Lively," a review of *Lives of the Poets: Six Stories and a Novella*, by E. L. Doctorow, *New York Review of Books*, December 6, 1984, 34.

97. Herbert Mitgang, "Finding the Right Voice," a review of *Lives of the Poets: Six Stories and a Novella*, by E. L. Doctorow, *New York Times Book Review*, November 11, 1984, 36.

98. E. L. Doctorow, *World's Fair* (New York: Random House, 1985).

99. David Leavitt, "Looking Back on the World of Tomorrow," a review of *World's Fair*, by E. L. Doctorow, *New York Times Book Review*, November 10, 1985, 3.

100.   Whitney Balliett, "Mel-O-Rols, Knickers, and Gee Bee Racers," a review of *World's Fair*, by E. L. Doctorow, *New Yorker*, December 9, 1985, 157, 160.

101.   Leavitt, "Looking Back," 3.

102.   Walter Clemons, "In the Shadow of the War," a review of *World's Fair*, by E. L. Doctorow, *Newsweek*, November 4, 1985, 69.

103.   R. Z. Sheppard, "The Artist as a Very Young Critic," a review of *World's Fair*, by E. L. Doctorow, *Time*, November 18, 1985, 100.

104.   Balliett, "Mel-O-Rols," 157.

105.   Edmund White, "Pyrography," a review of *World's Fair*, by E. L. Doctorow, *Nation*, November 30, 1985, 594–95.

106.   "Fiction," a review of *World's Fair*, by E. L. Doctorow, *School Library Journal* 32 (February 1986): 102.

107.   Robert Towers, "Three-Part Invention," a review of *World's Fair*, by E. L. Doctorow, *New York Review of Books*, December 19, 1985, 23–24.

108.   Phoebe-Lou Adams, a review of *World's Fair*, by E. L. Doctorow, *Atlantic Monthly* 256 (December 1985): 119.

109.   Mary C. Erler, a review of *World's Fair*, by E. L. Doctorow, *America*, March 8, 1986, 193.

110.   D. Keith Mano, "That Trivial Finesse," a review of *World's Fair*, by E. L. Doctorow, *National Review*, March 14, 1986, 54–55.

111.   E. L. Doctorow, *Billy Bathgate* (New York: Random House, 1988).

112.   Anne Tyler, "An American Boy in Gangland," a review of *Billy Bathgate*, by E. L. Doctorow, *New York Times Book Review*, February 26, 1989, 1.

113.   Peter S. Prescott, "Getting into Dutch," a review of *Billy Bathgate*, by E. L. Doctorow, *Newsweek*, February 13, 1989, 76.

114.   Barbara Hoffert, "Fiction," a review of *Billy Bathgate*, by E. L. Doctorow, *Library Journal*, February 15, 1989, 176.

115.   Tyler, "An American Boy in Gangland," 46.

116.   Michael Freitag, "The Attraction of the Disreputable," *New York Times Book Review*, February 26, 1989, 46.

117.   Paul Gray, "Attentive to Mysteries," *Time*, February 27, 1989, 76.

118.   Paul Gray, "In the Shadow of Dutch Schultz," a review of *Billy Bathgate*, by E. L. Doctorow, *Time*, February 27, 1989, 76–77.

119.   Gary Wills, "Juggler's Code," a review of *Billy Bathgate*, by E. L. Doctorow, *New York Review of Books*, March 2, 1989, 3–4.

120.   Alfred Kazin, "Huck in the Bronx," a review of *Billy Bathgate*, by E. L. Doctorow, *New Republic*, March 20, 1989, 41–42.

121.   Terence Rafferty, "World's Apart," a review of *Billy Bathgate*, by E. L. Doctorow, *New Yorker*, March 27, 1989, 112–14.

122.   Paul Stuewe, "Of Some Import," a review of *Billy Bathgate*, by E. L. Doctorow, *Quill Quire* 55 (April 1989): 22.

123.   Chilton Williamson Jr., "An Amphibian Journey," a review of *Billy Bathgate*, by E. L. Doctorow, *National Review*, May 5, 1989, 53–54.

124.   John Leonard, "Bye Bye Billy," a review of *Billy Bathgate*, by E. L. Doctorow, *Nation*, April 3, 1989, 454–56.

125.   Melvin J. Friedman, "Boy in Gangland," a review of *Billy Bathgate*, by E. L. Doctorow, *Progressive*, August 1989, 38–39.

126.   Michael Wood, "Light and Lethal American Romance," a review of *Billy Bathgate*, by E. L. Doctorow, *Times Literary Supplement*, September 15–21, 1989, 997–98.

127.   Boyd Tonkin, "A Round Table Story," a review of *Billy Bathgate*, by E. L. Doctorow, *New Statesman & Society*, September 15, 1989, 37.

128. John Sutherland, "Shakespeare the Novelist," a review of *Billy Bathgate,* by E. L. Doctorow, *London Review of Books,* September 28, 1986, 26.

129. Marvin J. LaHood, "English: Fiction," a review of *Billy Bathgate,* by E. L. Doctorow, *World Literature Today* 64 (Winter 1990): 111.

130. Donald E. Pease, a review of *Billy Bathgate,* by E. L. Doctorow, *America,* May 13, 1989, 457.

131. E. L. Doctorow, Jack London, Hemingway, and the Constitution: Selected Essays: 1977–1992 (New York: Random House, 1993). In England, the book was titled more simply Poets and Presidents: Selected Essays, 1977–1992 and was published as a Macmillan paperback.

132. Janice Braun, "Literature," a review of *Jack London, Hemingway, and the Constitution: Selected Essays: 1977–1992,* by E. L. Doctorow, *Library Journal,* September 15, 1993, 74.

133. Alice Joyce, "Literature," a review of *Jack London, Hemingway, and the Constitution: Selected Essays: 1977–1992,* by E. L. Doctorow, *Booklist,* September 15, 1993, 118.

134. Donald Lyons, "Books in Brief," a review of *Jack London, Hemingway, and the Constitution: Selected Essays: 1977–1992,* by E. L. Doctorow, *National Review,* December 27, 1993, 72.

135. Stephen Fender, "The Novelist as Liar," a review of *Jack London, Hemingway, and the Constitution: Selected Essays: 1977–1992,* by E. L. Doctorow, *Times Literary Supplement,* May 27, 1994, 20.

136. E. L. Doctorow, *The Waterworks* (New York: Random House. 1994); hereafter cited in the text as *TW.*

137. Fender, "The Novelist as Liar," 20.

138. Laurel Graeber, "Left Out by Edith Wharton," a review of *The Waterworks,* by E. L. Doctorow, *New York Times Book Review,* June 19, 1994, 31.

139. Ibid., 31.

140. Donna Seaman, a review of *The Waterworks,* by E. L. Doctorow, *Booklist,* April 15, 1994, 1485.

141. Barbara Hoffert, a review of *The Waterworks,* by E. L. Doctorow, *Library Journal,* April 15, 1994, 111.

142. Walter Goodman, "Adrift in Old New York," a review of *The Waterworks,* by E. L. Doctorow, *New Leader,* June 6–20, 1994, 35.

143. Ted Solotaroff, "Of Melville, Poe and Doctorow," a review of *The Waterworks,* by E. L. Doctorow, *Nation,* June 6, 1994, 784–85, 789–90.

144. Simon Schama, "New York, Gaslight Necropolis," a review of *The Waterworks,* by E. L. Doctorow, *New York Times Book Review,* June 19, 1994, 1, 31.

145. Paul Gray, "City of the Living Dead," a review of *The Waterworks,* by E. L. Doctorow, *Time,* June 20, 1994, 66.

146. Luc Sante, "The Cabinet of Dr. Sartorius," a review of *The Waterworks,* by E. L. Doctorow, *New York Review of Books,* June 23, 1994, 10–12.

147. Malcolm Jones Jr., "A Gothic Tale of Horror in Old New York," a review of *The Waterworks,* by E. L. Doctorow, *Newsweek,* June 27, 1994, 53.

REVIEWS
◆

Novel of Old West
[Review of *Welcome to Hard Times*]

S. E. B.

Welcome to Hard Times by E. L. Doctorow is a novel about a small town in the barren West at the close of the last century, in which the author uses the stark and elemental background of the frontier as an unconventional stage for presenting the timeless strategy of the strength of destructiveness and the weakness of good will.

The tale revolves around a bad-man who destroys the town of Hard Times in one day, casually and cruelly; a mayor who is too weak to kill the bad-man but who is hopeful enough to rebuild the town, and a woman of easy virtue who waits, in terror and hatred for the return of the bad-man. Despite the familiar setting, the author puts aside the shop-worn sentiment and melodrama of the usual western novel and uses the conventional framework for the creation of a serious literary structure.

Reprinted with permission from the *Springfield Sunday Republican,* September 18, 1960, 5.

A Realistic Western
[Review of *Welcome to Hard Times*]

OSCAR LEWIS

The town of Hard Times was located somewhere in the Dakotas during the latter part of the last century: a straggling line of tents and false-front wooden shacks that sheltered, among other things, a carpenter shop, an Indian's cabin, a general store, and a combination saloon, gambling joint and brothel. As the story opens, the spot is playing unwilling host to a ruthless killer and all-round badman who speedily reduces the place to a shambles and rides off again, without a hand having been laid on him.

After such a beginning, few readers of Westerns will have much doubt as to what's coming next. For obviously this is yet another of the hell-raising, free-shooting horse operas that have entertained generations.

During the early stages, the present yarn faithfully follows that tried and true formula. The book's "hero"—who is also the narrator—is the unofficial mayor of the place, a timid soul who lacks the courage to thwart the badman, and who goes about patiently bringing the dead town back to life, all the while looking ahead to the day when he will again meet the destroyer and redeem himself in his own eyes and those of the townspeople. So far, so good. But from there on in, things begin to go wrong. It grows clear that, for all his good intentions, Mayor Blue is not the stuff of which heroes are made, and although in the end he slays his tormentor, he fails in everything else— including his dream of making Hard Times a permanent town—and his story ends on a note of complete frustration.

While it is unlikely that habitual readers—and viewers—of Westerns will find "Welcome to Hard Times" altogether to their taste, the novel nonetheless serves a worth-while and long overdue purpose by showing the other side of the shield; namely, that in the West as elsewhere virtue is not invariably triumphant, and that not every embryo town hopefully planted beside Western rivers or trails or foothill streams was destined to grow and

Reprinted from *New York Herald Tribune*, January 22, 1962, 280.

prosper. Many hundreds of such places, having served their purpose, withered and died and, like Hard Times, vanished from view.

Here then is a Western with a difference, one that not only makes interesting and often exciting reading, but should prove a wholesome corrective to those too long exposed to the brand of Wild West fiction purveyed in the magazines and radio and on the TV screen.

[Review of *Welcome to Hard Times*]

John T. Osborne

Into the small town of Hard Times in the Dakota Territory rides a Bad Man from Bodie who proceeds to kill and destroy, finally burning down the town. No one really opposes him, for the Colt revolver does not make all men equal. Blue, the Mayor and professed coward, Molly, a revenge-crazed prostitute, and Jim, a young lad whose father was killed by the Bad Man, share a sod hut for the winter. In this environment hate, fear and hope clash. The arrival of a Russian with three prostitutes to provide entertainment for miners in a nearby camp encourages Blue. Through his efforts the town is rebuilt, but the Bad Man reappears. Destitute men from the played-out mine assist in destroying the town again. This is a well-written, above-average adult western novel. Recommended for all public libraries. [Ed. note: Because of Mr. Osborne's broad recommendation, we think some libraries should know that for sheer brutality graphically portrayed this novel is close to those of Spillane.]

Reprinted from *Library Journal*, September 1, 1960, 2956.

The Menace [Review of *Big As Life*]

GWENDOLYN BROOKS

One day a gigantic, nude man and woman arrive in New York. They lean against the horizon. They are beautiful, burnished, odorous and they have a powerful effect on the town, which proceeds to tumble over itself, to huddle, to pray. The town cries NO.

What can be done? Consultation, defense command, intellectual research, jetliner, helicopter, and practical philosophy are brought to bear. The President, the Cabinet, and the governors of New York, New Jersey, Connecticut, and Pennsylvania are interested, make suggestions.

Through the screen of hysteria we see most plainly Wallace Creighton, a professor of history at Columbia University, jazz bass king Red Bloom and Red Bloom's love, Sugarbush. These people inch their way through the violence, death, blanks, and quavers of their predicament and emerge, shredded, with new creeds. Thoughtful Creighton is at first convinced that the new people are endurable, that they are overwhelmingly repulsive and subtly dangerous; for there is the possibility of mysterious and awful infection, and even though it is discovered that an hour of "normal" time is a month or two of giant time, there is the certainty that eventually the nameless ones will become aware of their small oppressors and will simply stamp them out. But after considerable mullings and veerings, Creighton decides that the invaders have become actually necessary, that they are stimulating the beginning of a "real history," that the net result may be "nice" for posterity, may improve the prospects of that little son Red and Sugarbush are expecting. To tamper with them might "touch some nerve, some key connection." Red, although still awed after a year of the mighty presences, declares that it will be all right if the big beauties remain. He can no longer imagine their non-existence. "I think if you take them away, they'll still be there."

As for Sugarbush—her creed is comprised of Red, "love" with Red, housework, the coming baby, and making-the-best-of-things. In Essential Woman we meet the solving heart of things, the blood of this book. Making-the-best-of-things is E. L. Doctorow's recommendation. It is a good recommendation, so we water down our regret that his characters and style are servants to his message.

Reprinted from *Book Week*, July 10, 1966, 17.

[Review of *Big As Life*]

ANONYMOUS

A kind of space-age Evelyn Waugh: a pair of giants 2,000 feet high suddenly materialize in New York harbor; the resulting panic is intensified rather than quelled by a blundering military and by a scientific establishment interested only in accumulating sacred data. Though the giants can move only inches a week, earthling society is so bogged down in Parkinsonian inefficiency and pure narcissism that it can not resolve the problem. The three principal characters (the chief one called Bloom, a name that is becoming a commonplace in the recent American novel) huddle together as the social order disintegrates, and Doctorow's dead-pan manner in this second novel turns from satire to tenderness and human concern. A performance closer to James Purdy than to Orwell and Huxley, but in a minor key. For libraries with large holdings in the modern novel.

Reprinted with permission from *Choice*, November 1966. © by the American Library Association.

[Review of *Big As Life*]

Malcolm M. Ferguson

This fantasy novel (sub-species, disaster story) has neither memorable details nor turn of plot to warrant comparison with *Brave New World* or *1984*. It is reminiscent of the Orson Welles' radiocast of an H. G. Wells story, back in 1938 when the voices of the announcers alone caused panic. Here two passive, gigantic statues rising unaccountably out of New York Harbor have the same effect. Lacking a rampant King Kong or other monster lethally at large, the novel loses its direction. There are hints of *Dr. Strangelove* here, too but lacking the humor (as sight gags in the movie) and the situation resolution of that movie. Most libraries can pass this up, perhaps checking to be sure they do have the more memorable yarns in this genre.

Reprinted from *Library Journal*, April 15, 1966, 2086.

Lion's Den
[Review of *The Book Of Daniel*]

PETER PRESCOTT

•

The original Daniel, you remember, was an uneasy man—a Jew who lived by his wits in the court of the Chaldean kings. These kings had no more use for Jews and intellectuals than have most governments in history, but (even as kings go) they were a stupid lot, sharing a baroque taste in dreams and executions while demanding instant obedience at the sound of the cornet, sackbut and dulcimer. In such a political climate, what is Daniel's role? He works for himself, of course, and for his coreligionists. He may be, as the Dartmouth Bible suggests, "a Beacon of Faith in a Time of Persecution"; he may be something of a fanatic, too, a man angry at being trapped in a role fashioned for him by the state. Perhaps, seeing himself clothed in scarlet one day and tossed to the lions the next, Daniel has a certain sense of irony. We will never know. Irony is not the tone of the Old Testament.

The narrator of E. L. Doctorow's novel is the victim of certain stupidities and ironies of postwar America. This Daniel is the son of a Jewish couple who, in 1954, were electrocuted for stealing atomic secrets for the Russians. The Rosenberg case of course: Doctorow uses it fully, with significant variations, but the genius of his story is that his concern is with the heirs of the Rosenbergs, the heirs of the political pessimism and paranoia of the early 1950s. The execution of his parents has not so much scarred Daniel's life as it has become the controlling framework of his existence, of his split perspective on himself and on the world.

Dodging between first- and third-person narrative, Daniel tells two stories concurrently: how, in 1967, he tried to save his younger sister Susan from mental breakdown and suicide and, in an intricate series of flashbacks, the story of his parents' ordeal. Paul and Rochelle Isaacson, as Daniel sees them, were pathetic, useless people consumed by rage and dogma, willing to use people to further Communism, which they thought would "justify their poverty, their failure, their unhappiness . . . they rushed after self-esteem." Communism allowed them to transform "envy into constructive outgoing hate"; like a religion, it was "some purchase on the future against the terrible life of the present."

Pious: Were the Isaacsons guilty? Doctorow taunts us, hinting both ways, but their legal guilt is not the point. If guilty, they were ineffective. "They *acted* guilty," a reporter said; they "had to have been into some goddamn thing." And they were: they were into their own joylessness and pious excuses for "wanting a new world of socialism without want." They were victims of a society that needed victims and, following family tradition, they were exquisitely able to make victims of their children. Above all, the Isaacsons were self-destructive. Daniel torments his wife and child—"We're not nice people," he says—and Susan torments Daniel, telling him that she remains true to the Isaacson cause; Daniel is the betrayer. Daniel, the victim, agrees.

It is a hard novel to read. Doctorow never slackens his intensity. He continually shifts scenes, characters and time; he pauses for lectures on history: the reader is constantly beginning again. But every scene is perfectly realized and every part feeds into the whole—the themes and symbols echoing and reverberating—and I was not far into the book before I was wholly caught up in it.

Struggle: It is a purgative book, angry and more deeply felt than all but a few contemporary American novels, a novel about defeat, impotent rage, the passing of the burden of suffering through generations and "the progress of madness inherited through the heart." It is a novel about Daniel's struggle for detachment, his need to put a distance between himself and his story. We know he will never make it, in spite of his taking fixes from history. Daniel's suffering is the matter of this story, though he hardly recognizes it, and Doctorow, in a ferocious feat of the imagination, makes that suffering appallingly real. There is no question here of our suspending disbelief, but rather how, when we have finished, we may regain stability.

So much of what Doctorow accomplishes might, with less skill, have been melodramatic or sentimental. He avoids, for instance, the trial scenes he might have made sensational; in fact, he refuses all our vulgar expectations. The Isaacsons might have been sweet martyrs, but Doctorow clearly does not like them: they are rich in humanity but poor in spirit, and the politics of Doctorow's book is far more complicated than is the kind of fictional propaganda that requires martyrs. The overriding tone of this contemporary book of Daniel is ironic. Irony is sometimes used to fend the reader off—of Paul Isaacson, stumbling into the electric chair, Doctorow writes: "the chair would kill him but at this moment it was his only support." Irony is also used to fix a position: the Isaacsons looked toward a future which rejected them; the New Left, bored by the Isaacsons, literally closes the book on them when SDS activists take over the library at Columbia where Daniel is writing his story.

The year is not half spent, and a better American novel may yet appear, but I wouldn't wait for it.

Wrestling Society for a Soul
[Review of *The Book of Daniel*]

STANLEY KAUFFMANN

This is less a review than a celebration. E. L. Doctorow has written the political novel of our age, the best American work of its kind that I know since Lionel Trilling's *The Middle of the Journey.* Doctorow could hardly be less like Trilling in style or temper, but that's part of the point; it helps to make this novel the quintessence of the '60s, as Trilling in 1947, fixed the political '30s.

The time of the book, the "present" time, is mostly 1967, between Memorial Day and Christmas. Daniel Lewin, twenty-seven, is a graduate student at Columbia, and this book is (and is not!) what he writes instead of a dissertation. He's the son of Communist parents, Bronx Jews, who were executed at Sing Sing in the early 1950s for conspiring to steal atomic secrets for Russia. He has a younger sister. The book is built on his attempts to find like truth about his parents, about himself in relation to them, and on his relations with his sister in her attempts to regain sanity.

The premise is only one of the potentially troublesome elements in the book that Doctorow converts into triumph. The Rosenberg parallel might have been a mere gimmick. (Trilling, triumphing likewise, based a major character on Whittaker Chambers.) There is no tricky plot. And most certainly it's not a forensic novel about whether the Rosenbergs were really innocent or really guilty. This is an artwork about the *idea* of the Rosenbergs and people like them, how they came into being in this country, why their trial was needed, what their legacy is, and the intertexture of that legacy with the social-political climate today. I haven't looked up the facts of the Rosenberg case; it would be offensive to the quality of this novel to check it against those facts. This is a work of historic and psychic currents.

The parents were named Isaacson. (Nothing has been chosen lightly in this book, including names. The first Isaac, we remember, was nearly sacrificed to his father's beliefs.) They were first-generation Americans, he a radio repairman with a tiny Bronx shop, she the daughter of a crazy old woman who wrote Bintel Briefs to a Yiddish newspaper, recounting persecution in Russia and fierce struggle on the lower East Side.

From *The New Republic,* June 5, 1971, 25–27. Reprinted by permission of THE NEW REPUBLIC, © 1971, The New Republic, Inc.

After the Isaacsons' execution, their two children, fourteen and nine, were adopted by a Boston law professor and wife named Lewin. The book begins with a trip that Daniel and his young wife and baby make to Massachusetts, to join the Lewins in a visit to the mental hospital where his sister is confined. She was taken there after cutting her wrists in a Howard Johnson's ladies room nearby. The book ends—one of the three endings that are proposed—with the sister's funeral. In between we are pressed to a kaleidoscopic vision of the present and the intermingled past, of political history as it applies to the Isaacsons, of the fires of this century as they burn to and through the borders of all our lives.

A second triumph of Doctorow's is the form of the book. Daniel, the "author," often says that he hates the idea of sequence. The temporal urge of this book is toward simultaneity, not only of time planes but of different viewpoints. Not only are the present and various pasts closely interwoven but also various views of Daniel himself, who is seen in both the third and first persons—sometimes in successive sentences. As with many modern sensibilities, Doctorow has fractured seamless sequence because he felt, evidently, that the turbulence which bred and surrounds Daniel is always present with him, all of it, all the time. Doctorow's cascading form sweeps along with it occasional thematic variations, one of them a "True History of the Cold War" in the shape (says the author) of a raga.

Another important part of the method, throughout the book, is the consciousness that the book is being written. For instance: "I suppose you think I can't do the electrocution. I know there is a you . . . I will show you that I can do the electrocution." And then Doctorow-Daniel does it, unforgettably. This now-familiar consciousness of art in the making of art, this attempt to fix the act of creation as part of the finished work, can be both disarming and enriching, as it is here. "Nothing up my sleeve" adds to the magic, for the modern consciousness that is suspicious of magic.

(In fact, I wish Doctorow had used this method in one "straight" section: the climactic meeting between Daniel and his parents' accuser, years after their death, in Disneyland at Christmas. The irony of the setting and season might have lost its slightly pat touch if Daniel had capitalized on the Disneyland aspects of the meeting.)

A third triumph is that this novel's untraditional form has not subverted traditional fiction values. Doctorow might have thrown all his creative energy into glittering sequences and—like some contemporary writers, including some good ones—might have asked the fulfillment of the design to *be* the work. But he achieves other ends as well.

Character. Every character in this book, major or minor, is sharply visible, has a voice—even a peripheral character like the Isaacsons' Negro janitor, the black man whom these society-changing Communists, these Jews who have known persecution, are quite willing to relegate to a bare cot in the cellar; and who is symbolically waiting. Place. Every setting, every occasion has an essence, an odor: a dusty radio-shop window of the '40s, a Yippie pad in the East Village (where, fifty years before, Daniel's grandmother had struggled!), a Paul Robeson concert in the late '40s, a Washington Peace March in 1967. Drama. Every sequence is handled by a dramatist, is understood to its *conclusion*—just one example, the Dickensian episode in which the Isaacson children flee the children's center, while their parents are in jail awaiting trial.

And everything in this scintillating, yet deeply mined book feeds its theme. Here is an approximation of that theme. Political radicalism was brought to the US by late 19th-century immigrants, many of whom were East European Jews. Previous political impulses in this country had usually been comfortably meliorist, often theologically based. With increasing socio-economic pressures, partly caused by those very immigrants, the European ideologies that the immigrants brought with them became more and more germane. Therefore it's idle to speak of those ideologies as European concepts imposed on America: those immigrants, and their progeny, now are part of America, and the very changes caused by their interfusion have placed their ideologies among the American antecedents and options.

In its reaction against those ideologies, not an entirely deplorable reaction *in itself*, the US has gone through several spasms of purge, cruelly antithetical to our constitutional premises. One such spasm was the Red spy hunt of the late '40s when this country needed victims to console itself for the fact that Russia was getting the bomb.

This novel faces up squarely and intelligently to the Jewishness of its subject. Jews had been persecuted, Jews are historically avid for social justice, Jews had less at stake in Anglo-Saxon-cum-Yankee traditions and rewards. Jews were in big cities mainly, cities were trouble spots, Jews were troublemakers. Doctorow refuses to blink any of this. On the contrary, by plunging his hands into the nettles, he plucks out the flower. By confronting the matter in fullest human resonance, he transforms parochialism into universals. His Jews become prototypical.

Out of all this background, partially in reaction against it, come many of today's revolutionaries. (No longer so markedly Jewish, by any means.) Their anti-intellectualism has its roots in impatience with the Bach-and-Shakespeare radicals of the past. Pop culture and pot culture are a reproof of all that Parnassian pipe-smoking culture that, in their view, merely mirrored the oppressive society at a different angle. Socially and psychically, too, there have been both connection and change. Doctorow shows us how pervasively sexual the Isaacson marriage was. Daniel inherited that sexuality, as he inherited radicalism, but has rejected his parents' "respectability," as he rejects formal ideology. A bizarre sex episode with his wife in a moving car is a declaration of continuity and independence.

And beneath the large theme that underlies the book is the even larger contemporary crisis in consciousness: the crisis of faith in rationalism, the faith so hard-won in the last few centuries; the resurgence of the Myth of Unreason because the Myth of Reason has not only failed so far to bring the promised grace but may have become a habit-forming narcotic. One need not subscribe to this belief, as for the most part I do not, to see its power in this novel. (Congruent belief is hardly necessary in art. I'm not a Catholic royalist, yet I think Evelyn Waugh's trilogy is the best fiction produced by World War II.)

"Existential" revolution, since 1967, has shown defects in dynamics, but Doctorow dramatizes the forces that produced it, along with the opposition to it—chiefly, the ingrained American hunger for innocence, a hunger that always gets vicious when frustrated. Fundamentally, the novel implies, the new revolution grew out of a break with a formal ideology that had its own innocence. Daniel's parents accepted the roles that society imposed on them in the prosecution; more, they accepted the roles that the Party imposed on them. (There is a masterly courtroom scene, imagined by Daniel, in which a mere exchange of glances reveals an intra-Party collusion.) The book chronicles a long break with acceptances, both conservative and radical. The end, the third and final ending, leaves the facts of the Isaacson case still mysterious for Daniel, but the forces that grew out of the radical past swerve until they reach the Columbia library—spring of 1968!—where he is writing.

E. L. Doctorow is forty, a former editor for book publishers, and the author of two previous novels that are not comparable with this work. His *Book of Daniel* is beautiful and harrowing, rhapsodic and exact. Like all good artists dealing with such subjects, Doctorow does not give answers but is not content only to pose questions. At one point Daniel says of his father: "He wrestled society for my soul." The line might be a motto for this fine book.

The Music of Time
[Review of *Ragtime*]

R. Z. SHEPPARD

"Divided between power and the dream" is the way F. Scott Fitzgerald saw it in his luminous projection of lost innocence, *The Great Gatsby*. In *Ragtime*, E. L. Doctorow plays a dazzling variation on that theme in a slightly earlier era: the final days of America's privileged childhood.

His novel is carefully framed between 1902 and 1917, surrounding the robust, unambiguous patriotism of Teddy Roosevelt and the complex, brooding morality of Woodrow Wilson. It was Winslow Homer time, when, as Doctorow writes, "a certain light was still available along the Eastern seaboard." Eccentrics still putter in their garages and produce inventions without the aid of research-and-development bureaucracies. Henry Ford's new assembly line and Albert Einstein's peculiar idea that the universe is curved crack the dawn of the modern age. Before long, Doctorow notes, painters in Paris will be putting two eyes on one side of the head.

Like ragtime, the jazz form made famous by Scott Joplin, Doctorow's book is a native American fugue, rhythmic, melodic and stately. "It is never right to play ragtime fast," said Joplin, and the same can be said for reading it.

Yet the book never stands still for a moment. Story lines constantly interweave; historical figures become part of fictional events and fictional characters participate in real history. In ways both fantastic and poetically convincing, the members of a suburban upper-middle-class family combine and change in the undertow of events. As if Clarence Day had written *Future Shock* into *Life with Father,* Doctorow's images and improvisations foreshadow the 20th century's coming preoccupation with scandal, psychoanalysis, solipsism, race, technological power and megalomania.

Harry Thaw empties his pistol into the face of Architect Stanford White, the lover of Thaw's showgirl wife Evelyn Nesbit. White goes to his grave and Thaw to an insane asylum. But Doctorow has his own plans for Evelyn. Down from her red velvet swing, she drifts to the immigrant slums of New York's Lower East Side, where her social consciousness is raised by anarchist

Reprinted from *Time*, July 14, 1975, 64.

Emma Goldman. Sigmund Freud confronts the pleasure principle at Coney Island and cannot get back to Vienna fast enough.

A black musician turns violent revolutionary after his new Model T is vandalized by jealous whites. Harry Houdini, the immortal escape artist, cannot slip from his mother's apron strings. He is also a man incapable of political thought because, in Doctorow's moving phrase, "he could not reason from his own hurt feelings."

Elsewhere, J. P. Morgan and Henry Ford meet secretly to discuss their beliefs in reincarnation. Morgan has spent millions harvesting civilization's mystic wisdom. Ford, in his ready-made suit and L. L. Bean shoes, notes dryly that his occult education came from a 25¢ booklet ordered from the Franklin Novelty Co. of Philadelphia. It is the same organization that will buy moving-picture flip-books from a penniless Jewish immigrant. The peddler will end in Hollywood as Baron Ashkenazy, producer of those Rosetta stones of American nostalgia, the *Our Gang* comedies.

Literal descriptions and interpretations make many novels sound better than they are. With *Ragtime,* just the opposite is true. Its lyric tone, fluid structure and vigorous rhythms give it a musical quality that explanation mutes. In Doctorow's hands, the nation's secular fall from grace is no catalogue of sin, no mere tour de force; the novelist has managed to seize the strands of actuality and transform them into a fabulous tale.

Mingle With the Mighty
[Review of *Ragtime*]

RUSSELL DAVIES

According to his publisher's brochure, E. L. Doctorow has been nourishing the following ambitions for his latest book: "I want *Ragtime* to be read by people who do not normally read books. It has been my dream for years to write with high seriousness and yet to find an unselfconscious audience, to be accessible to people who work in factories and garages." What can he possibly mean by such a condescending and repellent utterance, except that he wishes to sell a great many books? What is an "unselfconscious audience," and if it exists, what are its peculiar virtues? Chiefly, I presume, an unawareness of what it requires from art, and an incapacity to call upon its own notions of aesthetic wholeness—resulting in an inability to resist the literary product so self-consciously aimed in its direction by Mr. Doctorow. The astonishing implication that people who work in factories and garages not only see great literature as inaccessible, but even find the "high seriousness" of a Doctorow terrifying enough to require dilution is an insult we must hope the literati of shop-floor and forecourt will themselves rebuff, by reading something else.

For this "high seriousness" of Mr. Doctorow's is a joke. There is no denying his commercial success: a quarter of a million hardback *Ragtimes* sold in America alone; paperback rights handed over for £900,000; film rights signed away to Dino de Laurentiis. But to achieve this, Mr. Doctorow has had to "break out of the little world of personal experience which has bound the novel" (his own words) and create a simple-minded, whimsical, socio-historical pageant that comes nearer to qualifying as a comic-book than any unillustrated volume I have ever seen. The background is America, in the early 1900s, and the technique consists of dropping a few imagined personages into a nation otherwise populated by known historical figures. Houdini, Pierpont Morgan, Booker T. Washington, Emma Goldman, Ford and Peary are prominent among the mythological, or semi-real, heavies; Mother, Father, Mother's Younger Brother, and "the boy" (Mother and Father's son) make up the unnamed family that heads the cast of imaginees. Mr. Doctorow wastes no time in getting the two groups to mingle. On page 7, Houdini's Pope-

Reprinted from *Times Literary Supplement*, January 23, 1976, 77.

Toledo Runabout automobile butts a telegraph pole outside the Mother/ Father place, and off we go into make-believe. "As it happened," our unembarrassable author confides, swinging on into Chapter 2, "Houdini's unexpected visit had interrupted Mother and Father's coitus." The very least of the family's troubles, as things turn out.

But first Mr. Doctorow must have his fun; his team of mythmakers must be put through their hoops. Ford and J. P. Morgan exchange portentous apocryphal banter on Egyptology and reincarnation; they form the Pyramid Club, a secret society of which they are the only two members, and of which, indeed, only you and I and Mr. Doctorow, and 250,000 hardback-buyers, have ever heard. Harry K. Thaw, killer of the architect Stanford White, flaps his penis through his prison bars, distracting Houdini, who, in an opposite cell, is staging a bravura escape from Murderers' Row. "Houdini was to tell no one of this strange confrontation," confides Mr. Doctorow, its inventor, adding cutely: "People who did not respond to his art profoundly distressed Houdini." Freud, another of Mr. Doctorow's cartoon giants, is made to arrive in New York with Jung, and to visit Luna Park with his disciple: "The dignified visitors rode the shoot-the-chutes and Freud and Jung took a boat together through the Tunnel of Love." So much for dignity: Mr. Doctorow can make a kid of anybody with his childish and useless irony.

Meanwhile, and worst of all, Evelyn Nesbit (the wife of Harry K. Thaw, and the cause of the scandalous murder) is falling under the spell of another "genuine article," the anarchist Emma Goldman, who sees in this fallen woman a fit recipient not only for her doctrinal barrage, but also for a spot of astringent massage. The bespectacled old orator sets about the delicate mondaine with a will, and a lively consciousness of the modern American male's taste in titillation. "The first thing is to restore circulation, Goldman explained as she rubbed Evelyn's back and buttocks and thighs." First things past, the treatment progresses: "Her eyes were closed and her lips stretched in an involuntary smile as Goldman massaged her breasts, her stomach, her legs. Yes, even this, Emma Goldman said, briskly passing her hand over the mons." The writing is just getting frankly masturbatory ("Evelyn put her own hands on her breasts and her palms rotated the nipples. . . . Her pelvis rose from the bed as if seeking something in the air") when suddenly the closet door flies open, and a male figure bursts out, helpless with lust. It is Mother's Younger Brother, who is in love with Evelyn, and has heard all:

> He was clutching in his hands, as if trying to choke it, a rampant penis which, scornful of his intentions, whipped him about the floor, launching, to his cries of ecstasy or despair, great filamented spurts of jism that traced the air like bullets and then settled slowly over Evelyn in her bed like falling ticker tape.

Even if Mr. Doctorow had not reserved his most resourceful writing for this orgasm (there is no livelier word-work in the book, regrettably), I think I should always remember this passage as the perfect flowering of the *Ragtime* method: two persons who once existed but probably never met ("my answer is that they have all met now," writes Doctorow in the accursed brochure) are engaged in a ritualized lesbian caress when a third figure totters noisily out of Doctorow's imagination to spray the unhistorical scene with sperm. The ticker-tape image is the final touch of instant all-American hyperbole which makes this chapter end a small classic of cheap grandstanding.

The story that eventually issues from the mass of capricious juxtapositions turns out to concern Coalhouse Walker, a fictitious ragtime pianist and former associate of Scott Joplin. Walker's car is savagely vandalized by a bunch of envious racist firemen (in the Mother/Father neighbourhood, naturally) and his campaign of vengeful terrorism sets up a thoroughly modern hostage-style siege melodrama. The climax arrives when the Coalhouse gang, augmented by the ubiquitous Mother's Younger Brother in blackface, is holed up in J. Pierpont Morgan's palace, which they threaten to detonate, objets d'art and all, with explosives pinched from Father's fireworks factory. Booker T. Washington is called in to reason with the insurrectionists in a ludicrous biblicalese presumably patterned after his public speeches: "I will intercede for the sake of mercy that your trial shall be swift and your execution painless," he tells them, privately. But he fails. Coalhouse succeeds in gaining a hollow victory when his car is labouriously rebuilt, outside the beleaguered premises, by the redneck fire chief; and the shooting-down of Coalhouse at the moment of surrender supplies a token-tragic end for the token-tragic black. Despite this Attica-style execution and the damning telegram from Morgan that precipitates it ("Give him his automobile and hang him," comes the message), the book is not so wholeheartedly anti-Big-League-Capitalist that the empire-building spirit cannot ride again in the final chapter. There is another fictional running character all set to rescue it: Tateh, a talented Jewish-Latvian socialist who rises from penury in a subplot to sudden success in the new film business, and ends the book by marrying Mother. (The Mother/Father relationship has failed to survive the shock of Younger Brother's participation in the Coalhouse plot, and his later death in Mexico. Besides, Father was drowned on the Lusitania.)

I am at a loss to say how this most wooden of jigsaws has come to be regarded as a powerful and impressive novel—unless it be by that uncontrollably spawning common consent that takes over when the American public realizes a publicity campaign has got too big to face failure. The breathless American reviews offer only the repeated clue that *Ragtime* is "fun to read." It cannot be the style that accounts for this, whatever Stanley Kauffmann, of the *Saturday Review,* may say ("written exquisitely" is what he did say). It is true that Mr. Doctorow achieves a kind of grinding readability, by dint of keeping his sentences short, and starting them with subject and verb, except where a little subordinate clause intrudes for variety's sake. But his excursions into fine, or at least risky writing are beyond parody. "Spring, spring!" he is capable of baying at the start of a chapter. "Like a mad magician flinging silks and coloured rags from his trunk the earth produced the yellow and white crocus, then the fox grape, the forsythia flowering on its stalks . . ." etc. (I particularly liked the response of one of Mr. Doctorow's humanoids to this abundance: " Grandfather stood in the yard and gave a standing ovation." How else?) Mr. Doctorow on relationships is confusing: "What bound them to each other was a fulfilled recognition which they lived and thought within so that their apprehension of each other could not be so distinct and separated as to include admiration for the other's fairness." On baseball he is delight-fully traditional: "the leather-covered spheroid" is what he calls the ball. On Emma Goldman's grip he is devilish ("it was a grip of iron"), and on Harry Thaw, destructive: "He had the wide mouth and doll eyes of a Victorian closet queen"—a pronouncement in which one catches the authentic derisive tone of a present-day author studying an old photograph of his victim.

There is no fun in all this. Nor do the incidentals maintain a fun-contin-uum, for all that Mr. Doctorow has larded his text with provocative one-lin-ers ("Every feat enacted Houdini's desire for his dead mother") and dark hints of occultism like the "Warn the Duke" message Mother's boy passes to Hou-dini seventy-eight pages before Houdini meets the Archduke Ferdinand and 255 pages before the Sarajevo assassination.

No, the answer must be that the American readership really does relish the "audacious" tinkering with real lives for its own sake. One had thought that cynicism had advanced beyond this stage, but American citizens are apparently still under such pressure from their mythology that they will jump at the chance to see the system subverted. Their history is still so full of heroes that it is a mighty relief to see a few treated, however clumsily, with the disrespect they have always deserved. Our own quirky method of histori-cal inculcation, which results in half our past national figures being better known for their foibles than for the dimensions of their achievement, has dis-respect built into it; and that is why I see no great future for *Ragtime* here, and certainly no destiny for Mr. Doctorow as the British petrol-pump atten-dant's Balzac. He is intelligent enough to have realized, however, that the bicentennial programme for 1976 is bound to increase home demand for books of this kind.

Political Romance
[Review of *Ragtime*]

Hilton Kramer

The hosannas that have greeted E. L. Doctorow's *Ragtime,* elevating the book to instant commercial success and its author to literary stardom, have already prompted one early celebrant—Raymond Sokolov, writing in the Washington *Post*—to caution readers against the extravagant claims (his own included) being made on its behalf.[1] This excellent advice is unlikely to be heeded, however. Mr. Doctorow is in possession of a genuine literary gift, and readers who have despaired of ever being able to finish some of the more highly touted of recent "serious" novels have every reason to be grateful to a writer who does not spurn the traditional obligation to provide a clear and vivid narrative furnished with colorful characters and a significant theme. *Ragtime,* moreover, has the additional virtue—for there is no question that its audience regards this as a virtue—of endowing some of our more fashionable social pieties with a resonance that is positively mythic. Although the book's complex web of action is wholly confined to the placid atmosphere of turn-of-the-century America—another large element of its appeal, of course—and its story closes on the eve of America's entry into the First World War, heroic roles are exclusively reserved for women, blacks, and partisans of the Left. The villains in *Ragtime,* drawn with all the subtlety of a William Gropper cartoon, are all representatives of money, the middle class, and white ethnic prejudice. Does this make it sound a little more like 1968 than 1908? That, alas, is very much the point. It is no exaggeration, therefore, to say that the myth of the "bad" America that emerged with such virulent force in the 1960s has found its true laureate in the author of this stylish historical romance.

Is it splitting critical hairs to describe *Ragtime* as a romance rather than as a novel? Consider the tale it tells, and the language employed in the telling. Father, whose ample income derives "from the manufacture of flags and buntings and other accoutrements of patriotism, including fireworks," installs his family—wife, son, bachelor brother-in-law, and aging father-in-law—in the "stout manse" he has built in New Rochelle, in 1902, only a few clays before joining Peary's third expedition to the Arctic. There, though he proves "not the sturdiest member of the expedition" because of "the tendency of his extremities to freeze easily," Father—never given any other name in the narrative—has the good fortune to discover Esquimo sex ("They cohabited without even undressing, through vents in their furs and they went at it with grunts and shouts of fierce joy"), and even manages to sample a bit. Mother, a tower of strength and character beneath her period mask of demure and accommodating femininity, likewise discovers an alien race in the form of a "bloody . . . unwashed newborn baby," miraculously still alive, freshly buried among the flowerbeds of her New Rochelle garden. Both the infant and his instantly located mother ("She had a child's face, a guileless brown beautiful face . . . the color of dark chocolate") are immediately welcomed into the family manse, there to be loved and cared for until the fateful day when the black father, a splendid figure of a man who drives a splendidly appointed new automobile, wins the black girl's hand in marriage. Before these happy nuptials can be completed, however, our black hero—a ragtime musician of rising reputation—is cruelly harassed by a group of Irish immigrant firemen, who viciously vandalize the splendid new Model-T Ford. Seeking legal redress and failing to receive it from his white adversaries, this musician-hero goes underground, organizes a cadre of exemplary black guerrillas, turns terrorist, and, aided by the white bachelor brother-in-law, who in the course of serving Father's fireworks business has become an expert on explosives, occupies the Morgan Library in Manhattan with the threat of blowing up its priceless treasures if his demands—full restoration of his Model-T to its original condition—are not fully met. The white world quickly capitulates. The automobile, functioning here as a kind of *machina ex deo,* is restored to triumphant splendor (at J. P. Morgan's expense).

This is very far from being the whole story, however. There is the parallel tale of Tateh and his daughter ("The Little Girl in the pinafore"). Tateh is a young immigrant Jewish peddler, a socialist of course ("He looked at the palaces [along Fifth and Madison Avenues] and his heart was outraged. . . . On these wide empty sidewalks in this part of the city the police did not like to see immigrants"), who, without ceasing to be a loyal socialist, rises from the poverty of the Lower East Side to fame and wealth in the movie business, and thus proves worthy of winning Mother's large heart after Father's convenient demise. And into this elaborate scheme of converging destinies are introduced several famous historical personages: Evelyn Nesbit, fresh from the ordeal of Harry Thaw's shooting of Stanford White, takes philanthropic fancy to Tateh's Little Girl and suffers the attentions of Mother's volatile brother—not to mention those of Emma Goldman—before sinking into oblivion; Harry Houdini, interrupting "Mother and Father's coitus" on a Sunday afternoon, seeks aid for his chauffeur driven Pope-Toledo Runabout ("It had brass headlamps in front of the radiator and brass sidelamps over the fenders . . . The driver was in livery") at the New Rochelle manse; and so on, in ever widening arcs of fabulous improbability, and all recounted in a style of fastidious storybook simplicity.

"Doubtless the main difference between the novel and the romance," wrote the late Richard Chase in *The American Novel and its Tradition*, "is the way in which they view reality." Chase then went on to make certain distinctions that tell us a good deal, I think, about what sort of book *Ragtime* really is. "The novel," he observed, "renders reality closely and in comprehensive detail. It takes a group of people and sets them going about the business of life. We come to see these people in their real complexity of temperament and motive. They are in explicable relation to nature, to each other, to their social class, to their own past. Character is more important than action and plot, and probably the tragic or comic actions of the narrative will have the primary purpose of enhancing our knowledge of and feeling for an important character, a group of characters, or a way of life." By such criteria, certainly, *Ragtime* can scarcely be said to be a novel at all.

"By contrast," Chase wrote, "the romance . . . feels free to render reality in less volume and detail. It tends to prefer action to character, and action will be freer in a romance than in a novel, encountering, as it were, less resistance from reality." In *Ragtime,* as everyone knows, Mr. Doctorow plays so fast and loose with historical personalities that what Chase called "resistance from reality" is virtually nil.

Emma Goldman massages the breasts of Evelyn Nesbit, Houdini has a brief audience with the Archduke Franz Ferdinand, Henry Ford sits down to lunch with J. P. Morgan, and Freud flees America because of a paucity of public toilets. "The romance can flourish without providing much intricacy of relation," Chase wrote, and the relations that obtain among *Ragtime*'s many characters—whether "real" or invented—prove to be simple indeed and purely emblematic. "The characters, probably rather two-dimensional types," Chase wrote in a passage that exactly anticipates the quality of Mr. Doctorow's narrative, "will not be complexly related to each other or to society or to the past. Human beings will on the whole be shown in ideal relation—that is, they will share emotions only after these have become abstract or symbolic. . . . Character itself becomes, then, somewhat abstract and ideal, so much so in some romances that it seems to be merely a function of plot. The plot we may expect to be highly colored. Astonishing events may occur, and these are likely to have a symbolic or ideological, rather than a realistic, plausibility."

I have quoted from Chase's observations at this length because I think they go to the heart of Mr. Doctorow's book and tell us, too, something important about its reception. For what Mr. Doctorow has written in *Ragtime* is a political romance—it even has a happy ending of sorts: the underdogs triumph—and its plausibility is nothing if not ideological. The major fictional

characters—Father, Mother, Mother's Younger Brother, etc.—are all ideological inventions, designed to serve the purposes of a political fable. To be born
into the middle class is, in *Ragtime,* to be nameless and faceless, a cardboard
pawn identifiable exclusively in terms of stunted emotions and wasteful consumption. Only the black hero—Coalhouse Walker, Jr.—is accorded the dignity of a full name, or indeed, dignity of any sort. Members of the middle
class, miserable wretches that they are, may, of course, be reborn. Younger
Brother achieves this rebirth by allying himself with the blacks and eventually dying as one of Zapata's revolutionaries in Mexico, and even Mother is
allowed to escape her dismal bourgeois fate by marrying the newly rich Jew-
ish-Socialist movie mogul. Otherwise, to remain middle class is to remain
soulless. It is also to remain sexually underprivileged. In the world of *Ragtime,*
only the exploited, the abused, and the reborn enjoy good sex.

The historical personages who occupy so large a place in *Ragtime* are
similarly disposed of. The great Houdini, lacking political consciousness, is
revealed to be in a permanent state of Oedipal arrest. Morgan is portrayed as
little more than an avaricious crackpot, Freud an anti-American snob, Ford a
clever but malevolent yokel, and Booker T. Washington an ineffectual knave.
Emma Goldman, on the other hand, reigns in this fable as a woman for all
seasons, a pillar of libertarian virtue, and a model, naturally, of sexual fulfillment. One notes with a certain curiosity that, except for Houdini, Emma
Goldman played a vastly smaller role in shaping the actual course of American life in the 20th century than any of the other historical figures I have
named here. Is it any wonder, then, that she is accorded the lion's share of
virtue in this tale of national malfeasance? To have had a hand in shaping
American life in the 20th century to any appreciable degree is, in *Ragtime,* a
crime not easily forgiven. Penance is called for, and punishment meted out—
Mr. Doctorow is, in his way, a harsh moralist. Bourgeois America is consigned
to eternal damnation in this book, and its antagonists elevated to political
sainthood.

Still, the great appeal of *Ragtime,* though owing much to the way its author
has turned the political debacle of the '60s into a mythical retroactive triumph, does not lie primarily in its rehearsal of radical pieties. These, after all,
are now the common property of hordes of writers—in the movies and the
theater and television, and in our major newspapers and magazines, no less
than in the novel—for whom the myth of the "bad" America is an unques-
tioned article of faith. What distinguishes Mr. Doctorow's use of this myth is
something else—his gift for combining it with the picturesque. *Ragtime* is, in
effect, a kind of story-teller's flea-market. It abounds in vivid description of
all those turn-of-the-century objects and styles, from the bathing costumes
worn by Mother and Father on the beach at Atlantic City to the furnishings
of their home in New Rochelle to the precise accessories adorning the auto-

mobile driven by Coalhouse Walker, Jr., that triggers the book's climactic scene of confrontation , which now command such high prices in the antiques business and inspire such wide-spread longing, imitation, and parody in the chic world of bourgeois consumption. The stern realities of Mr. Doctorow's political romance—its sweeping indictment of American life, and its celebration of a radical alternative—are all refracted, as it were, in the quaint, chromatic glow of a Tiffany lamp, and are thus softened and made more decorative in the process. Everything in *Ragtime,* even its politics, is expertly wrapped in the scenery of nostalgia, a strategy that has the effect of rendering its essentially adversary spirit almost sweet to the taste. The irony of this picturesque method—or is it only dishonesty?—is to be found in the way Mr. Doctorow flatters and exploits the sensibility of the very class he seeks to subvert. We are given every opportunity to savor the delectable aesthetic surface of the *Ragtime* era, and every encouragement to detest the class responsible for its existence. In the end, I suppose, Mr. Doctorow is secure in the knowledge that he can have it both ways, for there is nothing his middle class readers so much relish nowadays as an assault on their integrity suitably embellished with signs of their superior taste.

Perhaps it is this skillful exploitation of the picturesque, which ministers to a fondness for the beauties of a lost world even while instructing us on its moral depravity, that accounts for the most astonishing aspect of the book's reception: the almost complete unanimity with which its earliest reviewers agreed to ignore its patently political purpose. (An important exception is Greil Marcus's brilliant analysis, "'Ragtime' and 'Nashville': Failure-of-America Fad," in the *Village Voice,* August 4, 1975.) I do not believe, however, that this remarkable feat of misperception can be ascribed to the crude exercise of simple stupidity—though on the subject of the abysmal standards that currently characterize the book-reviewing profession, I would be among the last to suggest that stupidity can be wholly discounted as a consideration. No, I think we have to look for the source of the misperception in some larger fact of our culture—in the fact, that is, that our culture is now so completely permeated with the myth of American malevolence that an ambitious political romance like *Ragtime,* which distorts the actual materials of history with a fierce ideological arrogance, is no longer in any danger of being recognized as having a blunt political point. The reviewers who are responsible for making this book a phenomenal success are, in this sense, at one with the audience to which it is addressed: an educated class that has grown morally obtuse about the world in which it lives and prospers. What Richard Chase said of the romance as a literary genre—"likely to have a symbolic or ideological, rather than a realistic, plausibility"—also describes, in the case of *Ragtime,* the cherished illusions of its readers.

Notes

1.   "Some novels," Mr. Sokolov wrote, "are almost thrust upon us, declared instant masterpieces from all sides and then slip from view. Remember William Styron's *The Confessions of Nat Turner*? As someone who helped mount that six-day wonder's success, I am now unable to reread Styron's softheaded book without embarrassment, and so I am feeling leery about praising *Ragtime* to the rooftops along with the general chorus of reviewers" (*Book World,* July 13, 1975). Mr. Sokolov promptly recovered, however, and rejoined the chorus.

[Review of *Drinks Before Dinner: A Play*]

L. F. KORNBLUM

In his first play Doctorow eschews psychological drama of character and action in favor of "a theatre of language . . . a theatre of ideas," in which his characters, who are deliberately lacking in individuality, discuss philosophical ideas in long monologues. The result is a very static and fairly tedious play. One of the guests at a Manhattan cocktail party suggests, "Let's not have the evening we all expect to have," and at gunpoint he forces the conversation around to the sterility of life and the imminence of the end of the world. While many of the ideas are clichés, the rhetoric with which they are presented is interesting, and the play probably makes better reading than viewing. Important as a work by the popular author of *Ragtime* and *The Book of Daniel,* but not a necessary addition for general drama collections.

Reprinted from *Library Journal* 104 (June 15, 1979): 1353.

[Review of *Drinks Before Dinner: A Play*]

ANONYMOUS

Pretentious, ponderous, and dull are words that well describe E. L. Doctorow's *Drinks before dinner*. In his introduction (which is far more provocative and dramatic than the play it strives to illuminate) the author announces his intention to abandon the theater of psychology and biography in order to align himself with the theater of language and ideas. As it is, having read the play, one senses that in making the shift he has simply abandoned the theater itself. Doctorow has failed to recognize that any play, even a play of ideas, must be more than a text in dialogue form. The "language of the theater" consists of nonverbal as well as verbal codes. By ignoring the fact that stage imagery and visual metaphor are every bit as important as verbal imagery, Doctorow has created a heavily rhetorical monologue disguised as a play. *Drinks before dinner* also lacks the commitment and passion requisite for bringing its ideas to full theatrical life. Even with all these reservations, however, the drama should still be of considerable interest as the first published play of a distinguished American author.

[Review of *Drinks Before Dinner: A Play*]

Martin McNamee

In his introduction, E. L. Doctorow warns future directors and actors about his play's "rhetorical and some times incantory language." He "prefers a hundred words to one gesture, with a text that neglects the ordinary benefit of characterization."

Doctorow admits that *Drinks Before Dinner* "does not solicit conventional theatrical sentiment." Unfortunately his willingness to state this does not change the fact that he is correct.

The action, or lack of it, takes place in a New York apartment during the ritual cocktails before dinner. Edgar, one of the guests, decides not to have the typical dinner party everyone anticipates. As he says, "I won't survive it." To support his rhetorical musings and perhaps ensure an audience, Edgar withdraws a handgun from his jacket.

Yet after this revelation very little action occurs. There is dialogue, at times a monologue, between Edgar and the rest of the dinner party. At one point Edgar ties the guest of honor to a chair. Edgar is assured of a captive audience; unfortunately the playwright does not have the same trick at his disposal. He could use it.

The author prefaces his work with an introduction, which, written after the play's initial run at the 1978 N.Y. Shakespeare Festival, is the work's saving grace. Doctorow expounds on his theory of language as a rhetorical mode and "the rhythm of repetition." He first investigated this aspect of language after discovering the similarities between Gertrude Stein and Mao Tse-tung!

Doctorow also notes the differences between his theatre of language and the American theatre, "in which the presentation of the psychologized ego is so central."

Doctorow's work is not so much a drama as it is an experiment with language. "The language preceded the intention." Those seeking such experimentation will be satisfied. Those seeking more will be disappointed.

Reprinted from *Best Sellers* 39 (October 1979): 262.

82

Breaking the Rules
[Review of *Loon Lake*]

ALAN BROWNJOHN

The rules about what constitutes the indispensable essence of a *novel* are cruelly simple, and have not been altered by any of the strange and elaborate guises the form has been given. Write a novel backwards, slice it and shuffle it, have a heavy authorial presence breathe down its neck, print it as lists of its own semi-colons and indefinite articles, call it "a fiction"—it still has to have people, places and plot. And the first of these is plot; because anything happening entails the necessity (such is our anthropomorphising habit) that it is happening to something that resembles people, in something that is very like a place. In other words, you cannot abandon plot and proceed just with either (or even both) of the other two, and still hope to write a novel; but you might just achieve something with plot on its own. Paradoxically, it may be a sign of high skill if you *do* write a very good novel with a minimum of plot (and more of this later, since Marilynne Robinson's first novel is a case in point). But if you write a bad one on that basis it can be a most damaging sign of inexperience, or naivety, or charlatanism, and a lot of academic theorists will like it, provided you have done it in the right way. Now, more than ever, an ability to effect an ingenious concealment of vacuity seems to be the essential prerequisite of the bad novelist with high pretensions.

Which is why so infinitely researched and elaborately unfurled a "fiction" as E. L. Doctorow's *Ragtime* inspired a fair bit of mistrust. Could it be that underneath it all there was, simply, very little? That a long book with more well-knowns than unknowns may be pyrotechnically dazzling, but doesn't, in the end, tell you more about an era and a place than a novel populated by unknowns, like *A Passage to India,* or uncanny resemblances, like *A Dance to the Music of Time*? Not to mention *Bleak House,* or *Women in Love,* or Angus Wilson's *No Laughing Matter.* But even the sceptics seem to have been held by the plot of *Ragtime;* and so they will be with *Loon Lake,* which deserves for several reasons a more levelheaded and more generally favourable reception than its immediate predecessor. Two of the reasons are the "serious"

Reprinted by permission from *Encounter*, May 1981, 86–87.

one that it comes to grips with its era (the 1930s) in an altogether more subtle and purposeful way, and the mundane one that it is a better story.

Joe Korzeniowski (but we do not know his full name until very late on) jumps a train out of his deprived and submissive existence in Paterson; a nasty place in this novel, but celebrated differently in William Carlos Williams' long poem (and can this choice of a place be coincidence?). "Joe of Paterson" ends up at Loon Lake, a Gatsby paradise carved out of the wild by the wealthy manufacturer F. W. Bennett. There he finds a failed, alcoholic "poet-in-residence", Warren Penfield, who came originally from an evicted miner's family and nurtured the intention of killing Bennett, who owned the mine. Abandoning his scheme of vengeance, Penfield has stayed at Loon Lake, to fall in love with Clara, the girl friend of a union-breaking gangster. Joe of Paterson steals Clara, lives with her in a sleazy apartment in a factory city in Indiana, gets a job in a (Bennett) car plant, is lucky to escape when a union friend is murdered by the company hit-men who have used him—and rises mercurially to realms of unimagined wealth and power.

The narrative of *Loon Lake* is divided between Joe and Penfield. There are dashbacks and delays in this unfolding of the plot, as well as various cryptic interpolations which are only explicable as the pieces of the puzzle are slowly brought together. There are also some scenes of garish viciousness which primarily seem to be there because the ethos of the modern novel appears to stipulate them. Yet the story moves surely and grippingly, out of the depressed childhoods of the two men, into the fiercely-guarded and sinister splendours of Loon Lake, and away again into the industrial badlands. We are always convincingly, and poignantly, connected with the sheer physical detail of this American Thirties world of brute despair and meretricious dreaming.

With Warren Penfield the dream fails because his feeble resolution and slender talent cannot measure up to the moral enormity of the Bennett empire which quietly absorbs him. With Joe the dream is destroyed in its own banal fulfilment. The last computer print-out of Joe's biography is a catalogue of his achievements in the world to which his careless machismo has admitted him: ending with CIA man, company director (Pennsylvania steel and Chilean-American copper), respectable "Trustee of Miss Morris' School for Young Women" and Master of Loon Lake. This is final, and damning, but of course not explained enough: Joe has risen too fast after outwitting the Jacksonstown police when under interrogation for suspected murder. But it is part of Doctorow's skill to make these allegorical wanderings of Warren and Joe part of so vivid a past world that its implied links with the present leave the reader incredulous. . . .

The American Dream in Fragments
[Review of *Loon Lake*]

SAUL MALOFF

The last page of E. L. Doctorow's new novel, *Loon Lake,* is composed entirely of a biographical digest-of-sorts, set out coldly and emptily, void of life as any computer printout or Who's Who entry. It is a skeletal "life" of Joseph Korzeniowski, the protagonist-narrator, from his origins in a working-class "ethnic" family in Paterson, New Jersey, to the year 1936, his astonishingly knowing eighteenth and the year (a turning point of course for America and the world) in which most of the novel's pivotal action is centered. But though the novel itself concludes in 1936, the barebones life is swiftly foretold in highly detailed confidence to the year 1975.

Having changed his name to Joseph Paterson Bennett in 1941 under this sponsorship of his patron F. W. Bennett, robber baron, who has amassed an immense industrial fortune as well as an immense estate in the Loon Lake district of the Adirondacks, we learn that en route to becoming F. W.'s surrogate son—appropriating not only Bennett's name but his fortune, estates, board directorships, trusteeships, club memberships, virtual identity, his very skin seemingly—he had embarked, after the close of the novel and with its certification, so to speak, on what is almost a parody of one version of American upper-class Wasp career: Williams College (varsity letters in lacrosse and swimming, ROTC, "Most Likely to Succeed" and incidentally an honors degree in Political Science), an Air Corps commission, OSS leading to a career in CIA and eventful elevation to its higher echelons, two failed marriages, an Ambassadorship, the ultimate possession of the lordly fiefdom of Loon Lake—a paradigm of American success.

None of this is absorbed into the narrative, or even foreshadowed by other events; and while all of it is historically plausible, none of it, it may be argued, is artistically inevitable, or necessary. Given these antecedents, Doctorow seems to be saying, we can securely prophesy these developments, among others which lie within the range of American possibilities of that time and place.

Reprinted from *Commonweal,* November 7, 1980, 627, 629–30. © 1980 Commonweal Foundation.

Hardly a typical American life, but in a special sense it is a representative one. "Joe of Paterson," as he refers to himself (as if in repudiation not only of his parents but of his ethnic and class affiliations through them), lives out a variant of primary American fantasy, derived in the main from movies and books. Rather the converse of fantasy, a mockery of the fantasy: Doctorow is not writing light-hearted picaresque but a moral fable full of shadow and foreboding. What does a vigorous, energetic, smart, ambitious eighteen-year-old fresh out of high school (Paterson Latin, we learn on that abundant last page) who is not notably fastidious about ways of hustling a living do in the year 1936, a time not exactly overflowing with choices? First he gets out fast—out of the old neighborhood, of town, of family, all of them gone and forgotten the moment he leaves, not a tear shed, an awkward embrace enacted, not a backward glance. Out to the open road, the American romance of the road, and whatever may turn up next, so long as it isn't a life just like his father's, only elsewhere.

And what turns up next is that fairytale fantasy of childhood and ancient dream of disconnection from personal and social ties, that American dream of absolute freedom in the wild—the traveling carnival; only this one, in which he serves as roustabout and factotum, is grim and sordid, mysterious, threatening, owned by a sinister, ugly, menacingly silent, rapacious character whose season ends in a ghostly moonlit scene of grotesque horror. The carnival's main attraction, the Fat Lady—cretinous, elephantine, a dumb mountain of meat set up for the kill, yet somehow made touching, almost delicate and lyrical by a beautiful feat of the author's sympathetic imagination—is made to take on all comers, the leering, bestial yokels pouring out of the nearby hills in the end of night for the murderous bloodbath, while the owner calmly rakes in the price of admission, the biggest gross of the season, a bundle that Joe, fleeing the scene with the owner's wife, manages to come by and which he throws to the wind in a seizure of moral revulsion. So much for the romance of "running away from home and joining the circus."

Almost at that very moment he witnesses in a fleeting tableau another image of pure American fantasy: the lonesome train hurtling by in the night through the wide vistas of virgin American territory bound for strange, far-away places. Only this train, the stuff of American folklore, will decisively change and ultimately determine the rest of the boy's life. The romantic vision is perfectly fulfilled: this train is a private train, an imperially luxurious private train running a private track through forests and into the mountains to the Loon Lake fastness where the party of guests will disport themselves for a weekend of royal pleasure. In a lighted compartment of the flashing vision the boy sees standing before her dressing mirror, appraising herself closely, a beautiful naked girl. And then the apparition is gone, vanished into the depthless American night.

Only not quite: the bewitched boy of the romantic legend must follow the enchanted maiden; he can do no other but respond helplessly to the siren's summons. Only in this anti-romantic version she is a mobster's moll, a house-gift for the host, and the mobster is the infamous Tommy Crapo, whose entrepreneurial specialty is strikebreaking and union-busting—a highly marketable enterprise—with a little killing on the side should that regrettable necessity arise; and Bennett, the lord of the manor, whose week-end guests have more typically included moguls, kings, artists (Chaplin among them), has had and now has mutually profitable business relations with Crapo and his thugs and gunmen.

Now all this, in conveying the impression that *Loon Lake* is a conventional novel unfolded along traditional narrative lines, is grossly misleading. As readers and admirers of *The Book of Daniel* and *Ragtime* know, Doctorow is nothing if not a greatly accomplished, enormously skillful and resourceful, stylistically strong and subtle, highly venturesome novelist, who disdains conventional modes while disdaining even more the blandishments of mere chic (though in some of the pointlessly unpunctuated passages he succumbs) and the empty gestures of what passes for the avant garde. Doctorow's new novel employs strategies of discontinuity, splintering, fragmentation, and certain innovations—novelties perhaps is a better term—as the governing aesthetic principles. Fragmentary intimations and retrospective views, recurring motifs and passages, sudden shifts and leaps in perspective and narrative voice, time and place, events left suspended only to be unexpectedly resumed later, the surprising intrusion of (deliberately) awful prosy verses, the work of Warren Penfield, a shambling, disheveled, besotted poet who is a kind of court retainer and clown, a man who has come there years before to kill Bennett (with good reason) and stayed to accept his patronage—all these and other devices and mannerisms exert a shattering pressure on the narrative surface, resulting in a fiction of parts, segments, shards, crystals. Piecemeal, at wide intervals, we learn that Penfield goes off on what is intended as a round-the-world airplane trip with Bennett's wife, a celebrated flyer, and they will disappear into the blue; that the boy will make his way out of Loon Lake with his trophy Clara and will lose her again to Crapo, and after that take up with the child-wife of one of Crapo's spies who is murdered not by the union organizers he has betrayed but by his employer, and that he will in the midst of their flight to California and its promises of a new life desert her, abruptly abandon her and her child, disappear while she sleeps and return to Loon Lake and his patron and the waiting future.

The danger for the novelist is that the multifaceted mariner, so ornate and elaborate, so contrived and self-conscious, so pervasive and inescapable— that the manner, the technical apparatus of the novel, can overwhelm the wonderfully imagined fiction itself, leaving little more than the performance, the virtuosity, the dazzling display; and it is only Doctorow's high seriousness, artistic conscience and powerful gifts that prevent such sundering and dissolution. *Loon Lake* is a work of marvelous fragments and noble intentions, and it is unmistakably the work of a formidable writer, clearly one of the very small band of novelists here or anywhere, with a claim on our most serious attention. But we are asked to take too much on faith, asked in fact to collaborate in the act of creation: a notation is not a life, an anecdote is not a myth, a dip in the lake—even a triumphantly strong swim in the shimmering waters of Loon Lake in full view of the formerly omnipotent, now aged and diminished "father"—is not a ritual rebirth. If, finally, *Loon Lake* fails to attain the reverberant wholeness and coherence of the fully achieved work of art, it is the kind of superb "failure" which exposes the hollowness and glitter of most literary success.

Singing the Same Old Songs
[Review of *Loon Lake*]

PEARL K. BELL

• • • E. L. Doctorow, who was born in the same year as Richler—
1931—did not publish his first novel, *Welcome to Hard Times,* until 1960. Fifteen years later, Doctorow's fourth book, *Ragtime,* brought him the kind of
success that serious novelists rarely enjoy. Not only was *Ragtime* a huge seller,
but it was virtually canonized by the critics, and the few dissenting voices—
Hilton Kramer's in these pages, Greil Marcus's in the *Village Voice*—were all
but drowned out by the hallelujah chorus proclaiming *Ragtime* a masterpiece
that provided a stunningly fresh assent to the radical disaffection with America which engulfed the society during the Vietnam war. By wrapping his ideological fable for the 70's in a deceptively pretty turn-of-the-century package,
Doctorow pandered to every modish piety of his own time—America the
Decadent, the sexist repression of women, the racist oppression of blacks, and
the sinister power of American imperialism—while seeming to be engaged in
nothing more than a charming exercise in nostalgia for the vanished simplici-
ties of yesteryear.

But it took a while for the polemical design of the book to yield itself
with unmistakable clarity. What was remarkable about the book's initial
reception, as Hilton Kramer observed, was the reviewers' seeming blindness
to the novel's political objective, which he attributed to the fact "that our culture is now so completely permeated with the myth of American malevolence
that an ambitious political romance like *Ragtime,* which distorts the actual
materials of history with a fierce ideological arrogance, is no longer in any
danger of being recognized as having a blunt political point."

If the reviewers had looked back at *The Book of Daniel,* the novel Doctorow published four years before *Ragtime,* they would have realized that no
matter what disingenuous games he played in *Ragtime* with historical figures
manipulated as literary inventions, or with the domestic appurtenances of
middle-class New Rochelle at the beginning of the century, this writer
regards himself above all as a political novelist. *The Book of Daniel* was an
account of the Rosenberg case as told by their grown son, who is certain of

their innocence, and unequivocally committed to a conspiratorial view of his parents' trial and execution and of the "totalitarian society" that singled them out for martyrdom. In his didactic zeal to spell out these convictions, Doctorow expanded the Rosenberg drama with ironic lectures on such things as "The True History of the Cold War" and the hidden function of Disneyland as a training ground for the control of potentially dangerous crowds. Though the political argument of *The Book of Daniel* would hardly have been offensive to liberal readers of 1971, the style was more devious and self-consciously literary than the simple declarative rhythms of *Ragtime,* and failed to exert the direct appeal of the sugar-coated ideological tale that, four years later, opened the floodgates for E. L. Doctorow.

But what does a novelist do for an encore when such phenomenal success is behind him? It is a recurrent problem in American literary culture. Some novelists are struck dumb by extravagant celebration, but others, like Norman Mailer and William Styron, accept that the onus is now on them to come up with something new and different. So with Doctorow, who has now written a novel, *Loon Lake,* that is remarkably unlike anything he has published before. Yet not even by the most generous standards can it be called a remarkable novel. It is difficult at first to get any clear sense of what he is trying to do, and the mannered incoherence and stylistic confusion are in sharp contrast to the sleek, bright assurance of *Ragtime.* Though *Loon Lake* takes place in the 1930's, during the American Depression, and deals in several chapters with the labor strife of the period, the political themes one might expect are almost always sounded with weary indirectness, and only at the very end—on the very last page, in fact—can we fully grasp Doctorow's polemical intentions.

The narrative proper covers several picaresque years in the life of a young roughneck from Paterson, the son of wretchedly poor mill hands, who runs away from home, joins a gang of hobos, becomes a carnival roustabout, and stumbles accidentally onto Loon Lake, the vast Adirondack estate of the steel tycoon F. W. Bennett. One of the old industrialist's toys is a gangster's moll who sneaks out of Loon Lake with Joe, and the two settle down for a while in a steel town owned by one of Bennett's many companies. She leaves him, and Joe goes back to Loon Lake, is taken in by the old man, and that is literally the end of the story, except for a fraudulent last page whose extraordinary revelations have no plausible connection with the rest of the book. Doctorow makes only perfunctory stabs at endowing any of the characters with a semblance of life. If Joe is deliberately conceived as a cipher, like the cardboard figures of *Ragtime,* we are given no hint, until the end, of the idea, political or otherwise, he is meant to embody.

It is not the thin story, however, that betrays the desperation behind this baffling performance, but the ostentatious structure Doctorow has devised to fatten his undernourished tale. The adventures of young Joe are repeatedly interrupted by mysterious computer printouts supplying biographical data on the various characters or offering elaborate rationales for the sins of capitalism. Eventually we realize what lies behind this printout device: the ubiquitous computer that knows all and tells all is Doctorow's symbol for the dehumanized technology of a military-industrial world, the tyrannical machine that overwhelms its operators and reduces the entire culture to unfeeling statistics: the computer becomes the mechanical master of a mechanical world devoid of justice or human emotion.

In addition to the all-knowing computer, Doctorow also strews the narrative with elaborate verbal tricks, puns, pseudo-poetic doodling, and signals leading nowhere. For instance, in the computer-printout biography that concludes *Loon Lake,* we are told for the first time that the full name of the hero is Joseph Korzeniowski. This jolts us awake, since Korzeniowski was the real name of Joseph Conrad, but since there is not the remotest connection between Doctorow's novel and Conrad, the name must be taken as a whimsical in-joke signifying nothing. The book is full of incomprehensible pranks like this, dropped into the story at random to lend it an air of experimental, "modernist" daring. There are also run-on sentences, stream-of-consciousness monologues, typographical games, and every so often ruminations in the author's own voice about strikes, the Depression, the Ludlow mine disaster of 1914, and the irredeemable rottenness of American civilization.

If a good deal of this seems familiar, it is no accident. The unacknowledged ghost of John Dos Passos—the brilliantly innovative Dos Passos of *U.S.A.*—haunts just about every page of *Loon Lake.* Doctorow's computer biographies are a weak imitation of the portraits—of business magnates, political leaders, labor heroes, intellectuals, and scientists—that Dos Passos juxtaposed against the unheard and unremembered lives of the poor in Depression America. But while the Dos Passos biographies convey a living sense of history through the men who shaped and changed the American scene, Doctorow's printouts provide only unassimilated facts that have no bearing on a unique historical moment. Doctorow's Joe, the poor but ambitious mongrel who grabs whatever life throws in his path, has more than a few counterparts in *U.S.A.* And Doctorow's failed poet, Warren Penfield, is in many respects reminiscent of Dos Passos's Richard Savage, the spoiled idealist and poet corrupted by the main chance. The impressionistic commentaries of the "Camera Eye" in *U.S.A.*—the voice of Dos Passos—are also paralleled in Doctorow's ironic and bitter soliloquies, written in the monotone of computer language, indicting "the industrial Western democracies" for "the tendency of legislation to serve the interests of the ruling business oligarchy the poisoning of the air water . . . the obscene development of hideous weaponry the increased costs of simple survival the waste of human resources. . . ."

In such passages the computer is turned into an ideological instrument tapping out its message about the evils of present-day American society, but they sound like nothing so much as a throwback to the agit-prop radicalism of the 1930's. Doctorow is determined to resist any counterrevolutionary suggestion that anything has changed for the better over the course of the last half-century. But since he fails to enrich his judgment with anything like the immediacy Dos Passos achieved with his technical experiments, *Loon Lake* conveys little more than the author's hortatory ineptitude.

For it is only on the last page of the novel that Doctorow finally reveals the key, and by then it seems more preposterous than illuminating. The ubiquitous computer is hauled in for one last sinister printout, and as it taps out the bare facts of Joe's life, we learn that he was adopted by his capitalist benefactor, went to an Ivy League college, and served in the OSS during the war. As the computer clacks along, disgorging its data, we finally come to the kicker: "Appointed organization staff Central Intelligence Agency 1947. . . . Continuous service Central Intelligence Agency to resignation 1974. Retiring rank Deputy Assistant Director." And—aha!—there we have it, the worm in the apple, the hidden theme of *Loon Lake:* the corruption of the American working class by the evil forces of wealth and power.

Clearly Doctorow has nothing new to add to his old radical litany. Trapped in the simpleminded futility of his political dogmas, he is doomed to sing the same old songs over and over again.

Doctorow's "Hit" Is a Miss
[Review of *Loon Lake*]

ANTHONY BURGESS

The excitement caused by *Ragtime* five years ago was so great that, long before its European publication, we who live on the Mediterranean were itching to get hold of a copy. Summoned to Hollywood for a script conference, I made straight for a Los Angeles bookstore and bought one. Jet lag abetted my decision to read the book before even making amicable contact with my temporary masters at Universal. I was, of course, disappointed. Literary reality has never yet lived up to literary expectation. But that E. L. Doctorow was a genuine experimentalist I did not doubt. The aim of *Ragtime* was as purely aesthetic as that of *Ulysses:* The joy lay in the manipulation of the crass elements of history. Houdini and Scott Joplin and Freud and Jung and certain of their less reputable contemporaries were drawn into a kind of ballet. Bernard Shaw had done something similar in his *In Good King Charles's Golden Days,* but Doctorow's achievement didn't seem derivative.

Rereading *Ragtime,* I find that most of the initial impact has been blunted: Literary shocks are subject to the law of diminishing returns. I find, too, a certain vacuity of literary display. What once seemed verbally startling is now revealed as mostly tinsel. But that Doctorow was superior to most of his American fellow-novelists in his concentration on fiction as form, not as a vehicle for special or ethnic preaching, is made very clear. A rereading of *Welcome to Hard Times* and *The Book of Daniel* has confirmed Doctorow's special status. *Loon Lake* exhibits a new formal direction. It is a difficult book and I don't think it is a successful one. But it is a very honorable attempt at expanding the resources of the genre.

Set in the prewar Depression period, the novel concerns a young man whose name is finally revealed as Joseph Korzeniowski, though he is a.k.a. Joe of Paterson (New Jersey) and changes his name legally to Joseph Paterson Bennett. This name change symbolizes fulfillment of the American dream, since Joe's elected nominal pseudofather is the great automobile magnate Bennett, master of a mansion on Loon Lake. Joe himself, according to the capsule biography that comes at the end of the story, achieves the identical

Reprinted from *Saturday Review* 7 (September 1980): 66-67.

mastership, but the narrative explicitly presents only the years of struggle—
two years. In 1936 Joe works in a traveling carnival, obtains a job on Loon
Lake, moves to a Bennett automobile factory, and becomes involved in union
trouble; by the end of 1937 he is enrolled in Williams College and heading
for a distinguished career. His career is paralleled by one less distinguished—
that of the poet Warren Penfield, whose reminiscences of an exile in Japan
form a counterpoint to Joe's narrative and who achieves the sinecure of Poet
in Residence at Loon Lake, thus swimming into Joe's spatial orbit, or it may
be the other way round.

The paronomastic possibilities of the historical term Depression have not
been lost on Doctorow. This is a depressed and depressing story, not really
much modified by learning Joe will triumph. Depression forbids overmuch
coherence. Doctorow's prose patterns eschew punctuation of the regular
kind: "I would sell pencils on the sidewalk in front of department stores I
would be a newsboy I would steal kill use all my cunning but never would I
lose the look in my eye of the living spirit, or give up till that silent secret
presence grew out to the edges of me and I was the same as he, imposed upon
myself in full completion, the same man with all men, the one man in all
events. . . ." There is a faint odor of John Dos Passos, abetted by the bio as
well as the radical tone, or subdued hysteria, of the narrative. There is also a
kind of verse:

> Commingling with me she becomes me
> Coming she is coming is she
> Coming she is a comrade of mine
> Comrades come all over comrades
> Communists come upon communists
> Hi Hi.

Here the Com motif is more musical than logical. You travel from orgasm to
political organization along an arbitrary morpheme. It is Doctorow's way.

Sometimes whole patches of *récit* are presented in *vers libre:*

> She strode off down the trail toward the big house
> and they were not to see her again that day
> neither at drinks which were at six-thirty
> nor dinner at seven-thirty.
> But her husband was a gracious host
> attentive to the women particularly.
> He revealed that she was a famous aviatrix
> and some of them recognized her name from the newspapers.

Under the shifting verbal patterns—which draw attention to themselves
more blatantly than is usually considered seemly in a novel—characters stir
(including the famous aviatrix) and sometimes rise to dominate the flow, so

that we become aware of them in the traditional cinematic way, forgetting the technique of their presentation.

But Doctorow will not permit us to settle into a comfortable read for long. Apart from his abrupt transitions, there is the tendency to confuse us by not separating the imagined from the actual. "The light is blinding. I become my own size and break her open like an egg." But, we are told, "You are thinking it is a dream. It is no dream. It is the account in helpless linear translation of the unending love of our simultaneous but disynchronous lives." The gloom and violence are occasionally irradiated by such cerebral conceits. "The story of Noah is the religious vision of cloning." Try that on your alto flute.

I am happy to learn that *Loon Lake* is already a popular book, in that it is a Book of the Month Club choice and eighty-odd thousand copies have already been printed. Happy because, whatever the faults of the work (nearly always the admirable faults of the overreacher), serious students of the novel must recognize here a bracing technical liberation, and such a recognition is being forced upon a readership probably happier with *Princess Daisy*. The bulk of our popular fiction is the work of either cynics or simpletons. The serious novelist's problem is to be uncompromising and yet to find an audience. Doctorow has found an audience and nothing could be less of a fictional compromise than *Loon Lake*. Like most writers who consider the craft to be primarily an exploration of the nature of human consciousness, he is brought up against such damnable problems as the validity of memory, the truthfulness of the senses, and, more than anything, the ghastly dilemmas of style. And, behind the epistemological agonies, there rests that basic obligation of all but the French anti-novelists—to invent living personages and a convincing space-time continuum to hold them. Doctorow's characters—Joe, Penfield, Clara, even the grotesque Fat Lady of the carney—are alive, unrefracted by the often wayward medium. That *Loon Lake* breaks new technical ground and yet possesses so many of the traditional virtues of fiction must be accounted its peculiar distinction.

New Jersey Joe
[Review of *Loon Lake*]

NICHOLAS SHRIMPTON

The trouble with Doctorow is that he's twice the man you expect him to be. In part he's an aesthete, concerned to have fun with the form. But, simultaneously, the author of *The Book of Daniel* is a dourly political novelist who writes serious books about American economic and social history. Such an unusual combination of interests, inevitably, runs him headlong into a deep-rooted critical prejudice. Our otherwise indecorous age has a surprisingly acute sense of narrative decorum. Modernist formal experiment is assumed to belong to the novel of sensibility, to the exploration of the interior life. On the other hand, though few of us care to be Socialist Realists, we retain a sneaking belief that political fiction should be plain, precise and pellucid. Doctorow's novels challenge these easy assumptions.

Not all of his difficulties with the English critics, however, can be attributed to an ossified sense that formal East and thematic West must necessarily be poles apart. Making the twain meet is a tricky business and he hasn't always brought it off. *Ragtime* set out to provide a syncopated saga of American life between 1902 and 1917, linking its rapid snapshots of real events with some faint family history and a Marxist conception of the inevitability of war. In America it caught the bicentennial mood and triumphed in the nostalgia market. From the more dispassionate British viewpoint it seemed, like any scrapbook, scrappy.

Loon Lake shows a similar formal daring and exploits it to rather greater effect. Where *Ragtime* offered a linear, historical panorama, the new novel cuts a vertical swathe through American society in a single year, 1936. At one moment our hero is hobnobbing with a coal-baron in a luxurious hunting lodge. At the next he is out of work and freezing in a Mid-West industrial slum. The eccentric handling of the time sequence, and the frequent shifts of narrative viewpoint make these vertiginous alternations all the more striking. Loons, as English readers may not initially realise, are birds which hunt fish by diving into lakes. Doctorow's exploration of the body politic is here conducted by a constant process of diving and rising.

Reprinted from *New Statesman* 100 (October 31, 1980): 27. © New Statesman, 1999.

The action begins at the bottom of the pond—in Paterson, New Jersey, where Joe Korzeniowsky is a working-class boy having trouble with his parents. He runs away to New York and tricks his way into a job. But after committing a clumsy theft he is obliged to take to the road, and eventually becomes that most romantic of figures, a roustabout for a travelling circus. Hearn Brothers Carnival, however, is no Dickensian image of the life of the imagination, and Sim Hearn is a world away from Sleary. Instead, this is the book's most extreme example of economic exploitation. At first we are made to feel that the freaks exhibited in Hearn's human menagerie have been rescued from more miserable lives in homes and institutions. But as the season draws to an end (and as the novel's fragmented narrative structure belatedly releases the crucial information) the Roman nature of this circus becomes clear. Hearn prostitutes his exhibits to the warped tastes of his customers. The final engagement is a commercial gang-bang in which Fanny the Fat Lady is murdered in the ring.

Though Joe runs in disgust from this gross demonstration of man's calculating inhumanity to man, the very woods into which he flees have become the property of some not dissimilar capitalists. He finds himself at Loon Lake, the country retreat of a coal and car baron called F. W. Bennett. Here the pattern of exploitation is more elegantly repeated. Joe is engaged as a servant and falls in love with Bennett's mistress Clara. But when Joe runs away with her his poverty rapidly obliges him to take a job in one of Bennett's own car factories. Ground down on the line, he is finally beaten up and falsely accused of murder by company agents.

Violent though such ploy may seem, Doctorow's image of capitalism is less the jungle than the web. The riding and boating and enlightened literary patronage of Loon Lake are shown to be indissolubly connected with the sweat and grime of the Autobody Plant. Characters who appear in one guise in the sunshine of the country estate reappear in another in the gloom of industrial Jacksontown. And the way in which the time sequence of the story is broken, shuffled and redeployed involves not only a perpetual mingling of the two extremes of Bennett's life, but also a perpetual mirroring of its cruelty in the brutal glass of the circus.

Doctorow's formal innovations, in other works, are here a mode of intensification rather than complication. Though his methods may seem oblique, he is actually driving home some familiar parallels by violent juxtaposition. And though his purposes may seem detachedly historical, his final page asserts a sudden contemporary relevance. Joe, having unexpectedly become Bennett's adopted son, goes on to enjoy a successful career as an agent of the CIA. A second lifestyle, that of an unsuccessful poet called Warren Penfield, provides a counterpoint in the form of a kind of spiritual picaresque. But in the end its effect is marginal. *Loon Lake* remains a strong but simple book. The feverish haste of *Ragtime* has been cured. But Doctorow's narrative sophistication and political engagement still await a corresponding subtlety of thought.

[Review of *Lives of the Poets: Six Stories and a Novella*]

C. G. STORMS

Consisting of six short stories and a novella, E. L. Doctorow's *Lives of the Poets* continues the formal experimentation Doctorow began in *The Book of Daniel* (1971) and continued in *Ragtime* (1975) and *Loon Lake* (1980). As the stories' characters move from childhood to maturity and learn about the realities of death, sexuality, and loneliness, Doctorow portrays, as he has in earlier works, the ways in which these characters impose a fictive order upon experience. In the novella, the imaginary author of the stories tells how he has left his wife in order to live and write in a Manhattan apartment. As he describes his own life and the lives of his friends, the images and themes of the earlier stories emerge, revealing how the material for the artist's fiction is gathered in his experience and transformed in his imagination. *Lives of the Poets* is a bold formal experiment, and it includes some sharply focused satire on failed marriages, middle-aged crises of confidence and the social life of New York literary society. However, Doctorow's portrayal of the individual's transformation of experience into art is less compelling than in some of his other works, notably *Ragtime* and *Loon Lake*. The stories in *Lives of the Poets,* in fact, seem more interesting in their economy and the starkness of their images than the novella. Still, this book is skillfully written and in no way diminishes Doctorow's well-established literary achievement. For students (community college through graduate) and general readers.

Reprinted with permission from *Choice*, March 1985. © by the American Library Association.

The Creative Muse
[Review of *Lives of the Poets: Six Stories and a Novella*]

PETER S. PRESCOTT

The distinguishing characteristic of E. L. Doctorow's work is its double vision. In each of his books he experiments with the forms of fiction, working for effect that others haven't already achieved; in each, he develops a tone, a structure and a texture that he hasn't used before. At the same time, he's a deeply traditional writer, reworking American history, American literary archetypes, even exhausted subliterary genres. It's an astonishing performance, really; about the only thing a reader approaching one of his books can be sure of is that Doctorow won't give him quite what he expects.

"Lives of the Poets" works in a way I've never seen attempted before. It can be read as a collection of short stories, or as a novel, or as both at once. Again, Doctorow embraces one of the hoariest of literary themes: the peculiar vulnerability of a writer transmuting fragments of his own experience into fiction. It's hard to imagine how anything new can be wrought from such material; half the unpublishable novels rejected by editors today—and too many of those published—deal with just this subject. Yet Doctorow brings it off triumphantly, in part because he never shows us his writer writing and because he says nothing directly about the process of writing fiction. Instead, he shows us how a writer's mind works.

Six short stories precede the novella from which the collection takes its name. The novella should be read last, but it may be useful to consider it first, for it invites us to infer that its narrator, known only as Jonathan, is the author of the other stories. Jonathan is a husband and a father; he has two houses and yet he has taken an apartment for himself in Soho. There perhaps he will write, or welcome his mistress, should she return from roaming the world. "I am doing this," he says, "to find out why I'm doing it." At 50, Jonathan is undergoing a full-dress midlife crisis; he's concerned now with matters that never trouble the young. He's thinking about the Zeitgeist, entropy and the "doom of commitment . . . this drift through the blood of my obsolescence." Everything seems to be winding down: his body succumbs to bumps and stiffness his friends are falling out of marriage and talking too much about it. "Whatever happened to discretion? Where is pride? What has caused this decline in tact and duplicity?"

Yet Jonathan is far from despair. He senses in the city around him signs of renewal. Though Jonathan never comments on his work, the reader can recognize certain phrases, images and turns of thought that Jonathan has already altered to serve the six preceding stories. In creating the fictional Jonathan, Doctorow creates the fiction that he has made art out of his life; the truth is, he has created a life to account for the fiction.

Wounds: If the novella is Doctorow's "Odyssey," an epic voyage through its narrator's sensibility, full of unplanned detours and moral dangers, the stories, too, are about migrations of different sorts. Each has its own style, its own place, its own time, yet there's a unity as well. Each is written with the utmost economy and restraint; in each, Doctorow is looking for open wounds in the heart—he takes us where the hurt is. Against his will, a boy is obliged by his aunt to forge letters from his dead father to his grandmother, who is unaware of her son's death. Another boy (which is to say another fragment of Jonathan's experience put to use in fiction) discovers his mother making love to his tutor; unable to cope with the experience, the boy betrays his mother to his father. In a third story, reminiscent of those in "Winesburg, Ohio," Doctorow exposes the loneliness of a seemingly vivacious young woman on the verge of a nervous breakdown.

One of Doctorow's narrators observes that Houdini had a routine: "getting out of the kind of straitjacket to break the heart." The image serves a precise purpose in the story, but it's a metaphor, too: all these stories are about straitjackets to break the heart. Better than any fiction I know, "Lives of the Poets" illuminates the sources from which fiction springs.

[Review of *World's Fair*]

JANET WIEHE

World's Fair is a nostalgic fictional memoir of life in New York City in the 1930s as observed by a child who recounts his first nine years. Interspersed in Edgar's narrative are chapters by his mother and his older brother, Donald, whose realistic perceptions underline the innocence of Edgar's own. The family faces hard times as the father's business fails, Donald leaves home, Edgar's senile grandmother dies, and Edgar is hospitalized with a burst appendix. But the World's Fair (Edgar wins free admission in an "American Boyhood" essay contest) holds promise for the future; and his experience there offers Edgar the recognition that he's growing up, finding his place in the world. In a mellow and moving novel, Doctorow re-creates in careful detail both a specific historical era and a childhood universal in its pleasures and its great desire to "catch up to life . . . [to] comprehend it."

Reprinted from *Library Journal,* October 15, 1985, 101.

Fiction
[Review of *World's Fair*]

The 1930s was a turbulent time for America: the Great Depression, left-wing politics and the growing concern over the rise of Hitler in Europe. As seen through the eyes of nine-year-old Edgar Altschuler, these events provide a backdrop for the more intimate story of his own family and how they coped while living in the Bronx. They serve a symbolic purpose as well as a historical one. On his first visit to the fair, Edgar is enthralled by industry's vision of the future—safe, secure and prosperous cities, speedy and cheap transportation and modern invention to make life easier. On his second visit, he sees that the exhibits are constructed of gypsum whose paint is peeling and that the displays are really toys. Reality has altered Edgar's perceptions—he is growing up. Edgar's chapters are randomly interspersed with his mother Rose's recollections and a few by his older brother Donald to give a seemingly simplistic view of life that is actually a rich narrative of history, political and personal values and points for discussion. A remarkable book for perceptive readers.

From *School Library Journal*, February 1986. Reproduced, with permission, from *School Library Journal* Copyright © By Cahners Business Information A Division of Reed Elsevier Inc.

Looking Back on the World of Tomorrow
[Review of *World's Fair*]

DAVID LEAVITT

World's Fair" by E. L. Doctorow is a peculiar hybrid of novel and memoir. Its hero, like Mr. Doctorow, is named Edgar, and grows up in the Bronx in the 1930's; his parents, like Mr. Doctorow's parents, are named Rose and Dave; his brother, like the author's brother, Donald. The family's last name is Altschuler. One is reminded of Renata Adler's novel "Pitch Dark," in which the heroine, Kate Ennis, must choose a name similar to, yet slightly different from, her own and decides on Alder; in both these works, the naming strategy seems to be a kind of tipoff, a way of telling the reader that the book at hand will unapologetically combine fiction and memory.

By flaunting the artificial line dividing the true from the imagined, Mr. Doctorow not only suggests in "World's Fair" that the process of remembering is by definition a process of invention, he rejects altogether the notion that imagination and memory are ever pure of each other. His purpose in "World's Fair" seems to be to create a work that succeeds as oral history, memoir and novel all at once. Unfortunately, these disparate genres don't always make the best of bedfellows, and until its breathtaking final 100 pages, when it becomes most fully novelistic, Mr. Doctorow's new novel seems as peculiar a mix of brilliant vision and clumsy self-indulgence as the fair it so artfully describes.

"World's Fair" is told almost exclusively from the first-person point of view of young Edgar Altschuler, following the course of his childhood from early infancy through the age of 9, and ending with Edgar's visit to the magnificent World's Fair of 1939 in Flushing Meadow. As is appropriate to such a point of view, the large events surrounding Edgar—World War II, his father's bankruptcy, the slow burn of his parents' marriage—fall to the background and the narrative focuses on the schoolyard, park and living room which form the centers of a young boy's life. Edgar's mode is primarily recollective, and

Reprinted from *New York Times Book Review*, November 10, 1985, 3, 25.

the story moves forward through time with all the fluidity of memory, stopping along the way to focus on the finely honed *tableaux vivants* of life in the Bronx during the Depression: a visit to a kosher butcher, the fall of Edgar's pensive, Yiddish-speaking grandmother into senility and rage and the delectable pleasure of buying a roasted sweet potato from a pushcart vendor on the street. Edgar is smart, adventurous, slightly vain, a passionate observer of the world around him, and in much of "World's Fair" the older Edgar describes that world in language that is both hypnotic and wonderfully precise, skillfully articulating the inarticulate passions of childhood. In one particularly memorable passage, Edgar watches his brother, Donald, and some of his friends build a backyard igloo:

"As they slowly built the igloo up on an ever decreasing circumference, I watched with a sense of the anti-material oppositeness of the thing; bit by bit, it was eliminating itself as an idea from the light of the sun. I felt that what was being built was not a shelter, but some structured withdrawal from the beneficence of the lighted day, and my excitement was for invited darkness, the reckless enclosure, as if by perverse and self-destructive will, of a secret possibility of life that would be better untampered with."

This is dazzling prose—the sort of writing on which Mr. Doctorow has built his reputation in such works as "Ragtime," "The Book of Daniel" and "Lives of the Poets"—and it exemplifies the richness of much of this novel. There is wonderful description, later on, of the wrecked Hindenberg zeppelin ("They were not supposed ever to touch land, they were tethered to tall towers, they were sky creatures; and this one had fallen in flames to the ground") a skilled and revealing portrait of Edgar's gentle, somewhat dopey father (his "was a peasant vision, a thing of funny papers and dialect jokes"). But what is one to make, then, of prose as artless and imprecise as this description of Edgar's visits to the home of his friend Meg and her mother, a "ten cents a dance" entertainer?

"When the mother wasn't home, or when she went out while I was there, I was disappointed. The visit became less interesting. She smiled when she saw me. She had large eyes, widely spaced, and a wide mouth. She was very kind. Sometimes she joined us in our games. She would sit on the floor with us, and we three would have a good time."

This kind of prose, characterized by stunted or run-on sentences, narrative slackness and a blurring rather than a crystallization of detail, becomes increasingly predominant as "World's Fair" progresses, and contrasts shockingly with the hallucinatory, Whitmanesque elegance of the rest of the novel. One suspects that Mr. Doctorow is trying to recreate here the rhythms of speech, the sound of oral history, but instead has lapsed into prose that seems merely lazy.

Another problem the author comes up against—particularly in the first half of the book—is the unwavering narrowness of his recollecting protagonist's point of view. While young Edgar's perspective on the world can give rise to some magnificent descriptive passages, much of the family ritual he evokes has a kind of archetypal quality, and as a result seems disembodied. The finely drawn Passover seder, for instance, suffers from its detachment from any story; it is presented as the exemplary, average seder, and hence its inclusion in the novel seems to be more the result of nostalgic recollecting than a true narrative impulse. Too much of young Edgar's remembrances, moreover, consists of tedious description of radio and movie serial plots ("The Shadow" and "Zorro"), and tired adolescent fantasy: "I knew that if I had the power to be invisible I would go into the girls' bathroom at P.S. 70 and watch them pulling their drawers down," he tells us, then goes on to fantasize what comic-book heroics invisibility might allow him to achieve. This is overdone material to which Mr. Doctorow brings little fresh light.

As if to compensate for sticking so closely to his child-narrator's point of view, Mr. Doctorow punctuates the novel with a kind of fractured commentary offered first by Rose and then by Donald. These interpolations suggest a larger, more adult perspective on the world Edgar describes, but unfortunately there just aren't enough of them. Rose's narration stops abruptly a quarter of the way through the novel; Donald's is limited to two short monologues. The voices in which they speak, moreover, are halting and imprecise, not the tones of people conversing or telling stories as much as the awkward, faux-sophisticated voices that people affect when talking into tape recorders. One suspects that this quality of oral history is exactly what Mr. Doctorow is trying for here—all of Rose's and Donald's remembrances are addressed to a "you" who is presumably Edgar himself—but to what end is hard to see; difficult to read and short on specific detail, these passages seem the revelations of uncomfortable people remembering under duress.

It is, in fact, only in the novel's last third, when Edgar finally goes to the fair, that Mr. Doctorow achieves the descriptive fullness and sense of narrative intention that initially seem so elusive. Edgar's meticulous accounting of the World's Fair, which he visits twice, is dizzying in its specificity, revealing the fair as a peculiar combination of noble utopian intent and vulgar sideshow. (The mother of his friend Meg works at the fair wrestling with "Oscar the Amorous Octopus.") To young Edgar, even the crudest corner of the fair is wonderful, as Mr. Doctorow demonstrates in this scene in which Edgar buys Meg a ring from a human giant's finger:

"I held out one of my dollars. The large hand gently took it from me. I was surprised at the humanity of this commerce. The giant hand deposited a half dollar in my palm. Some sort of sound, like distant thunder, issued from him, and then found tone. He was chuckling. The giant removed a ring from his enormous finger and lifted her arm and slipped the ring over her hand and onto her wrist."

Mr. Doctorow conveys perfectly the extent to which a fair becomes a world unto itself, into which a child can become utterly absorbed: "As the evening wore on I forgot everything but the World's Fair," Edgar tells us. "I forgot everything that wasn't the Fair as if the Fair was all there was, as if going on rides and seeing the sights, with crowds of people around you and music in your head, were natural life, I didn't think of my mother or my father or my brother, or of school or the Bronx or even of keeping my wits about me and watching my step." It is this sense of removal from the real world—perched, in 1939, between the Depression and war—that the fair was designed to offer, and Mr. Doctorow communicates this idea by focusing on a single detail from the World of Tomorrow—a diorama showing a utopian city of the future:

"And then the amazing thing was that at the end you saw a particular model street intersection and the show was over," Edgar exclaims, "and with your I HAVE SEEN THE FUTURE button in your hand you came out into the sun and you were standing on precisely the corner you had just seen, the future was right where you were standing and what was small had become big, the scale had enlarged and you were no longer looking down at it, but standing in it, on this corner of the future, right here in the World's Fair!"

The tragedy was, of course, that the "corner of the future" was an illusion, just as the fair was an illusion; a thing of paper and metal. Still, Mr. Doctorow insists upon the nobility of the fair's intention, just as he insists upon the nobility of his young protagonist, and of the era he lives in—an era which, for all its hopelessness, nonetheless had the imagination and faith to erect and enjoy such a monument to farsighted unreality. Such a penchant for imagination and faith in a Bronx-born child of immigrants, Mr. Doctorow suggests, is the seed of the future he will grow up to inhabit—a future that will prove to be as glamorous and unreal as the miniature World of Tomorrow at the fair, and at the same time as tragically self-deluding as the imperfect world outside the utopian enclosure at Flushing Meadow.

At the very end of "World's Fair," Edgar, in imitation of the fair's organizers, plants his own personal time capsule in Claremont Park, then walks home practicing the "vetriloquial drone" he is trying to learn from a book called "Ventriloquism Self-Taught." It's not hard to wonder if Mr. Doctorow means to suggest in this final image that fiction-writing itself is a kind of ventriloquism, a matter of throwing a voice out and listening for it, seeing how similar or how different it is from the voice with which one normally speaks. Biography or oral history need employ no such trickery; they can get by on the power of plain speaking.

And that, perhaps, is why "World's Fair," as an amalgam of these genres, has a fractured and inconsistent feel to it. Its structure is that of an autobiography, beginning at the beginning and moving through the life of its protagonist with the thoroughness of a catalogue; but where a work of biography derives its imperative from the significance of the life it describes, in a novel, it is the author, not the subject, who must provide the reader with a sense of what to read for; we, as readers, expect from a novel an organizing principle more substantive than chronology, and implicit sense of direction and occasional clues, no matter how vague, that we're moving toward some revelation. And that is what seems to me to be wrong with "World's Fair"; only in its last third, where it becomes most fully novelistic, does this oddly shaped book achieve a sense of purpose and offer the rich rewards readers have come to expect from Mr. Doctorow's work. Until that point, the reader feels as if he were listening to young Edgar in the park, practicing his ventriloquial drone: a child chattering to himself, and only sometimes achieving the compelling thrown voice of true fiction.

Pyrography
[Review of *World's Fair*]

EDMUND WHITE

The very modesty of E. L. Doctorow's new novel is its most daring aspect, but it's a dare that pays off. In so many autobiographical novels the writer is tempted to gift himself with nearly perfect recall and to turn his early experiences into signs of his own later genius. Doctorow avoids these temptations and sticks close to memory, its gaps and haziness as well as its pockets of poetic lucidity. He never divines in his Jewish middle-class Bronx childhood of the 1930s the extraordinary eloquence and wisdom he was later to win for himself.

Doctorow trusts his material. He also trusts his recollections, no matter how incomplete they may be in some places. This is not a book about the deceptions of memory. In some slight instances the narrator's brother or mother, who are both given their turn to speak, may correct the facts as presented earlier, but the corrections are only a question of five dollars more or a year older. This is a novel in which the brick buildings and the summer light arc as intense, as substantial and as present as in a Hopper painting.

The sentences are short, the presentation straightforward, the chronology strict. The narrator seldom indulges in psychological speculation about his past self or his parents' motives. The epic ordinariness of people's lives is the meat of this novel. That this ordinariness should apply to the story of a Jewish kid who is often ill, who fears the local hoodlums, who overhears his parents' late-night quarrels only proves how heterogeneous American life is. There is no norm; the rule is nothing but the exception. At the end of the novel the teen-age hero places in a contest by writing an essay on the typical American boy. The one-paragraph essay concludes that the typical American boy is kind and "cooperates with his parents. He knows the value of a dollar. He looks death in the face." This disarming, oddly satisfying sequence sets the tone for the book.

Along the way the author examines the phenomenology of everyday life. Any book in which a young person is being inducted into the mysteries of

Reprinted with permission from the November 30, 1985 issue of *The Nation*.

adult life permits us to take a slow, puzzled look at conventions usually too close to be seen. With a sure touch Doctorow renders the conventions as well as the landscape against which they occur. We catch glimpses of a Woman With a Past (a childhood sweetheart's affable pretty mother). We overhear echoes of rancor from the in-laws who think their daughter-in-law is a Spendthrift and in any event Not Good Enough (the maligned woman is the boy's mother). From the boy's point of view we learn that his happy-go-lucky father, always so jaunty and elegantly turned out, is gambling away his music store business. And we share the narrator's dismay when he discovers that his beloved older brother is flunking out of college. At the same time the decline of the family's fortunes is marked by their successively smaller, cheaper apartments.

But the problems are not overplayed. Juxtaposed against the family gloom are bright set pieces that record the weight and wonder of the visual world: the coal truck ("the great smoking avalanche of black stone"); the wake of the passing water wagon ("In the raging course of water flowing swiftly along the curb I tossed a Good Humor ice cream stick"); the kids' success in building an igloo (noting its "structured withdrawal" into the "invited darkness"); the fish store and drug store (the latter with its "large glass jars of red and blue liquid").

The characters themselves are as clear as if they had been etched out of wood with fire—that old-fashioned summer-camp technique of pyrography. Particularly memorable is the Yiddish-speaking Grandma who has attacks of madness during which she thinks her daughter is poisoning her and prays that an army of Cossacks will mow her evil children down. The older brother is a mild, sensible guy, competent in the small things of life; a less observant writer would have missed him altogether. Doctorow's gift is to make his outlines firm and dark, burned into the wood to stay.

When, as a boy, the narrator first studies Christian art, his untutored response reveals how weirdly sadistic those paintings can seem. With the objectivity of youth he sees the representations of Christ on the Cross as pictures of "scraggly bearded men almost naked and looking very pale with their eyes rolled up in their heads and their arms stretched out on wooden posts and with nails in their hands and feet." On every page the narrator is constructing the anthropology of twentieth-century America.

Doctorow has rooted his vision in a particular moment, place and social milieu. His attention to detail, however, never becomes just an excursion down memory lane. Mere lists of names, products and now-vanished sights can have the unwanted effect of making the past seem somehow amusing, quaint, absurd (absurd for not being up-to-date), and that approach leaves the past spayed and clawless. Doctorow finds feelings that are deep in the settings of a more innocent past. His past purrs and hisses and is capable of scratching deep enough to draw blood.

Time-Encapsulating
[Review of *World's Fair*]

T. O. TREADWELL

E(dgar) L. Doctorow, the son of Rose and David Doctorow, was born on January 6, 1931, and spent his early childhood living in the Tremont neighbourhood of the Bronx. The central character of *World's Fair* is a boy named Edgar, whose parents are Rose and David, whose birthday is January 6, 1931, and who lives in Tremont for most of the period covered by the narrative—from 1934 to 1941, though with flashes backwards and forwards. The book seems, therefore, to be a Portrait of the Artist as a Young Man, though, as with Joyce's novel, the relationship between fiction and autobiography is ambiguous, finally resolvable only by the author himself.

Both *World's Fair* and Joyce's *Portrait* have as their subject the gradual extension of an individual consciousness from pure self-absorption, outward through an awareness of the reality of other people and relationships, to a sense of the complexity of the world and the place of the self in it; both novels begin with infantile bed-wetting and end with their narrators' determination to embrace the multiform experiences of life and, by implication at least, to turn them into art. Doctorow's prose at moments becomes so Joycean that it flirts with parody, as in the five-year-old Edgar's epiphany on a Brooklyn beach:

> Beyond any name's recognition, under the shouting and teeming life of the world's public on their tribal Sunday of half-nude ceremony, was some quiet revelation in me of unutterable life. It was inspired in this state of clarity to whisper the word *scumbag*. It was as if all the sound had stopped, the voices, the reedy cry of gulls, the sirens and the thunderous surf, for that one word to be articulated to illumination. I felt through my fingers the sand pour of bones, like some futile archeologist of a ground-up mineral past.

But while Stephen Dedalus has to undergo the trials of adolescence and young manhood before grasping his destiny, Edgar's quest for a sense of himself and his place in the world reaches its climax at the age of ten. Doctorow's

Reprinted from *Times Literary Supplement*, February 14, 1986, 163.

symbol for this goal is the New York World's Fair of 1939, with its centre-piece, the Futurama, a giant mechanical model of the city of the future which offers a thrilling and optimistic vision of adult possibility. But the World's Fair also incorporates a grim exhibition of freaks and monsters, and a tawdry burlesque show where Edgar faces the fierce and upsetting power of sexuality. Multiple meanings, it turns out, reside in Doctorow's title. *World's Fair* moves Edgar towards the great exhibition of 1939 as a symbol of adult acceptance; but it is also much concerned with questions about the fairness of the world in terms both of beauty and equity.

Doctorow conveys childish fearfulness and uncertainty with great skill: Edgar's bafflement in the face of the forces that motivate the adult world around him is reflected in his sense of the horror and cruelty lurking in nursery rhymes and religious iconography. As he grows older, the boy becomes aware of tension in the relationship between his parents and between his mother and his father's family. Death occurs both in the family and, with shocking randomness, in a street accident, while reports of the persecution of German Jewry by the Nazis become less abstract when Edgar is mugged by antisemitic louts in the East Bronx. But though his world can be a frightening place, this novel also succeeds in rendering the richness of the child's experience, his sense of loving and being loved and the familiar artefacts and comforting rituals of his everyday life. In the end, Edgar achieves the "World's Fair" twice, once as a consequence of his affection for a serenely beautiful little girl, the second time as a reward for his performance in an essay competition on the theme of the typical American boy; as lover and artist, he enters the glittering world of the future.

For the adult Doctorow, *World's Fair* also functions as a way into the past. In the final pages of the novel Edgar and a friend, inspired by an exhibition at the World's Fair, construct a time capsule from a mailing tube and bury it in Claremont Park in the Bronx. In this they place, among other items, Edgar's Tom Mix Decoder badge, an "H" Hohner Marine Band harmonica, and two Tootsy Toy lead rocket ships, trivial objects from a middle-class boyhood in the New York of forty-five years ago. Their recovery in this novel suggests that *World's Fair* is itself a time-capsule, an evocation of the spirit of a lost era through a rendering of the texture of its daily life, but that life as seen in childhood, when the ordinary surfaces of things are at their most threatening and wonderful. Doctorow's chronicle of a child's experience is often comic, and never patronizing or coy. By narrowing its focus to the life of one family, *World's Fair* offers a profounder sense of the past than the elaborate historical fantasizing of Doctorow's *Ragtime* (1975), and it communicates its themes the more effective by dropping the stylistic extravagances of *Loon Lake* (1980). Doctorow's portrait of the artist when young may not be in Joycean class—not to be Joyce is, after all, no disgrace—but it is a considerable achievement.

[Review of *Billy Bathgate*]

Barbara Hoffert

Having grown up poor but ambitious on the Bronx's Bathgate Avenue during the Depression, young Billy is now being educated in the ways of the world. But his is no ordinary education, for Billy is a gangster-in-training employed by the notorious Dutch Schultz. As the story moves fluidly from the violent underworld of New York City to the playgrounds of the rich, Billy falls for "the Dutchman's" latest lady—a beauty named Drew Preston who eventually reciprocates his youthful passion. Soon Billy is questioning the actions of the mob he was so eager to join as he seeks to protect Drew from its vengeance. Though at times 15-year-old Billy seems far too precocious, even for a streetwise punk, ultimately we are made to feel his apprehension of the world: that "large, empty resounding adulthood booming with terror." An engrossing tale that successfully re-creates worlds gone by in loving and meticulous detail.

Reprinted from *Library Journal,* February 15, 1989, 175–76.

Huck in the Bronx
[Review of *Billy Bathgate*]

The Bronx-born gangster Arthur Flegenheimer, professionally "Dutch Schultz," not one of your nice Jewish boys, was killed on October 23, 1935, mown down in a New Jersey chophouse with his immediate entourage. This consisted of his accountant, a mathematical wizard known as "Abbadabba" Berman, and his bodyguard, "Lulu" Rosencrantz. Doctorow has added, invented, a taciturn, horribly perfect man-of-all-work, "Irving," who never killed anyone, but did many a preliminary job that enabled Dutch and company to kill and kill.

The "Dutchman" was big in policy (the numbers racket), beer (which he compelled saloons to buy even after Prohibition), and unions (the window washers and waiters). He had committed quite a few murders himself with spectacular brutality, and had ordered many more. Though there were rival gangs like Lucky Luciano's Mafia mob, that loved him not, Schultz might have lived beyond his 33rd year had he not, with his usual crazy rashness, plotted to have Thomas E. Dewey himself murdered. As Manhattan district attorney, Dewey was cutting the wide swath through New York gangsterdom that was to make him governor of New York and twice a candidate for president of the United States.

In his deliciously irreverent and quite wonderful novel about the life and death of Schultz, E. L. Doctorow has him murdered by Lucky Luciano's gunmen. In the novel, Luciano stands witness to Schultz when the latter has himself very cunningly converted to the Roman Catholic faith in order to impress the small upstate town where he is to stand trial for income tax evasion. Luciano is, in the novel, understandably alarmed by the thought of having Dewey murdered.

Dutch did not die all at once. Strange to relate, he lingered long enough for an amazing monologue to be taken down. This became famous in its own right and has often been featured as a literary curiosity; it is so unlike what you would expect of gangster Schultz at his end. William Burroughs wrote a

From *The New Republic,* March 20, 1998, 40–41. Reprinted by permission of THE NEW REPUBLIC, © 1984, The New Republic, Inc.

play, *The Last Words of Dutch Schultz.* Young professors of English, understandably looking for novelty, have found in Dutch's ravings a stream of consciousness "worthy of Joyce." "Please, mother! You pick me up now. Please, you know me." "I want to pay, let them leave me alone." Doctorow has kept some of the "last words," has invented others in the style of "A boy has never wept, nor dashed a thousand kim."

Doctorow has cleverly adapted and recast Schultz's last words to the services of his plot and somehow finds the thread of the ingeniously versatile style of his novel in these words. *Billy Bathgate* relates in *his* own words the adventures inside the Schultz gang of a 15-year-old boy who takes his last name from the once flourishing market street Bathgate Avenue in the Bronx. His Jewish father has skipped, his Irish mother is demented. He finds a kind of father in "Abbadabba" Berman, who reduces all existence to numbers, thus allowing Billy to dream that numbers can be changed to words. And Billy is understandably spellbound by the sheer hulking presence of Dutch Schultz himself, who in bulk exercises the kind of power over others that Billy comes to think of as another element of existence.

The book opens on a stunning scene in which Schultz's deputy "Bo" Weinberg, who has been disloyal to Schultz in the secret company of Luciano, is prepared for death by the inestimable Irving. (As Luciano says after Irving's death, "A man like Irving, you don't find his quality.") Irving is encasing Bo's feet in a laundry tub of cement, and tying him up to a chair every which way before Dutch pushes the helpless fellow into the dark night river. Bo, who has performed many a murder for Schultz, is insulting Schultz with every conceivable obscenity so that Dutch will shoot him and end his agony. But the usually rabid Schultz is quiet and restrained, for once. "You always had the words, Bo. You got more words than me, being having been to high school."

The scene is all too vividly narrated by Billy who, duly registering every instant of the horror—and of Schultz's day-to-day career—will come through to us as the Bronx's own Huck Finn. Like Huck, he is encased in a violence not his own. Like Huck, he is so sentient, self-dependent, and in a sense self-"educated" that he brings a special style of his own to the book. This is quite lyrical at times and amusingly overdrawn in a style that rises at times to Joyce and descends to the darling vernacular of Damon Runyon. Billy is his own man in every sense, and so (this is one of Doctorow's jokes) he alone finds the clues in Dutch's last words that enable him to discover the millions that Dutch stashed away. With these Billy grows up to become an Ivy League graduate, U.S. Army officer in World War II, and a corporate entrepreneur.

The plot is a fairy tale of sorts, and there is a joke in the plot. With Doctorow's usual irony about the moneyed goings-on in the upper levels of American society, he has Billy conclude that the gangster world is not untypical of, at least, corporate America. But more immediately the joke is in Billy's narrative style. This is perfectly straight and chillingly vivid in giving us Dutch's looming presence and murderous rages, but becomes "inspired," gives itself a lift, which is the sheer joy of reporting a Bronx kid's ascent in life, when Billy is in communion with his own feelings:

> I had counted off my time with Mr. Schultz by the killings, the gun shots and sobs and cracking skulls resounded in my memory like tolling bells, but something else had been going on all that while, which was the movement of money, it had come in and it had gone out all that time, as uninterrupted as a tide in its incoming and outgoing, as steady and unceasing as the quiet celestial system of the churning earth.

The handsome and usually dashing Bo Weinberg had been taken to the river with his latest flame, a young society beauty married to a rich homosexual who gets kicks out of moving in gangster society. Bo's fate is to Billy "the first inkling of how a ritual death tampers with the universe." Billy marvels at "the realm of high audacity that these men moved in, like another dimension." Describing the 1935 street life of a working-class neighborhood in the Bronx, Billy writes, "I was very moved by the sullen idyll of all this impoverishment." But coming on the shockingly easy relations between Bo's girl and her husband, who is introduced to us on a couch holding his lover's erect penis in his hand, Billy surmises, "It made things go easier, living on an explanationless planet."

The book is full of Billy's understandably affected style yet everything gets straight and deadly when he describes Schultz, in a "roar of rage" over the routine visit of a fire inspector to Schultz's nightclub, hammering the man to death on the floor. Schultz then cries, "Get this load of shit out of here," and the dutifully perfect Irving neatly doubles the body and crams it into a garbage can just as a carter—a private one, to pick up restaurant garbage—comes along on 56th Street.

As Huck is all country, Billy is all city. Each urban detail, right down to the hexagonal tiles on the park side of Fifth Avenue and the view from the El passing along Third, is wonderfully real to a boy whose gangster life gives him the whole city to take advantage of, and for all the risks, to be safe in. "The city has always given me assurances whenever I have asked for them."

Indeed it does. To the point where Billy, rounding out the fairy tale he has lived up from Bathgate Avenue, recovers Schultz's money. But—the Doctorow note—the money when recovered is clearly associated with junk and garbage. Though Dutch's gang is all gone, "Nothing was over, it was all still going on, the money was deathless, the money was eternal and the love of it infinite."

There are those who will bridle at the destined conclusion of the fable and the all too assured tone in which the grown and successful Billy identifies the slipperiness he has survived with the corporate America in which he now rules. Is it just Billy speaking here and not Doctorow? Bridle at the conclusion or not, it is all less serious in the end than what has come before. And if the conclusion is shocking, it is no less shocking because it is so amusing.

Bye Bye Billy
[Review of *Billy Bathgate*]

JOHN LEONARD

To the radical politics of *The Book of Daniel,* the revisionist history of *Ragtime* and the collective, elegiac American dream worlds of *Loon Lake* and *World's Fair,* E. L. Doctorow has added some amazing grace and made a masterwork. Though *Billy Bathgate* meditates on many matters—mobsters and orphans, the East Bronx and the Great Depression, the politics of sex and the psychology of class, "how a ritual death tampers with the universe" and "the amphibian journey" from desire to identity—think of it, like Horatio Alger's *Ragged Dick* or F. Scott Fitzgerald's *The Great Gatsby,* as a fairy tale about capitalism. And color it wonderful.

Of course, this capitalism is in its first stages of primitive accumulation, by extortion, murder and the numbers racket. The gangster Dutch Schultz dies of his failure to evolve into the higher, monopolistic forms. Dutch lacks the corporate vision of a Lucky Luciano. Still, like the church, the army, trade unions and professional sports, organized crime has always been a launching pad for the upwardly mobile. And dirty money is the medium through which young Billy in 1935 levitates out of boyhood and the Bronx into "a large, empty resounding adulthood booming with terror" and "even greater circles of gangsterdom than I had dreamed, latitudes and longitudes of gangsterdom." This is the modern world, where everybody lives alienated ever after.

Billy is a 15-year-old high school drop-out and amateur juggler. His immigrant Jewish father abandoned him in infancy. His immigrant Irish mother, who works in a laundry, is the neighborhood crazy. ("When I was little I thought all rugs were in the shape of men's suits and trousers. She had nailed his suit to the floor as if it was the fur of some game animal, a bearskin." Their apartment smells of burning wax, "the smoke of wicks" from guttered candles: "Now when I looked behind me into the kitchen it was illuminated with my mother's memory candles, this one room glittering like an opera house in all the falling darkness . . . and I wondered if my big chance hadn't a longer history than I thought.") Like any Horatio Alger hero, he

Reprinted from *Nation,* April 3, 1989, 454–56.

wants glamour, status, a destiny, "the mythological change of my station."
Just listen to him:

> there was something in me that might earn out, that might grow into the lin-
> eaments of honor, so that a discerning teacher or some other act of God, might
> turn up the voltage of this one brain to a power of future life that everyone in
> the Bronx could be proud of. I mean that to the more discerning adult, the
> man I didn't know and didn't know ever noticed me who might live in my
> building or see me in the candy store, or in the schoolyard, I would be one of
> the possibilities of redemption, that there was some wit in the way I moved,
> some lovely intelligence in an unconscious gesture of the game, that would
> give him this objective sense of hope for a moment, quite unattached to any
> loyalty of his own, that there was always a chance, that as bad as things were,
> America was a big juggling act and that we could all be kept up in the air
> somehow, and go around not from hand to hand, but from light to dark, from
> night to day, in the universe of God after all.

But fairy tales in the West tend also to be Oedipal. Billy wants a father,
too, and in gangsterdom he has his choice. There's bossman Dutch, born
Arthur Flegenheimer, all passion, energy, menace and "rudeness of power," a
sort of bad-seed Henderson the Rain King. And there's Abbadabba Berman,
the gang's accountant, a natural pedagogue, wise in his numbers, a dandy
even if a humpback in his "summer yellow double-breasted suit and a
panama hat."

Dutch is capitalism's past: social Darwinism. He moves in a "realm of
high audacity," "contriving a life from its property of danger, putting it
together in the constant contemplation of death," in "an independent king-
dom of his own law, not society's." The law, he says, "is the vigorish I pay, the
law is my overhead." Each hit's "a planned business murder as concise and to
the point as a Western Union telegram. The victim after all had been in the
business. He was the competition." And this laissez faire attitude toward the
morality of economic relations translates into an equally laissez faire attitude
toward the economy of moral conduct: "I like the idea of women, I like that
you can pick them up like shells on the beach, they are all over the place, little pink ones and ones with whorls you can hear the ocean." Even his sudden
conversion to Catholicism has this greed about it: "I give you my word I
couldn't be more sincere, Father. I brought it up, didn't I? I live a difficult
life. I make important decisions all the time. I need strength. I see men I
know take their strength from their faith and I have to think I need that
strength too. I fear for my life like all men. I wonder what it's all for. I try to
be generous, I try to be good. But I like the idea of that extra edge."

On the other hand, Abbadabba Berman is capitalism's future: the man-
agerial revolution. Having seen this future, he knows it belongs to Luciano.
It's like railroads: "You look at the railroads, they used to be a hundred railroad companies cutting each other's throats. Now how many are there? One

to each section of the country. And on top of that they got a trade association to smooth their way in Washington. Everything nice and quiet, everything streamlined." Besides, according to Abbadabba:

> At a certain point everyone looks at the books. The numbers don't lie. They read the numbers, they see what only makes sense. It's like numbers are language, like all the letters in the language are turned into numbers, and so it's something that everyone understands the same way. You lose the sounds of the letters and whether they click or pop or touch the palate, or go *ooh* or *aah,* and anything that can be misread or con you with its music or the pictures it puts in your mind, all of that is gone, along with the accent, and you have a new understanding entirely, a language of numbers, and everything becomes as clear to everyone as the writing on the wall.

It's Billy's juggling—of a barter economy of "two rubber balls, a navel orange, an egg, and a black stone"—that first commends him as a "capable boy" to a troubled Dutchman and Abbadabba. He insinuates himself into the Schultz gang as a bagman, go-between, good-luck charm, sorcerer's apprentice and spy. He'll be there for the tugboat murder of Bo Weinberg singing "Bye Bye Blackbird" in tuxedo and cement booties; the kidnap of Bo's upper-class inamorata, the fair Drew Preston; their grumpy hiding-out in Onondaga, upstate among farm foreclosures, till Dutch is tried for income tax evasion; the protracted planning, as if for Kitchener's advance on Khartoum, of a hit on District Attorney Tom Dewey; and in the men's room of the Palace Chop House in Newark on October 23, 1935, for the tabloid massacre: "Murders are exciting and lift people into a heartbeating awe as religion is supposed to do."

As in any fairy tale, the hero will scale a dark tower, in this case the fire escape at the Max and Dora Diamond Home for Children, "the black ladder of my love." He'll don various magic cloaks: the reversible satin jacket with the team name, Shadows, on it; the Little Lord Fauntleroy suit Drew makes him wear for his upstate Bible studies of "the desert gangs"; the polo shirt he puts on to tail Dewey. He'll rescue a fair maiden, though not without a qualm: "How could I be sure of anything if I didn't know everything, I wanted a moving shield around her, like a fountain of juggled balls, like a thousand whirring jump ropes, like fireworks of flowers and the lives of innocent rich children." And he'll find a buried treasure, "pirate swag," by deconstructing the last words, "an insane man's riddle," of the dying Dutch.

There's also an enchanted wood, a "sinking darkness of forest" where Drew and Billy walk "hand in hand like fairytale children in deep and terrible trouble." And a sacred cave, the cellar of the orphanage, where Arnold Garbage is in business "to love what was broken, torn, peeling. . . . To love what didn't work." And an evil wizard: "I was shown into a carpeted heavily draped bedroom that smelled of apples and wine and shaving lotion, a very atmospheric habitat that did not appear to include any open windows. And there propped atop the covers on a grand bank of pillows, in a dark silk robe, with the hairless legs of an old man protruding, was James J. Hines himself, the Tammany district leader." And a pair of gnomes, humpbacked Abbadabba and midget madam Mugsy, adding up the bill for an orgy "like a stunty little couple in a fairy tale, an old woodcutter and his ancient wife puffing their magic white weeds of smoke and child mystification and having a conversation in their language of numbers."

Why do you suppose gangsters show up so often in the novels of serious male writers like Doctorow, William Kennedy and Saul Bellow? Maybe because, to the immigrant trying to Americanize himself, one myth is as good as another—baseball, Hollywood, Tin Pan Alley, Murder Inc. Or maybe it's otherwise hard to think about our American romance with money—the unmentionable in Henry James, the ponderous obsession of Dreiser, the peculiar poetry of Fitzgerald. Lionel Trilling said somewhere that money is "the great solvent of the solid social fabric of the old society," the jumping beans of a new culture and a new status system. And surely its absence is an oppression. Yet, for the most part ours is a literature of loners and losers. We can't talk about serious money from the point of view of deerslayers, whaling captains, river pirates or the Lone Ranger—not even a private eye, not even Huck Finn. And so, sorting among pop icons, we arrive at the urban outlaw. We drop, as if by bathysphere, into the primordial greed and consult the original crab. We inquire into metastasis.

Doctorow has as much fun as Kennedy, and more than Bellow, among these low-lifes. He seems especially to enjoy their mannered violence, their arabesques. To be sure, he writes beautifully about everything from food and water to sex and horses, from corrupt unions to the country poor, from "the contours of the ocean bed" to "the contours of the white Miss Drew." As Billy levitates by money, Doctorow levitates by language, through circles of light and suspensions of childhood, the deepest chords and finest blood threads, on his way from the cityscapes "where we come out sliming . . . where we . . . make our tracks and do our dances and leave our coprolitic spires" to "the black mountains of high winds and no rain," where moral awareness waits in ambush.

But to the executions of a West Side numbers boss (in a barbershop, after the hot towel has been applied, "wrapping it the way they do like a custard swirl, so that only the tip of the nose is visible") and "Bye Bye" Weinberg (dainty "as some princess at a ball" on the tugboat, placing one foot at a time in the tub of wet cement, which "made a slow-witted diagram of the sea outside, the slab of it shifting to and fro as the boat rose and fell on the waves"), he brings such fierce relish, such lovely precision, that we either blush or gasp. The absurd is dignified.

And yet Doctorow obviously doesn't *like* these gangsters as much as Kennedy and Bellow seem to. It's as if, for all their "supernatural warrior spirit," they'd somehow let him down. Unlike the bootleg dreamer Gatsby, they don't know what to do with the money once they've got it: "It was all for survival, there was no relaxed indolence of [their] right to it." And so Doctorow takes the poetry of their money, their imaginative capital, and gives it to the white Miss Drew. For Doctorow, as much as for the smitten Billy, Drew Preston, half a tourist in the underworld and half Persephone, is what the magic of money is really all about. Which is why Billy must rescue her from a Dutch who "needed more death, he was using up his deaths so quickly now he needed them faster and faster"—like Third World markets. Of Drew, Billy rhapsodizes:

> I don't mean just her free access as a great beauty to the most advanced realms of power and depravity, she had chosen this life for herself when, perhaps for her same reasons of staring meditation, she might have chosen life in a convent, say, or to be an actress on the stage. I mean rather how she knew this place would be here. How familiar woods were to her. She knew about horses . . . about sailing and oceans too, and beaches to swim from with no crowds on them and skiing in the European mountains of the Alps and in fact all the pleasures of the planet, all the free rides of the planet that you could have if you knew where they were and had the training to take them. This was what wealth was, the practiced knowledge of these things so you could appropriate them for yourself.

This tiresomely insouciant Miss Drew, American aristocrat, golden girl, Daisy chain, "covered her tracks . . . trailed no history . . . would never tell her life because she needed no one's admiration or sympathy or wonder, and because all judgments, including love, came of a language of complacency she had never wasted her time to master." So what if "she took her clothes off to gunmen, to water, to the sun"? "Life disrobed her." And so on. This is why we kill our fathers. It's also an awful lot for any 22-year-old to have to carry around in any novel's scheme of things. No wonder she disappears. It's a vanishing act, like Alan Ladd's in *Shane*. The white Miss Drew seems to me to be not so much a woman, not even a Persephone, as a credit card, by means of which Billy is enabled to multiply his opportunities for social and erotic disappointment. In her, sex and money and Freud and Marx are more mixed-up than Leslie Fiedler, than Herbert Marcuse. And hard as it is to believe in *her*, the baby in a basket is impossible.

Never mind. Doctorow's whole point is to call into question the authenticity of Billy's identity-making, his juggling act. So much for the "metaphysical afflictions" that inspire "art, invention, great fortunes, and the murderous rages of the disordered spirit." The Dutchman dies, going out with a tantrum, a delirium. And so, too, does Abbadabba die, though *his* last words are the combination of a lock. And Billy sees, through a boy's eyes in the animal skin of grown-up language:

> I am resentful, I feel fatherless again, a whole new wave of fatherlessness, that they have gone so suddenly, as if there was no history of our life together in the

gang, as if discourse is an illusion, and the sequence of this happened and then that happened and I said and he said was only Death's momentary incredulity, Death staying his hand a moment in incredulity of our arrogance, that we actually believed ourselves to consequentially exist, as if we were something that did not snuff out from one instant to the next, leaving nothing of ourselves as considerable as a thread of smoke, or the resolved silence at the end of a song.

That's Doctorow talking, the Doctorow who improves Dutch's delirium—that mad death-bed pastiche William Burroughs arranged into a screenplay in *The Last Words of Dutch Schultz*—with a little Lear-like rage, some Molly Bloom and some Long John Silver. But he warns us:

> While this monologue of his own murder is a cryptic passion, it is not poetry, the fact is he lived as a gangster and spoke as a gangster and when he died bleeding from the sutured holes in his chest he died of the gangsterdom of his mind as it flowed from him, he died dispensing himself in utterance, as if death is chattered-out being, or as if all we are made of is words and when we die the soul of speech decants itself into the universe.

For Doctorow, language is the agency of moral awareness. Moral awareness is the content of any serious discourse. This works for a writer of his quality, and for Toni Morrison, and almost nobody else. Is it sufficient for Billy? His decoding of the Dutchman's "cryptic passion" will make Billy rich. (Happy is some other category.) But to do what? An adult Billy isn't saying. "Who I am in my majority and what I do, and whether I am in the criminal trades or not, and where and how I live must remain my secret because I have a certain renown." Among the several endings to this subversive fairy tale—a mother rescued from her "distractions," a lovely hymn to the Bronx that was, a surprise package from Persephone—we are encouraged to choose for ourselves the one we need. I found a bitter chocolate sadness in Billy's floating, his tumble in freefall, his vertigo among the memory candles. He tells us:

> I will confess that I have many times since my investiture sought to toss all the numbers up in the air and let them fall back into letters, so that a new book would emerge, in a new language of being. It was what Mr. Berman said might someday come to pass, the perverse proposition of a numbers man, to throw them away and all their imagery, the cuneiform, the hieroglyphic, the calculus, and the speed of light, the whole numbers and fractions, the rational and irrational numbers, the numbers for the infinite and the numbers of nothing. But I have done it and done it and always it falls into the same Billy Bathgate I made of myself and must seemingly always be, and I am losing the faith it is a trick that can be done.

America by the numbers: a counting-house.

It seems to me that Billy—like Bo Weinberg in concrete on the tugboat, like the window washers falling from the midtown skyscraper because they didn't pay their dues, like his own lost father in the long history of the big chance, like the Max and Dora Diamond orphans—is singing "Bye Bye Blackbird." Once upon a time he'd had a huge heart, our Billy, Billy Budd, Huck Finn, call him Ishmael; but they broke it forever.

Juggler's Code
[Review of *Billy Bathgate*]

GARRY WILLS

In sentences with nicely clutched transmissions, a long limousine runs, one night in 1935, onto a New York pier, where it smoothly transfers its human cargo to a short tugboat. A boy of fifteen, leaping by impulse onto the boat, is about to undergo the crucial event of his life. He will watch a man die in the muted ritual of one of Dutch Schultz's "necessary business murders." The gangster is going to kill one of his own hired killers, Bo Weinberg. Billy, the boy looking down from the boat's rail, sees "a lighted pucker of green angry water." Schultz, entering the cabin below him, has turned on its light. Going inside himself, he watches preparations for the murder by "the almost-green shards of one work light." It is more frightening to be thrown about on a vibrating boat than to lie in the sand at night, like Nick Carraway, thinking of the green light that beckoned Gatsby over the water. Nick, already an adult, meets a Gatsby who has covered up his criminal past. Billy, a streetwise boy but still a boy, meets Dutch Schultz at the height of his lawlessness. Yet Billy is in some ways less dazzled than Nick by the glamour of the man beyond rules.

In the dingy Bronx neighborhood where Billy lives, there is not much for a teenager to do but shoplift with impunity, since the neighborhood has "a precinct house of cops whose honor it was never if they could help it to breathe the air out-of-doors." What tames the cops is the presence in Billy's neighborhood of one of Schultz's beer warehouses. Though Prohibition has been repealed, Schultz conducts his beer business as a matter of compelled purchases, contriving to make even lawful activity unlawful. Schultz does not just break this or that specific law; he exists in a realm whose contours are not related to any other government's. Billy, like the other boys on his street, dreams of entering that magic realm—and his charmed life lets him in.

Billy is a natural athlete, though not a team player. A runner and acrobat, a sleight-of-hand artist, he has worked longest on one specialty—juggling two rubber balls, an orange, an egg, and a stone. The different weights

From *New York Review of Books* 36 (March 2, 1989): 3. Reprinted with permission from *The New York Review of Books*. Copyright © 1989 NYREV, Inc.

and shapes of the objects make for constantly varying hefts of muscle, conformity of fingers. The trick is not only to juggle them smoothly enough to suggest that they are all the same, but to cover up the fact that this is difficult. Thus the better he gets at it, the less can any audience but himself appreciate Billy's performance. Schultz, in one of his rare visits to the beer drop, happens to see Billy doing this trick. Billy, suspended in the enjoyment of his own achievement, observes Schultz and chooses the moment when, before Schultz turns away, he should *feign* observing him and pay tribute by sailing each of the objects off into the air behind him. *He* is now the ball thrown up for future juggling—though Schultz, at this first encounter, just laughs and gives him ten dollars.

Emboldened by the gift, Billy seeks out Schultz at the center of his numbers operation. Billy gets in by a ruse, but one that is self-defeating, since it shows that he knows too much about the center. Luckily, "Abbadabba" Berman, the mathematical wizard who invented Schultz's numbers system, reads properly the boy's admiring effrontery and takes him on as a messenger, to be groomed for higher service.

Berman is all calculation and control, but he *has* nothing to control apart from Schultz, who is all appetite and impulse. Berman is no more like Schultz than an orange is like a rubber ball; yet only by the smooth interplay of these two can the Realm be maintained. Billy is determined to insert himself as another heterogeneous element into their system, not knowing himself whether he is a rubber ball, to bounce out of it again, or an egg. Wizard and king, Berman and Schultz groom him for "investiture." He learns the etiquette of their court, more willful in its rules than society at large, yet with the heat of personal encounter behind each ritual move. Billy's apprentice role gives him more intimacy with his leaders, and less responsibility for their actions, than any other gang member has. But each mark of favor is a new danger. The first two murders Billy sees Dutch commit unsettle (and thrill) him, but he can escape the *internal* burden of the witness because one murder is so carefully planned that delegates commit it and the other is so sudden, in one of Schultz's earthquake angers, that it seems more a natural accident than a human act.

But the third murder is different. Billy only witnesses this one by slipping onto the tugboat unbidden. This time, Schultz is methodical, almost didactic, in his observance of the forms (encasing the victim's feet in concrete). And this time there is another witness who is not part of the gang— Bo Weinberg's society girlfriend, picked up with him by accident. And this time, finally, while Dutch takes the woman downstairs to rape her, Billy talks to the victim, and is given a moral imperative—to protect the woman.

Schultz finds that Bo Weinberg's woman, Drew Preston, is morally incapable of being raped. She anticipates outrage. This makes Billy's job of protecting her more difficult, since she has no *sense* of danger in her refined experiments with dangerous people. So far, money and youth and beauty have kept her invulnerable. She thinks they always will. The uneducated but streetwise Billy knows better than that. "What do we have to be protected from?" she asks. "The likes of us," he answers. He is afraid for her as well as for himself when Schultz takes the two of them north to corrupt the New York State district where he is about to stand trial. After the uprooting night of murderous travel on the water, they are moving inland, taking their civilized diseases to the Indian ("Onondaga," the town, with its statue, named after the man). Billy remembers musing as they drove:

> I had never been out of it [the city] before, never had the distance, it is a station on the amphibian journey, it is where we come out sliming, it is where we bask and feed and make our tracks and do our dances and leave our coprolitic spires, before moving on into the black mountains of high winds and no rain.

Schultz, raining money on the natives, turns Onondaga into Hadleyburg, though members of the gang feel out of place in the country. Bill at first argues the "this was American too" to a doubting mobster, but he is dismayed when he finds that "there was nothing to do but good"; he will later decide that "the country had damaged my senses." Schultz, the benevolent local patron, soon has bankers, policemen, and preachers eating out of his hand. He ingratiates himself by, among other things, sending Billy to Bible class, where he hears about "the desert gangs, their troubles with the law, their hustles and scams, the ways they worked each other over, and the grandiose claims they made for themselves."

In Onondaga, site of Part Two of the novel, Billy learns to use a handgun at the local police range, and gets to know Bo Weinberg's woman. Drew Preston, cultured, amoral, not only comes from a different world but seems of a different species. He tells her, in a passage at the very center of the novel, about his pledge to Bo Weinberg. We finally hear the conclusion to the story begun on the opening pages, the story of that night on the tugboat, how the dying gangster extracted from Billy "the first act of mercy in my life."

In Part Three, set in Saratoga during the races, Billy has to redeem his pledge and protect Drew, though that goes against the entire gangster training he has submitted to. "Yet what was any of this speculation [about saving her] but the symptom of my own state of mind? I would think of nothing like this if my conscience was clear and I was intent only to advance myself." Billy must go against the conscience prescribed for him by the gang as Huck Finn defies the conscience instilled in him when he saves Nigger Jim. In Onondaga Billy and Drew form an alliance while serving Dutch and Abbadabba, just as Huck and Jim serve and see through the King and the Duke.

Doctorow, like Twain, like Dickens, sees adult possibilities in "the boy's book"—the tale of an orphan, not yet socialized into ordinary adult life, who acquires an outlaw mentor. This formula, at its best, combines psychological subtlety (the study of formative experiences undergone in a state of peril), with social criticism (the "normal" looks odd if not crazy when seen from outside). Thus Billy, outside accepted moral systems, must create his own code of responsibility, as Huck does. And Schultz, by stripping the pretense from preachers and bankers and the police, only "corrupts" Onondaga by re-creating the conditions of the original settlement, when Onondaga's land as well as his name was seized, so that his story could be distorted into the myths of "ordinary" life.

Schultz wants not only to corrupt Onondaga but to incorporate it, to eat it and to have it too, including all its values and assumptions. So he decides to join the Catholic Church, to have any "extra edge" it might give him: "I don't understand Latin, but I don't understand Hebrew neither, so why not both?" But he must keep his first "edge" too: "This mustn't get to my mother—Irving, your mother neither, the mothers shouldn't know this, they wouldn't understand." Drew is only amoral. Dutch is panmoral; he wants in on all the games in town. He is the American "consumer" in many senses, subject only to his own voraciousness. He endorses by destroying. Death even attends the ceremony of his baptism, which Doctorow puts to brilliant plot use: the Italian who comes to that event as his literal "grandfather" recognizes Drew and knows now who killed Bo Weinberg. The scene with which we began works out its logic in Dutch Schultz's death at the end.

Drew, acting as Billy's sister/aunt/mother, dresses him up for the various Huck Finn charades of respectability in Onondaga, while in secret (especially from Schultz) she becomes his lover. Twain, like Dickens, observed the sexual conventions of Victorian fiction, which meant he had to make "boy" mean the oldest possible *pre*pubescent. Doctorow, released from such constraints, makes Billy the youngest possible *post*pubescent, one who has known sex before he meets Drew. His "girl" in the neighborhood lives in an orphanage (and is named, with a flirt at Twain, Rebecca—"Becky" in his mind). Drew, Billy knows, is both below and above anything so ordinary as "love." He has to forge entirely new kinds of relations to other people, as he forges his unique sense of responsibility. He does not save Drew because he sleeps with her (the erotic "wanes pathetically in terror"), but to honor his own pledge. In the same way, he accepts the fatherly guidance of Abbadabba Berman, yet he knows instantly when Berman is trying to kill Drew, and he knows there will be no regret on Berman's part if he succeeds.

The unpredictable Schultz could kill Billy at any time; but predictably, wanting it both ways, Schultz would certainly regret it afterward. In fact, during his rambling deathbed monologue, overheard by others, Dutch leaves Billy clues to the places where various treasures are hidden. The boy's book devices extend here even to touches of Robert Louis Stevenson, as Billy undertakes a final hunt for "pirate swag."

This is Doctorow's first superbly constructed novel. The first-person narrator reassembles boyhood impressions, moving back and forth over the year of his gang activity with easy recall yet with an adult's remembering vocabulary. The tone is consistent, convincing despite a lingering tendency to the precious—adverbs like "worklingly," wordplays like "culled cash, or cold cash, and then it turned into a gold cache." Doctorow has previously used an arch third-person narrator (in *Ragtime*), or a Kerouacian first-person (in *Loon Lake*). He has not been able to sustain the first-person tone, so he alternates narrators (not only in *Loon Lake* but in *World's Fair*). Even in *The Book of Daniel,* the first-person narration was interrupted by dissertation notes and other intrusive gimmicks. But here the story flows; the dialogue is mainly filtered through the narrator's memory, continuous with everything else recalled; sentences glide on for a page and half at a time with no sense of effort. The prose is itself charged with the "three-dimensionality of danger" Billy finds in Dutch Schultz's presence. When, for instance, he picks up his first gun, Billy muses:

> As Mr. Schultz told me later in a moment of reminiscence the first time is breathtaking, you have this weight in your hand and you think in your calculating mind if they only believe me I will be able to bring this thing off, you are still your old self, you see, you are the punk with the punk's mind, you are relying on them to help you, to teach you how to do it, and that is how it begins, that badly, and maybe it's in your eyes or your trembling hand, and so the moment poses itself, like a prize to be taken by any of you, hanging up there like the bride's bouquet. Because the gun means nothing until it's really yours. And then what happens, you understand that if you don't make it yours you are dead, you have created the circumstances, but it has its own free-standing rage, available to anyone, and this is what you take into yourself, like an anger that they've done this to you, the people who are staring at your gun, that it's their intolerable crime to be the people you are waving this gun at. And at that moment you are no longer a punk, you have found the anger that was really in you all the time, and you are transformed, you are not play-acting, your are angrier than you have ever been in your entire life, and this great wail of fury rises in your chest and fills your throat and in this moment you are no longer a punk, and the gun is yours and the rage is in you where it belongs and the fuckers know they are dead men if they don't give you what you want, I mean you are so crazy jerking-off mad at this point you don't even know yourself, as why should you because you are a new man, a Dutch Schultz if ever there was one.

Performing himself to us in this way, Billy is always the juggler inside and outside his own action, making it look easy. He throws himself out of his little world into Dutch Schultz's hurricane of adult strivings, "translates" himself into that foreign mind. Yet the same ability that let him launch himself out of his own first ambit makes him maintain a disengagement from the criminal mind he enters. In a nation that thinks of itself as having a special destiny, he can only stay true to his own sense of balance by refusing to be absorbed in the communal myths of destiny—that of the gang as well as of "one's country." He remains the only one who can appreciate his own performance, can be the juggler and the juggled, the judge and the judged.

Books in Brief
[Review of *Selected Essays*]

DONALD LYONS

E. L. Doctorow is little known as critic or essayist—and with good reason. This exiguous assembly of prefaces and assignments is unstartling: Jack London was "a workaday literary genius/hack"; Hemingway was tormented; Orwell's *1984* is concerned with "the political manipulation of reality through the control of history and language." In this salad bar of limp banalities, there is not a fresh thought, a crisp phrase, or a morsel of original research. His King Charles's head is the wickedness of the Cold War: "I was a high school student in 1946 when Winston Churchill made his Iron Curtain speech in Fulton, Missouri," is his version of its origin. At Kenyon in 1948, "I thought of the late Franklin Roosevelt as the real President and so was rooting for his one-time Vice President Henry A. Wallace, an idealist running on a third-party ticket with leftist backing and getting his comsymp head handed to him." The sentence is a classic—from the ingenuousness of "idealist" through the fuzziness of "leftist" to the demotic snarl of "comsymp." The dreariest thing about this book is its inability ever to rise above generic comsympsprach.

From *National Review* 45 (December 27, 1993): 72. © 1993 by National Review, Inc. Reprinted by permission.

[Review of *Selected Essays*]

ALICE JOYCE

Doctorow's freethinking inclinations and eloquently noted concerns for the global universe illuminate diverse topics. He approaches the American literary tradition from various angles, looking at the men behind the classics. Dreiser's *Sister Carrie,* London's *Call of the Wild,* and the posthumous work of Hemingway all provide material for Doctorow's incisive and provocative views. But these essays are far more than a series of literary studies. Also included are a trenchant assessment of Reagan's presidency (taken from a commencement address by Doctorow) and additional commentary on the performance of other recent presidents. Whether Doctorow is reflecting on the Constitution's sacred status or looking back on James Wright at Kenyon College, the mind of a great humanist is apparent on every page.

Reprinted from *Booklist,* September 15, 1993, 118.

[Review of *Selected Essays*]

JANICE BRAUN

Doctorow (*Billy Bathgate; Loon Lake*) declares that he prefers to write fiction over nonfiction, but he does the reader a great service by using "his own voice" in these 14 essays on literary, political, and historical topics. Highlights of the collection are an extraordinary essay on the subjectivity of fact as opposed to the visionary nature of fiction ("False Document"); a sort of deconstruction of the Constitution; and a speech dated 1989 that deals damningly with issues of the Reagan/Bush era. The latter may irritate some whose political beliefs are not in accord with those of the author, but Doctorow's eloquent articulation to a commencement audience of that administration's legacy is admirable. These essays are, without exception, well-crafted, thought-provoking, and entertaining; highly recommended.

Reprinted from *Library Journal*, September 15, 1993, 74.

[Review of *The Waterworks*]

Donna Seaman

Doctorow's ninth novel is another variation on his favorite theme, New York City's delirious history, but it's an entirely different creature than its predecessors. Set in New York during the frenzied and cynical aftermath of the Civil War, this suspenseful narrative is told by an old, wry newspaper editor named McIlvaine. It all began with the disturbing, if not downright inconvenient, disappearance of McIlvaine's favorite free-lance writer. Moody, young and uncompromising, Martin could have been rich since his profiteering father amassed vast sums slave trading and selling shoddy goods to the Union army, but Martin objected to his father's venality and immorality and got himself disowned. His handsome young stepmother did no such thing, yet, when old Pemberton dies she is left destitute: the family fortune is nowhere to be found. Just before Martin vanishes, he tells friends that he has seen his allegedly dead father riding around in a white coach. McIlvaine turns to the one police officer he trusts, an uncommon man of uncommon height and shrewdness. As they begin their investigation, we are reminded of the Holmes-Watson team, but as this astonishing and ghoulish story unfolds, we also detect echoes of tales about mad scientists, vampires, and the pursuit of eternal life. Curiously, New York City itself becomes the central character. An "unprecedented life force," it seethes with the hectic hustling of street urchins, thugs, and corrupt officials. Doctorow revels in dramatic descriptions of the rapidly mutating cityscape while he dramatizes life's brutal pragmatism and our capacity for sinister acts. Gothic and penetrating, rooted in Poe and Melville, and crisply written, this is a rare treat.

Reprinted from *Booklist,* April 15,1994, 1485.

City of the Living Dead
[Review of *The Waterworks*]

PAUL GRAY

A beautiful widow left destitute by the will of her plutocrat husband. The surreptitious exhumation of a corpse while fog swirls in the phosphorescent light of early dawn. A treasure chest crammed with cash. Innocent children falling victim to a mad scientist in pursuit of the secret of eternal life. A brilliant, tormented young hero who says things like, "Either I am mad and should be committed, or the generations of Pembertons are doomed."

Now for something truly weird. These gothic, melodramatic flourishes appear not in the first chapter of the latest Stephen King novel but rather in E. L. Doctorow's *The Waterworks*. This is not entirely unexpected. The author of such luminous page turners as *Ragtime, World's Fair* and *Billy Bathgate* has made it a habit to surprise his readers with each new book. His central concerns—the unavoidable sway of historical forces, the insidious effects of the powerful upon the powerless—have remained constant, but he has chosen a variety of fictional voices and techniques to bring them to life. Even longtime readers, though, are likely to find *The Waterworks* Doctorow's strangest and most problematic invention so far.

The setting is New York City in 1871, although the story of what happened there and then is told at an indeterminate later date by a man named McIlvaine, who notes, at one point in his narrative, "I have to warn you, in all fairness, I'm reporting what are now the visions of an old man." A number of similar caveats are interspersed throughout the story, and taken together they add another level of mystery to the point he makes over and over again: he has been a witness to horror and lived to tell the tale.

Which, perhaps, begins as follows. As the city editor of the New York *Telegram* in April 1871, McIlvaine employs a number of free-lance writers, including his most talented, Martin Pemberton, the disinherited son of the late Augustus Pemberton, a millionaire whose death and funeral had made the papers the previous September. None of the editorial comments or public eulogies mentioned the true sources of the old man's fortune, although McIl-

Reprinted from *Time,* June 20, 1994, 66.

vaine the newspaperman knows what they were: Pemberton had run illegal slave ships out of New York harbor, with the connivance of Boss Tweed's ring, and had also profitably supplied Union troops during the Civil War with substandard goods—"boots that fell apart, blankets that dissolved in rain, tents that tore at the grommets, and uniform cloth that bled dye."

Now, Martin Pemberton tells McIlvaine and several others, he has seen his father alive, on the streets of Manhattan. The editor at first assumes that the disillusioned young man is speaking in metaphor, that he means his father's evil lives on in the rapacious city all around them. After Martin drops out of sight, McIlvaine begins to investigate and comes to believe the vision could have been true, that a white Municipal Transport stagecoach might actually have carried old Pemberton and other presumed deceased rich men through the teeming, oblivious streets of Manhattan. McIlvaine imagines Martin's impression of the passengers: "Their heads nodded in unison as the vehicle stopped and started and stopped again in the impacted traffic."

To find out whether and why the city he loves and thinks he knows includes the living dead, McIlvaine seeks the help of Edmund Donne, a rare honest captain in the municipal police, which has become, under Tweed, "an organization of licensed thieves." The trail these two follow—with powerful forces conspiring against them—leads sinuously through accumulating outrages: unexplained murders, a mysterious orphanage, missing millions in inheritances and a waterworks north of the city where very strange things are going on.

This chase is fascinating, although wildly implausible, but McIlvaine makes the worst of a good thing by insisting that what he reports has implications far beyond its particulars: "I would not have extended myself now, at my advanced age, if this were just the odd newspaper tale I had for you . . . of aberrant family behavior. I ask you to believe—I will prove—that my freelance, finally, was only a reporter bringing the news, like the messenger in Elizabethan dramas . . ." His story, the narrator says several times, is "far more than" the mystery of the Pemberton family.

This claim is asserted but never convincingly shown. The shocking, Poe-like tale at the center of the novel does not achieve the emblematic significance that Doctorow wishes it to have. It is simply too bizarre to stand for—or comment on—anything outside itself, particularly the entire City of New York and what McIlvaine calls its "roiling soul, twisting and turning over on itself, forming and re-forming . . ." The Waterworks is at its best when Doctorow stops McIlvaine's huffing and puffing about social significance and lets him get on with the business of telling an entertaining and sometimes truly haunting story.

A Gothic Tale of Horror in Old New York
[Review of *The Waterworks*]

MALCOLM JONES

All through E. L. Doctorow's latest novel, *The Waterworks*, you're likely to have the feeling that you've heard this tale—or better yet, seen it—somewhere before. There's the bright, smart-alecky young man who vainly tries to warn the world that evil is afoot. Add the keen-witted cop who unravels the mystery, the quivering ingénue girlfriend and a smirking villain. The last piece of the puzzle falls into place when, at the heart of the story, you find lurking a mysterious mad scientist named Dr. Wrede Sartorius. Doctorow describes the wily doctor, but why bother? You know he looks like Basil Rathbone. Or maybe Charles Laughton—any brainy bad guy who ever stalked a Hollywood back lot in the '30s. This is a sci-fi-horror movie masquerading as a novel, with every wisp of fog, every plot twist in place. It's a terrific piece of literary larceny.

Heisting has always been a habit of Doctorow's, from his first novel, "Welcome to Hard Times," where he borrowed from movie Westerns, to "Billy Bathgate," which reworked the legend of gangster Dutch Schultz. In none of these books has Doctorow tried to hide his tracks. Rather, he's taken history and its legends and used them like armatures around which he's wound new plots and themes. "The Waterworks" uses the hackneyed story of a mad scientist as an excuse to reinvent the New York City of 1871 and to explore the polar pull of ethics and experiment. When old Augustus Pemberton dies, he leaves his wife penniless and the world wondering where his fortune went. After his son Martin, an acerbic freelance literary critic, claims to have seen his father alive and then disappears himself, a newspaper editor named McIlvaine starts investigating. The secret he helps uncover involves helpless orphans, addled old rich men, a secret laboratory and the search for eternal life.

With that plot summary in hand, any late-show channel surfer could foretell the ending of "The Waterworks." But that hardly matters, because in stories like this, atmosphere is everything, and Doctorow is a master of atmosphere. New York in the late 1800s has lately inspired novelist Caleb Carr in "The Alienist" and movie director Martin Scorsese in "The Age of Innocence." But Doctorow's is the best version yet. In his artful hands, Manhattan becomes the book's most memorable character, its flawed hero. The gutter vitality of the grimy old city seeps through every page, malign but also magical: "A mansion would appear in a field. The next day it stood on a city street with horse and carriage riding by." It was "as if, with a mind of its own, the city was building itself."

Doctorow is not a first-rate thinker. What he has to say about the evils of power and unchecked ambition has been better said elsewhere. But he knows the art of storytelling inside and out, and in "The Waterworks" he weaves a spell of genuine creepiness. Reading this novel, one is reminded of that wonderful exchange in the 1934 Universal movie "The Black Cat," where the feckless hero exclaims, "Let's cut out this metaphysical baloney." To which Bela Lugosi murmurs, "Metaphysical, perhaps. Baloney, perhaps not."

Of Melville, Poe and Doctorow
[Review of *The Waterworks*]

TED SOLOTAROFF

In what used to be the canon of American fiction, there is a sharp break between Hawthorne, Poe and Melville and the post–Civil War figures such as James, Twain, Howells and Crane. The dark meditative tales and romances (what Hawthorne called "blasted allegories") suddenly give way to realistic stories and novels, and an intensely literary language drops a level to embrace the fresh current of the spoken idiom. One of the several fascinating features of E. L. Doctorow's new novel, which takes place in 1871, is that it settles in the mind like a kind of missing link in our literary evolution. Hints and glints of Poe are embedded in its twinned interests in mystery and science, its detective-story format, its necrological overlay, its protagonist—a brilliant, noir, disinherited literary journalist—its man-about-New York ambiance, even a mansion named Ravenwood.

The other figure who haunts the book's pages is Melville. Not the Melville who wrote the novels so much as the one who had ceased to do so, who would have been walking these harsh teeming streets on his way to his job at the Custom House, his moral imagination gripped between the evils of rampant industrialism and even more rampant corruption. Melville's provenance in *The Waterworks* is less a matter of literary traces than of a great shadow cast on Doctorow's moral imagination, urging him to see darkly and negatively all the way to the end of sanity and morality, and to make a distinctively American allegory of it, updated from the era of the New England oversoul and whaling industry.

At the same time, *The Waterworks* is controlled by a direct, reportorial realism that looks forward to the urban, industrial-age fiction of Crane, Upton Sinclair and Dreiser. The New York that it holds in its bifocal lens is both a factual and prophetic place, the young power-struck metropolis of the gilded age and at the same time a "panoramic negative print, inverted in its lights and shadows" of the postwar city for sale that had a centennial of sorts in the Ed Koch era. Doctorow's New York, with its horse-drawn traffic jams, its humming industrialized waterfronts, its real estate boom north of 42nd

Reprinted with permission from the June 6, 1994 issue of *The Nation*.

Street, is also a city of homeless veterans, ruined children, a cynical younger generation, a massively extortionate politics, a screaming press, a humming stock exchange, a plague of fires.

> It was a pungent air we breathed—we rose in the morning and threw open the shutters, inhaled our draft of the sulfurous stuff, and our blood was roused to churning ambition. Almost a million people called New York home, everyone securing his needs in a state of cheerful degeneracy. Nowhere else in the world was there such an acceleration of energy. A mansion would appear in a field. The next day it stood on a city street with a horse and carriage riding by.

Doctorow is a remarkable writer. He casts his imagination into a patch of American history and makes it his own turf, an accurately rendered, resonating "repository of myth," as he says in one of his essays. Viewed together, his novels form a highly composed vision of American history, its phenomena turned into firm images pointed in our direction. Mostly set in and around New York, each book is a kind of relay network between its time and ours, keeping our awareness in touch with American experience. For example, his narrator reports that as the sluice gates of the city reservoir, then at 42nd Street, are opened, "the water thunders in . . . as if it were not a reservoir at all, but a baptismal font for the gigantic absolution we require as a people."

Except for Gore Vidal, I don't know of another novelist who is doing this job, an enormously important one in an age when a sense of the past weakens and falls in value from year to year, so that the new is thought to reside in a trendy *pisher* culture (to use a precise Yiddish term).

Doctorow's sense of the past is more textured than Vidal's and less tendentious. He has a 20/20 social imagination that sees his subject steadily in its presentness to itself, and whole in its permanent implications. He also has an unusual versatility of voice that adapts from book to book, tuned to the representational demands and distinctive feeling of the material: the homely, earnest prose with an edge of twang in *Welcome to Hard Times;* the counterpoint of the personal and the objective, of rage and detachment in the political indictment of *The Book of Daniel;* the mix of the demotic and the elegant in the class novel of the Depression, *Loon Lake;* the sinuous lyricism of a prewar Bronx childhood in *World's Fair;* the clipped cadences of America marching into a new century of affluence and violence in *Ragtime;* and so forth. As a stylist, Doctorow has developed into the literary counterpart of Barry Bonds—he hits for both distance and percentage, runs the bases like a street thief and ranges all over his position in left field.

As Melville would say, *The Waterworks* is "an inside narrative." It is inhabited by the mind, imagination and soul of its narrator, the former city editor of the *New York Telegram,* writing some decades after the sensational events he witnessed but was unable to report at the time. The Tweed Ring is at the height of its power, its tentacles everywhere. A middle-aged bachelor,

McIlvaine lives for his work: "My newsman's cilia were up and waving. The soul of the city was always my subject, and it was a roiling soul. . . . As a people we practiced excess. Excess in everything—pleasure, gaudy display, endless toil, and death."

It takes an imaginative man to tend a roiling soul, and McIlvaine has been waiting since the passage of the dead Lincoln along a dumbstruck Broadway for the spawn of the assassination, "some soulless social resolve," to declare itself. He is thinking riots, another to add to the draft ones, as well as the gang riots, the police riots, the internecine Irish riots, the recent general strike riot he has witnessed. But what comes from Lincoln's grave, as he puts it, proves to be suitably spectral and macabre.

The young freelance book reviewer Martin Pemberton turns up one morning in his sardonic Union greatcoat and attitude (the War was fought by two confederacies; New York has no intellectuals, only newspapermen and clergy) to declare that his father, supposed to be some months dead, is still alive. At Columbia, Martin had discovered that his vaunted father, Augustus, had made much of his money in furnishing the Union troops with "shoddy" as well as in slave trading, so McIlvaine takes the young man's remark as another of his metaphors for their "city of thieves, mucous in its dissembling." Yet it soon turns out that Martin has seen his father not once but twice, both times riding in a white municipal stagecoach with a group of moribund old men in black coats and top hats. (Black and white are the primary colors of the literature the novel is bouncing off.) Shortly thereafter Martin disappears. His cilia waving like mad, the astute McIlvaine winds his way through the high and low life of the city in search of his guilt-ridden young rebel, who was last seen by his fiancée saying, "Either I am mad and should be committed, or the generations of Pembertons are doomed."

The shade of Poe shortly thereafter visits the novel in a more brilliant way. McIlvaine has turned to Edmund Donne, the one honest police captain in New York, who quietly leans upon Martin's friend Harry Wheelwright to tell what he knows, which is mainly of a nighttime trip to Woodlawn Cemetery to open Augustus Pemberton's grave. The darkness, the white mist, the prying open of the coffin, the effort to take heart, the shriveled figure within that is not Augustus but a small boy with a red bow and patent leather shoes: Well, Wheelwright's story does take one back to how scary Poe used to be. Watching Martin look down into the grave, Wheelwright "heard a moan . . . an awful basso sound . . . not in his voice at all but brought up from the lungs of a shaggy ancestry . . . a million years old." Doctorow's touch is quicker, more suggestive than the Master's, enabling the reader to frighten himself.

Poe's M. Maupin was the first of the gentlemen sleuths, his mind so detached and powerful that he needed only "ratiocination" and a bit of casual observation to solve the crime. Poe placed him in Paris because that's where gentlemen of genius amused themselves outwitting the bourgeoisie—in this case the diligent but shortsighted police. Doctorow's lanky, methodical, austere Donne is the professional law-enforcement officer of the democratic future. Instead of clues recollected in leisure, he depends upon knowing the city as though it were a village, on informers, on composite portraits of suspects (he is the first in the field here), on his gift for making witnesses conform to his expectation of them, and on his nose for paper trails. All of these are effectively deployed in the course of the hunt, most notably Donne's use of documents. Combing through the account books of the Tweed Ring (the first slip of the clasp) that had been given to McIlvaine by the dissatisfied City Sheriff, Donne notices an anomaly—a charter for a new orphanage for which no money has changed hands. Its physician is Wrede Sartorius, in whose Adirondacks sanitarium Pemberton *père* was reported to have died: its director is Eustace Simmons, Pemberton's erstwhile slave trader. The Home for Little Wanderers ties in with an informer's report of a child-buying ring—another anomaly, since the city streets provide so many children for the asking. All of which suggests an explanation for the boy that Martin and his friend found in the coffin.

From this point on, the novel is increasingly dominated by the figure of Dr. Sartorius. Though McIlvaine and Donne are pursuing him, he moves into the story like an advancing general, preceded by awed rumors, reports and skirmishes. A preternaturally gifted surgeon who arrived from Germany in time for the Civil War, he turned his field hospital into a laboratory for revolutionary techniques that could treat head wounds and restore joints, amputate a leg in nine seconds, an arm in six—no small mercy at the time. But mercy was not his motive; knowledge was. He was a pioneer as well in postoperative treatment, his theory and practice anticipating the work of Pasteur and Robert Koch. All in all, McIlvaine concludes in his circumspect way, Colonel Sartorius's army career was "brilliant and masterful and brave. It's important to understand this. . . . We are speaking of the noble lineaments of the grotesque."

When Donne arranges a police raid on the Home for Little Wanderers that Sartorius founded, it turns out to be a model of enlightened institutional child care. On the other hand, some of the children are missing and most are prematurely aged. Also, in a basement cell is the missing Martin Pemberton, near death and in a catatonic state.

Martin's relationship with Sartorius has been an intense one that follows the arc of a long spell. What drew him into it was the genius of the man, one of those who make "the world seem to exist for the sake of their engagement with it." After being abducted, he has spent months in the doctor's one-man research institute devoted mainly to extending the doctor's encyclopedic knowledge and incidentally to prolonging the lives of his father and the five other benefactors Martin had glimpsed in the horse car. Though he is soon aware of the connection between the orphanage and the huge, domed garden he beholds (in which the zombielike moguls waltz with deaf and dumb attendant concubines amid an array of erotic statuary while they await the injections and infusions that maintain them), Martin nonetheless is soon disarmed by Sartorius's presence and mission. His impressiveness consists not only in the learning and prowess that have brought him and his clients to the frontier of life's struggle with death but also in his awesome detachment from his own ego. In his Zenlike objectivity and curiosity, he is the ultimate embodiment of science for science's sake. He records his findings in meticulous Latin but is beyond even the need to publish them, though he likes having Martin around to talk to and allows him free run of everyplace but the treatment rooms. Eventually this attitude of amorality proves to be too much for the disciple; though willing to sit for an early version of an EEG, he balks at contributing bone marrow to the enterprise, and goes into a tailspin of conscience that ends in the cellar of the orphanage and his own zombielike state.

The novel's main focus of interest and claim to greatness is the character of Sartorius. His slim, resolute figure bestrides the modern era, one foot in his time, one foot in ours, Faust without Mephistopheles, or rather, a Faust whose Mephistopheles has become the power structure of the state, in this case the State of New York. For his enormously expensive program has been funded by the Tweed Ring, which built the orphanage and expanded the city's waterworks at Croton to create Sartorius's laboratory and human conservatory. This is the city's "soulless social resolve" that emerged from Lincoln's grave. When Tammany Hall is finally breached by a *New York Times* exposé of the magnitude of the take, and Tweed flees, he is last seen by a Cuban fisherman who reports that he was babbling about being the god of the city where "they have learned the secret of eternal life."

All of which may seem a bit too dated and mythy for the sophisticated, hard-headed reader of today to note the prophecy. Instead of eternal life we have Elisabeth Kübler-Ross and Sherwin Nuland, hospices and living wills and the increasingly portentous figure of Dr. Kevorkian: what a psychologist I know calls "Death Lib." But with a small adjustment of the lens, we can look all the way up the road to the nexus of science, money and politics that hove into view just the other day in the report that linked the debilities and pain found among veterans of the Gulf War to mass inoculations of esoteric and insufficiently tested antidotes for germ and gas warfare.

Which is not to say Doctorow is writing a cautionary tale for our times. As McIlvaine stoutly puts it, "We did not conduct ourselves as if we were preparatory to your time. . . . New York after the war was more creative, more deadly, more of a genius society than it is now." Also, his interests are metaphysical as well as political. The far side of his consciousness has a visionary edge, so that the horror of Sartorius's show is not only in its objective disruption of the natural relationship of the generations, which is but the next step of the common practice of child labor, but also in the rent it makes in moral consciousness itself, revealing the darkness and chaos of a universe that negates the understanding and faith of the human bond. In an extraordinary passage toward the end, McIlvaine, whose own soul has been permanently roiled by the events he has witnessed and suffered, dreams of Sartorius observing with terrifying intentness a child's boat struggling in a heavy sea that soon takes it under. The dream goes on to recapitulate and dramatize other images of the radical noetic experience that he has been given by "my darkbearded captain," who, like Ishmael's, has struck through the pasteboard mask of appearances. But though Melville went farther than any writer of his time in his negation and despair of the regnant ideology of spiritual optimism, he was still standing ankle-deep in the sea of faith. "O Nature and O soul of man! how far beyond all utterance are your linked analogies. Not the smallest atom stirs or lives on matter, but has its cunning duplicate in mind!" Sartorius has come out of the water and taken the next step. When we last see him, standing as calmly as ever against a background of maniacs in the asylum to which he has been dispatched, he dismisses McIlvaine's and the novel's final, awed question about his moral views with a brief lecture on biology that turns the page to the modern mind.

> The truth is so deep inside, so interior, it operates—if that can be said to be the verb—in total blindness, in the total disregard of a recognizable world that would give us comfort, or in which we might find beauty or the hand of God—a point where life arcs in its first sentient glimmerings . . . senseless and unalive, and quite . . . mindless . . . as it is in black space.

As in cosmology, so in ethics. Just before McIlvaine's interview with Sartorius, there is one with Dr. Sumner Hamilton, whose board of examiners has voted to commit their colleague rather than have him tried and hanged, alternatives to which Sartorius himself is indifferent. He "answered only the questions he felt deserved an answer. We ended up trying to formulate questions he respected." One of the pointed ones is whether Sartorius's defense of his deployment of scientific method suggests that his experiments would someday benefit schoolchildren as they did soldiers; to which he replies with a smile, "You're not suggesting, Doctor, that I am to be distinguished from you or your colleagues . . . or indeed anyone else in the city . . . in observing the laws of selective adaptation . . . that ensure survival for the fittest of the species."

According to Hamilton, who has read Sartorius's notebooks, no child died directly from or was even impaired by his procedures; they suffered only a certain devitalization of the will to live. But such temporizing is beside the point of the pioneer's position. The closer the knowledge of how contingent, mutable, "membranous" the physical organism is, the more, as Sartorius testifies, it "cleanses the natural scientist of ennobling sentiments, pieties which teach us nothing." As for his patients and donors, they are hardly more pathetic than people in society, "all of them severely governed by tribal custom, and a structure of fantasies which they call civilization" but is only a blind allegiance to electromagnetic impulses "that constitute the basis of our actual living."

The medical tribunal ends up feeling more implicated than judgmental, forced to admit that their genius, with his blood transfusions and hormone infusions and marrow transplants, has been developing a medical technology that is perfectly consistent with his previous achievements. So, too, is the enlightened orphanage and the highly civilized conservatory. Of course he went too far, Dr. Hamilton concludes—beyond sanity and morality, to be sure, but, after all, how firm are their boundaries? His crime was a matter of excess.

Which brings us back to McIlvaine's early formulation of New York as a city of excess, and to the modern fusion party of intellect and power. The narrative and thematic weave of *The Waterworks* is a powerful assertion of artistic strategy and tact. In dwelling on what it is saying, I have scanted what it is doing, notably growing a novel of deep, transitive ideas on the trellis of nineteenth-century genre fiction, complete with melodrama, domestic sentiment, a villain crushed by his own strongbox, and even an ending of two happy marriages. It is also, as I've suggested, Doctorow's own meditation on the great tradition of American fiction, and his own claim to his place in it as both a recipient and a contributor.

The Cabinet of Dr. Sartorius
[Review of *The Waterworks*]

LUC SANTE

In the course of his career E. L. Doctorow has made a subspecialty of constructing New York Cities, varied by historical setting as well as by architecture of genre and psychological weather. In *Ragtime* and *World's Fair* and *Billy Bathgate,* for example, the city is carnival and mountain range and obstacle course by turns, brilliantly colored and dangerous and exhilarating. The city he has erected in *The Waterworks* is in most regards the Manhattan of 1871, the oyster of the Tweed Ring, still fat from war profits but possibly hollow within, lurching its way into the modern era.

> You may think it stands to your New York City today as some panoramic negative print, inverted in its lights and shadows . . . its seasons turned around . . . a companion city of the other side.

This is the narrator speaking from somewhere just the other side of the century's turn, recalling in old age events he witnessed in his early middle years. The contrast he sees between his earlier and his later city is of course nothing compared with the city of the reader's present—or is it that 1871 is more like the present? The youth of 1871 are "a wary generation, without illusion . . . revolutionaries of a sort . . . though perhaps too vulnerable ever to accomplish anything." They make "little social enclaves of irony," wear bits of Civil War uniforms, are "of that postwar generation for whom the materials of the war were ironic, objects of art or fashion." Perhaps this is not so much the early modern city as the pre-postmodern city, in which the nascent industries are those of self-consciousness and artifice.

The germ of *The Waterworks* would seem to be an enigmatic sketch of the same title that appeared in Doctorow's 1984 collection *Lives of the Poets,* which here appears as a flashback. At the Croton Holding Reservoir, the massive Egyptian-styled structure that stood on the present site of the Public Library,

From *New York Review of Books* 41 (June 23, 1994): 10,12. Reprinted with permission from *The New York Review of Books.* Copyright © 1994 NYREV, Inc.

at Fifth Avenue and Forty-Second Street, a boy falls in the water and apparently drowns. As a crowd looks on, a bearded man rushes up, pulls the boy out of the water by his feet, wraps him in his coat, rushes downstairs and into a waiting carriage, which speeds away. Everyone has assumed the man to be a relative or a doctor rescuing the boy, until the terrified mother appears. It seems the man had come from nowhere and had returned there bearing the boy, for unknown reasons. In its sketch form the anecdote is unexplained and stands alone, with the fathomless clarity of a vision or a dream. In the novel it functions as a harbinger of unsavory revelations to come.

Its witness is a newspaper editor, McIlvaine. He conforms to a classic type of nineteenth-century narrator, fortuitously present for all the major events of the novel, but whose function within it is largely restricted to witness, with perhaps a sideline in introducing the other characters to one another. He is a bachelor, saturnine, slightly uneasy, given to vicarious passions, with a deliberative, ruminative voice that gives the book its ellipsis-laden style. The narrative begins with the disappearance of his favorite freelance writer, Martin Pemberton, a slight, nervous youth who writes devastating, career-puncturing book reviews (he has savaged not only the Boston sages, Holmes and Lowell and Longfellow, but another sort of literary critter, "a sporting man, a heavy drinker with a predilection for stripping to the waist in saloons and engaging in prizefight matches," although his name is not Hemingway, but then the reviewer's isn't Poe, either).

Pemberton is the estranged son of August Pemberton, a plutocrat whose piety and social responsibility poorly camouflage his outsize rapaciousness. Not only has he established, in a contemporary-sounding way, "a pattern of loyalty not to any one business, but to the art of buying and selling them," but he has been secretly a slave trader, persisting in the commerce as late as 1862.

Now the elder Pemberton has expired and been entombed with appropriate ceremony, but his son, before vanishing, has given several people breathless accounts of having seen his father in the flesh, not once but twice, aboard Municipal Transport stages. McIlvaine surmises that the son's disappearance and the father's putative spectral apparitions must be linked, and he gradually enlists a motley cast of accomplices to help him get to the bottom of the mystery. This crew seems to have stepped as much from a novel of the period as from the period. There is Martin's idealistic fiancée, herself the daughter of a rich man; his young, unworldly stepmother; his father's myopic old confessor; his Columbia roommate, now a rude but passionate realistic painter (who a century ahead of his time occupies "the top floor of a commercial ironfront on West Fourteenth Street, the equivalent of one large room, and with a bank of windows characteristic of the ironfronts," and who in the course of the story appears to invent a procedure that anticipates the police identikit sketches of the present); and, finally, the one utterly incorruptible member of the Police Department, who promptly takes charge of the investigation.

Elements of pastiche are never far from the surface of any of Doctorow's novels, and *The Waterworks* is no exception. He seems particularly fond of the boy's adventure novel; *Loon Lake* and *World's Fair* both suggest this genre, and *Billy Bathgate* might be his version of *Treasure Island*. *The Waterworks* owes its form to a mode slightly later than the period of its setting, the "scientific romance." Such is its flavor—cartoonish and cryptic, flatfooted and lyrical, slight and profound at once. After many travails our heroes, led by the stalwart Captain Donne, penetrate a seemingly unassailable barrier of silence, made possible by the financial manipulations of the Tweed Ring, and uncover a hidden world presided over by the mysterious Doctor Sartorius. In this realm unimaginably sinister depths are sounded, justified by the claims of pure disinterested science. This is a familiar state of affairs for the genre, and Dr. Sartorius is a familiar figure, recalling Wells's Dr. Moreau, Verne's Dr. Ox, Gustave Le Rouge's Dr. Cornelius, and a long line of twisted medicos down to Dr. Mabuse and Dr. Phibes, all of them descended from Dr. Frankenstein.

The genre is apt because it evokes the mingled enthusiasm and dread with which the symptoms of change were greeted in that vulnerable period, and maybe too because its contrivance matches the prevailing artifice of our time. But ours derives from overstimulation and panic; the innocent devices of the past risk seeming precious today. In the end, the novel's contradictions are not resolved. There is a chasm between surface and implication that threatens to swallow the reader, who cannot suspend disbelief and simultaneously indulge it to the same degree.

Dr. Wrede Sartorius is a German émigré, perhaps a "forty-eighter," a veteran of the Union Army, and a redoubtable medical pioneer. During the war he invented numerous surgical procedures, rejected the use of collodion dressings in favor of fresh air, devised a new kind of hypodermic syringe, successfully innovated with aseptic solutions, and generally represented an extraordinarily farsighted approach to infections and their remedies. Later in his career he turns out to have invented means for blood transfusions, dialysis machines, procedures for transplanting bone marrow, and, at the end, he is preparing to carry out heart transplants. He adheres to the prototype of the Romantic nineteenth-century scientist, appearing sinister in part because he is so far ahead of his time, and in part because he is so purely intellectual that he evades the pull of human feelings. Like many of his fictional predecessors, he has been assigned Faustian and Promethean attributes by an uncomprehending society.

The younger Pemberton is found languishing in a dungeon beneath a dubious orphanage owned by Dr. Sartorius. When he at length recovers the power of speech, he tells what happened after he dug up his father's grave and found a dead child in the coffin. Making contact with a known associate of the elusive Sartorius, who had been his father's physician at the end, he was knocked out in a saloon and recovered consciousness in a windowless sanctum, site of the doctor's laboratories. The doctor himself is not the monster he had expected, but a rational if bloodless savant who shows him around the plant and allows him to watch the procedures. It seems that his father, along with a half-dozen other rich old men, has signed most of his assets over to Dr. Sartorius in exchange for which he gives them a form of immortality, which turns out to be a bare vegetal existence, as creatures of social conventions. These formerly powerful men have in effect become automatons.

> While the orchestrion disk revolved and tined out its lumbering waltzes, boosted with automatic bass drum and cymbals, the creatures of the immortal fellowship danced in their black ties . . . with their caretaker women. It was a medley of the waltz tunes of the day, to which the old men, led by their cyprians, made their obedient slow shuffles . . . including my father, doing his dutiful dance in a way that absolved him in my mind of all his criminal cunning. He had foregone the dignity of death, as they all had. He was reduced to a vacant old man I could look in on.

But Martin somehow transgresses and, having seen too much, is condemned by the doctor and his henchmen to waste away on a pallet in pitch darkness.

For all the trappings of villainy that surround him, Dr. Sartorius is not the real bad guy here. He even has an alibi for the most serious charge that can be lodged against him—that he victimizes street children. Apparently all he does is extract "fluids" from them, and otherwise keeps them sheltered and fed; the corpses with which he replaces his undead plutocrats are those of victims of accidents, such as the boy at the reservoir. But he and his shadowy domain throws into relief the two invisible realms that bookend urban society and serve to define it. At one extreme are the urchins, omnipresent and yet unseen by the rest of the population; at the other are "men hidden, barricaded, in their own created realm behind the thick walls of the brownstones of New York . . . men who are only names in your newspapers . . . powerful, absent men." It is not even economics so much as a sort of alchemy that makes for their strange unequal equivalence, where the existence of each make possible the existence of the other. At one point the narrator says,

> I define modern civilization as the social failure to keep all children named. . . . Only where we have newspapers to tell us the news of ourselves . . . are children not assured of keeping their names.

It is as if the disembodied rich who populate the press were sucking away those names and hoarding them for their own use.

The Waterworks is crowded with such dualities, temporal, economic, moral, generational: art and science, soul and body, inner and outer, human and divine, and so on. This is fully in keeping with its period flavor. Allusion is likewise made to the "sunlight and shadow" motif prevalent in journalistic accounts of New York City at the time of its setting, a conceit that could sum up the city's dizzying and appalling contrasts, equally well for purposes of poetic shorthand or moral laziness. In that booming period, accounts of rag-pickers and nomadic children and anonymous murder victims could serve a perverse civic pride: New York had more of them than anyplace else. It seemed only fitting that the city with the most advanced systems of transportation and lighting should also possess the most horrifying crimes, the most bottomless destitution. Lurking just beneath this sort of smugness is the unexamined notion that progress is fueled by such horrors, depends on them for propulsion.

In the novel progress and civic evil are joined in the image of the waterworks, the city's circulatory system, the vast project of aqueducts, tunnels, and pipes that continue to link upstate reservoirs to the island city. The Croton Water-works in Westchester is identified as the central organ, around which "the ground . . . pulsed like a heartbeat," while the holding reservoir in the center of Manhattan is "a squared expanse of black water that was in fact the geo-metrical absence of a city." The metaphorical power of this occult system can be further appreciated in the light of a bizarre coincidence: another novel, issued by the same publisher in the same season, employs the same device. In Caleb Carr's elephantine penny-dreadful *The Alienist,* which takes place in 1896, a map of the city's water system furnishes the trajectory for an evil scheme. In that book, too, a major set piece takes place at the holding reser-voir, although its anatomical significance is different; it is "the *heart* of the city's water system, the center to which all aqueducts fed and from which all mains and arteries drew their supply."

In Carr's book the water system finds its bloody correlative within the symbolic order in the mind of a nineteenth-century Zodiac Killer or Son of Sam. In Doctorow's it is identified with the machinery of civilization, a mat-ter of considerable ambiguity. It is both the locus of possibly nefarious deeds and a marvel of engineering no less impressive today than it was then. Within its precincts Sartorius carries out his experiments, which are futuristic and quaint, morally questionable and straightforwardly inquisitive. His zombies may be bound to their antique convention of the afternoon dance, but the automated music supplied for the occasion does not seem far from the mode of the present, automatic bass drum and cymbals included.

This may be part of Doctorow's point, that progress is a slippery matter, that change does not move in a straight line, and that orders of succession are not to be trusted. Fathers can succeed sons—or so the elder Pemberton would have it, at least—and the present has little to teach the past. In McIlvaine's words:

> You may think you are living in modern times, here and now, but that is the necessary illusions of every age. We did not conduct ourselves as if we were preparatory to your time. There was nothing quaint or colorful about us. I assure you, New York after the war was more creative, more deadly, more of a genius society than it is now.

But, then, he goes on to cite the constituents of this genius: rotary presses, steam engines, gaslights. Just as every era believes itself superior to the past, so it also imagines that it holds the key to the future, which it does, but never in the way that it expects. The equivocal Sartorius is the man of the future, but not even McIlvaine at a remove of decades can quite appreciate this. Long before Pasteur and Koch, Sartorius believes that diseases are spread by germs. McIlvaine, in one of several lovely descriptions of the city streets, recalls a walk down Broadway:

> The air seemed suspended, unmoving, with a specific attar projected by each shop, store, restaurant, or saloon. Thus we walked through invisible realms of coffee, baked goods, leather, cosmetics, roasting beef, and beer . . . at which point, on no scientific authority whatsoever, I was willing to endorse the miasma theory of zymotic infection.

The sources of those odors have vanished as surely as the odors themselves, as surely the miasma theory itself. That which has thrived has been transmitted by germs unsuspected at the time, marginal phenomena and loony theories that turned out to possess the future. The city's genius resides in its capacity for breeding such germs. Meanwhile, change is the only real constant, as New York, of all cities, proves by its history. After ending his story with a couple of weddings, as in Dickens or a Russian fairy tale, Doctorow closes on a mirage: an empty, icy city on a winter Sunday, "as if the entire city of New York would be forever encased and frozen, aglitter and God-stunned." It is only in that city—the one under the snow-globe—that immortality can be achieved.

ARTICLES
◆

Doctorow's *Hard Times:*
A Sermon on the Failure of Faith

MARILYN ARNOLD

Because of *Ragtime* and its success as a motion picture, and because of his recent novel, *Loon Lake,* E. L. Doctorow is well-known across a broad spectrum of literate America. What is not always well-known, however, is that Doctorow had earlier tried his hand at western fiction. In a book called *Welcome to Hard Times,* he created what appears at first glance to be a rather standard, if artful, western tale, a frontier novel. The setting is predictable—treeless prairie town with a mining camp nearby. So are some of the characters: saloon women, sharpshooters, Bad Man, stage driver, immigrants, miners, and token Indian. The plot traces the destruction, rebirth, and final destruction of the town, and at the same time follows the protagonist's efforts at winning a woman. But for all its adherence to the standard western format, the book is disturbingly atypical. Its hero is uneven in his courage, running like a coward in his first encounter with the Bad Man from Bodie. Not only that, but he would rather keep books than fight outlaws. His lady is a pock-marked prostitute who would sell her soul to any man good enough with a gun to protect her. Doctorow said he wrote the novel because as a Hollywood script reviewer he had encountered so many bad scripts for westerns that he decided to try his hand at writing one.[1]

But the book is, in fact, a serious piece of fiction about a man who is creating fiction as he attempts to write history. It is about what happens to events as a man describes them, and what he realizes about the power of the past to perpetuate and repeat itself through its being established in historical records.[2] Doctorow uses the western town to reveal that truth by treating it as a microcosm for the rise and fall of civilizations. What may take centuries to be accomplished in another time and place can be realized in a single year in the West. A basic conflict in the book, then, is the battle between civilization and the wilderness, between order and disorder, with Blue, the protagonist, trying to make order out of chaos by recording deeds and transactions in his ledgers. But Doctorow does more than present Hard Times as a micro-

From *Literature and Belief* 3 (1983): 87–95. "Doctorow's *Hard Times*: A Sermon on the Failure of Faith" reprinted with permission of *Literature and Belief*.

cosm for civilization's cycling birth and destruction, and he does more than present Hard Times as the battleground for the clash between wilderness and civilization. He also explores the *reasons* for the destruction of cities and civilizations.

There is a subtle but unmistakable pattern of religious language, imagery, and structure running through the book, a pattern that, enhanced by its frontier content, suggests that Hard Times (and, by implication, civilization) falls because of the subversion of basic religious values. Almost every religious reference or image or concept in the book is somehow inverted or subverted until Hard Times and its inhabitants become a living mockery of the religious idea or impulse. And in this sense, the people of Hard Times become the abstraction called fate, become their own destruction. Blue seems finally to recognize this at the end when it strikes him that the Bad Man from Bodie, whom he had regarded as the embodiment of Hard Times's destructive fate, is only a man after all. He sweats, he bleeds. He did not destroy the town single-handedly. Not the first time, and not the last. It died from internal rot. The Bad Man simply lifts the lid and exposes the rot.

And, like the accounts of Biblical cities that were destroyed for their wickedness—accounts of Babylon, Nineveh, Sodom and Gomorrah—Blue's "gospel" details the human corruption that precipitates destruction. Blue's record-keeping is a mark of his civilizing impulse, but Doctorow indicates that it also has a religious function. As the town begins its cyclic upswing after the Bad Man's first catastrophic appearance, Blue takes hopefully to his record-keeping, commenting that the ledgers brought in for him by stage contained "enough paper . . . to write the Bible."[3] And so he writes it, a western bible. He writes the story of the demise of civilization as a result of individual corruption and the failure of faith, generosity, and charity to prevail against doubt, greed, and hate. And Doctorow describes that failure as a religious one.

Structurally, the book moves cyclically from death to rebirth and back to death, a scheme with obvious religious implications. It is, of course, the redemption myth carried a step too far, past the rebirth phase and once more into the death phase. Doctorow opens his novel with the first appearance of the Bad Man, an appearance which leaves several people dead and the town smoldering in ashes. When the Bad Man rides off, only a few people remain: Blue, the unelected "mayor"; young Jimmy Fee, son of the killed town carpenter; John Bear, a deaf-mute Indian who keeps mainly to himself; and Molly, the saloon woman whom the Bad Man had left for dead. Things look anything but promising; still, Blue is a man of faith. He has to hope in spite of himself. And when a few wanderers trickle in, Blue convinces them to stay and help him rebuild the town. The small group of them survive a bitter winter, and spring brings a semblance of rebirth. Just as Molly had risen like a phoenix from the town's ashes (an obvious redemptive metaphor), so does the town itself rise, rebuilt, significantly, of wood scavenged from a dead town some miles away.

When the first rain signals the end of winter, Blue steps outside the dugout he shares with Molly and Jimmy into what he calls "that new morning." His eyes are filled with the sun, "with a warmth of hazes, pink, pale green and yellow, and all over the flats white mists were rising like winter being steamed out of the ground." He exults, "I swore I could feel the earth turning. Everything was new in my sight." The few feeble structures that constitute the town appear to him "like a row of plants just sprung" (p. 112). Blue writes in jubilant recollection of that spring when "the hurts were healing in the warm sun and the expectations were nourished into life. A greenness of hopes grew up like the scrub along the rocks coming up green" (p. 114). Under the influence of a "deep gold sunlight" (p. 117), a sense of community begins to grow. More people arrive, love blooms between one shy miner and one of Russian Zar's saloon women, and even Molly begins to warm toward Blue. His language speaks of rebirth: ". . . it was as if we were two new people sprung from our old pains" (p. 132). As Molly and Blue experience their brief season of conjugality, she actually responds to him with "the shyness of a bride" (p. 133).

But that time passes. The story does not end with the redemptive miracle, but traces again the tumble into destruction and death. Blue realizes later that in one of their nights of love he and Molly reached a moment of perfection, a "ripeness," but "the earth turned past it." He knows now that "the best that can be is come and gone" (p. 139). Through Blue's increased understanding of events as he records them in his ledgers, in his "bible," Doctorow makes it clear that the rebirth of Hard Times is a sham. Blue observes repeatedly that "the earth turns and we turn with it"; human experience is a "mockery that puts us back in our own steps" (p. 199). Significantly, the Bad Man's name is Clay Turner. To Blue, he is an agent of Fate, an earth turner who comes a second time as the town again enters a death phase.

Doctorow also makes clear connections between the earth's turning— and taking Hard Times with it—and the absence of religious values among people in the town. While Blue fights for community and cooperation and applauds any sign of love or caring, the town's entrepreneurs think only of their personal security and prosperity. Molly's only concern is the cultivation of a gunman capable of working her vengeance on the Bad Man when he returns—and she knows he is coming. She plays up to the foolish crack-shooting Jenks and trains Jimmy to love violence. Zar's only interest is gold; and Isaac Maple, the scornful storekeeper, insists on cash for his goods and exploits his monopolistic advantage. Even Blue sacrifices human beings in order to achieve community, a home for himself. Only Swede seems selfless, and perhaps Adah, one of Zar's women. She makes several generous gestures, but they come to little in a hostile environment.

That what happens in the town is for Doctorow a subversion of religious values seems clear when we consider how religious allusions and language are used in the book. For one thing, there are a multitude of instances in which what appears to be simple profanity carries a double meaning and makes an unconscious comment on the spiritual state of the town. For example, when, in the midst of the first violent episodes, someone shoots the Bad Man's horse, Blue hollers angrily, "Who in hell did that!" (p. 9). Later on, begging Molly to leave after the return of the Bad Man, Blue uses language that carries an undertone of religious meaning: "Molly in the name of God listen to what I'm telling you!" Then he cries, "You want it to happen again? You think I can atone more?" (p. 199). Blue speaks of atonement, which in Christian theology is synonymous with redemption but which in Hard Times has been reduced to retribution or subverted to vengeance.

Perhaps more important are the reversals of the redemptive images associated with spring and hope for the town's rebirth. Bert Albany and his "Chinagirl" conceive a child in Hard Times, but they flee before it can be born. Blue observes, "No child has ever been born in this town, and that's the saddest thing I will ever know . . ." (p. 95).

Instead of an actual birth, the town provides an ugly mockery of a birth. Blue, who had felt at one time almost "married" to Molly, realizes in the end that it was the Bad Man, not himself, to whom she was figuratively wed. What she had wanted all along, even as she had dreaded it, was the Bad Man's return: "She'd been waiting for him, a proper faithful wife. Nothing mattered to her, not me, not Jimmy, just herself and her Man from Bodie" (p. 200). When Blue finally outwits the Bad Man and hauls him half dead to Molly's table, Molly falls on him to take revenge with her stiletto. As she jabs him repeatedly, she is "almost dancing with the grace of retribution." All along she had clutched the cross necklace given to her by the old Major who had favored her, but at the end she substitutes the cross-shaped stiletto for it. As Blue observes, when she has the Bad Man before her, wounded on her table, she has "no need to wave her cross for protection, a knife would do, the stiletto" (p. 212). Horrified at the scene, Jimmy shoots them both, at close range, his "instrument booming of birth," at "the moment Turner's arms had closed around Molly as if in embrace." The offspring of this unholy union is a devil who was once a boy named Jimmy; he rides off pell mell to become the next Bad Man from Bodie. In this excruciating perversion of conception and birth, there is even an ugly image of afterbirth. As Blue faints (his hand was over the muzzle of Jimmy's gun when it fired), he hears "people outside tipping over the water tank," making an "indecent gush" (p. 212).

In still other ways, Blue's hopeful accounts of spring and rebirth are mocked or inverted. In passages noted earlier, Blue had spoken of his hopes and those of the townspeople coming up like new plants after winter. But by the time he reaches the end of his account he is aware that the harvest of his hopeful planting is not life but death. He grieves, "I have farmed the crop of this country, the land's good yield along with Men from Bodie" (p. 211). Blue concludes sorrowfully, ". . . we can never start new, we take on all the burden" (p. 187).

Doctorow's book is structured not only around the cycle of nature's seasons and the destruction, reconstruction and subsequent destruction of Hard Times, but also around the cyclical birth and death of Blue's hope. That hope rises even in the winter when the little group huddled on the old town site make one feeble attempt at religious observance. They come together on Christmas Day for a drink of whiskey and a few hymns, and Blue takes heart. The whiskey going down is warm, spreading over him "like the sun," and he feels already that "better times" have come and that he and the others now have "a root on the land where there was nothing but graves a few months before" (p. 104). But that root, as we have seen, yields only more corpses. The holiday gathering ends abruptly after a greedy quarrel, and each celebrant returns to his quarters even more isolated and forlorn than before. The charity of the Christian gospel can make few inroads into Hard Times. Even at the end, however, in the midst of total destruction, Blue decides that he probably won't even try to muster the strength to burn the town because maybe "someone will come by sometime who will want to use the wood" (p. 215).

Doctorow further indicates the subversion of religious values through the language of paradox, irony, and inversion. We have seen this subversion operating on a broad scale in the book's events and themes, but it is underlined in incidental ways as well, especially through the character of Molly. For example, Blue perceives Molly's "sweet smile" to be "full of hate" (p. 35), and Zar notes that "she has sharp nails for a believer" (p. 43). And throughout the book Molly wears a wedding dress given to her by one of Zar's women, an ironic virginal symbol of her "wedding" to Blue and ultimately to the Bad Man. The prostitute-as-bride image is constantly before us. When, during the winter, Jimmy takes sick, Molly cuddles him against her breast in a mock Madonna gesture; but she blushes at it, says Blue, and "she kept looking at me as if she expected me to laugh at her" (p. 95).

Molly, as was noted earlier, is the phoenix who rises out of the town's ashes at the beginning, but at the end she is the purveyor of death. So bent is Molly on revenge that her prayers over the cross are understood to be vengeful, and she sacrifices Jenks, Jimmy, and even Blue (he finally becomes her "final fool," p. 205) to her desire. The mocking religious allusion is clear in Blue's observation that Molly "put her hook into him [Jimmy], a carpenter's son" (p. 211). Jimmy listens to Molly as though she were speaking "gospel" (p. 153) and "kept up his duties to her like a faith" (p. 159). And when she goes with Jimmy to put a cross over his father's grave (the Bad Man killed him in the first riot), they put it on the wrong grave and end up paying reverence to the one-armed Jack Millay.

Molly is not the only "preacher" in the book. Her "true husband," the Bad Man, is also something of a mock preacher. When asked what happened to the town, Blue replies, "Well a man come by preaching hellfire" (p. 39). He also observes that the Bad Man "wedded" him and Molly, just as a preacher might, and he realizes the second time the Bad Man appears that they will all soon be "suffering Turner, feeling his sermon." Blue himself also acts as a preacher, performing the wedding ceremony for Bert Albany and his bride, though he has no authority to do so. When Blue sets the trap for the preacher/Bad Man, however, he speaks of himself as one acting in "righteousness" who nevertheless infects the Swede with his "madness," and the two of them go about their deadly work "like penitents hurrying before God's wrath" (p. 208). And instead of making a barbed crown for their victim, they make "a bed of barbs" (p. 208) for him. Thus Blue, who had tried to promote the religious values of love and charity, whose foremost desire was for community and faith, not only bears the guilt for the deaths of those he lured into the town to settle, but also becomes an agent for Molly's retribution. He abandons his ideal and succumbs to violence. The man who had believed in the power of dialogue and community to hold out against evil takes up a gun and joins in the final death frenzy.

Doctorow's inversions and ironies are apparent in other ways too. At the Christmas "celebration," for example, Zar turns his own initially appreciative response to the singing of "Holy, holy, holy" into an irreverent joke as he compares it to the cry of coyotes, "Howly, howly, howly" (p. 105). In a town like Hard Times, too, Bert is thought to be crazy for falling in love, though for Blue it is something of a miracle, "a revelation" (p. 128). And the floor upon which the wedding dance is held seems to Blue to be "sanctified." Zar's saloon, as one would expect, has a false front, and the sign the citizens spread across the street to attract new settlers is a paradoxical announcement: "Welcome to Hard Times." The fact that Doctorow also chooses that greeting for his title suggests the centrality of paradox and inversion to his purposes. And then there is Blue's final heart-breaking revelation about the consequences of his faith: ". . . if I hadn't believed, they'd be alive today" (p. 214).

As further indication that in this frontier town religious values are subverted and destruction is therefore imminent, Doctorow describes Hard Times in hellish terms. In the wake of the Bad Man's first visit, the pitiful crying of Molly and Jimmy is accompanied by the moaning of the night breeze through the boards of John Bear's shanty "like an awful chorus of ghosts" (p. 30), and over the town "smoke still rose, blue now in the moonlight, and embers were glowing on the ground like peepholes to Hell" (p. 31). That winter Blue, Molly, and Jimmy live in a dugout, below ground, and as Blue digs it Jimmy asks him if he is preparing a grave. The whole scene is one of terrible desolation. Ruin is everywhere, and even Blue wonders what good could possibly come out of "this ashen townsite" where people resemble "phantoms" (p. 53).

Wood to rebuild the town is collected from a "ghost city" (p. 65), and Fee's buried body seems to say, "I ain't much for God" (p. 149). Again, too, the uttered profanities seem to emphasize the godforsaken nature of the site ("Blue, for God's sake let's leave this place!" p. 150). And after the town has begun to take shape, it is peopled with grotesques, outcasts, and the physically and spiritually deformed. Its chief customers are miners, men who work under ground. Blue notes that even when the wreckage of the town appears inevitable, people do not try to leave, but remain as if held by an implement of the devil, "stuck here like pigs on a pitchfork" (p. 193). As he concludes his "bible," Blue emits a groan that might have been made by his "ghost already in its hell before [he is] dead" (p. 211). And in Helga's mad eyes he imagines "all the eyes of those dead faces" (p. 211). Finally, the selfish human commerce of the hopelessly damned town is replaced by the "hum of enterprise" of infernal creatures—"buzzards, jackals, and vultures, flies, bugs, mice" (p. 213).

It seems clear, then, that Doctorow is doing more in this novel than chronicling the rise and fall of one fictional western town. Hard Times is representative of towns all over the West. As the government man who comes to charter it observes, "Over this land a thousand times each year towns spring up" (p. 142). More than that, as we have observed, Hard Times symbolically charts the rise and fall of civilizations. But more important still may be Doctorow's implicit analysis of why frontier towns, and, indeed, whole civilizations and societies, decline. Blue's record, written over his ledger accounts with the last of his strength, is a kind of bible which details the unfolding of events and conditions in Hard Times. Integral to that record is the language of inverted religious belief and principle. Even as it prospers, and perhaps partly because it prospers, Hard Times becomes again a hellish place where the religious values of love and faith are subverted. Having bred its own fate, the town turns out of its phase of rebirth and once more into its phase of death and destruction. Its end was thus in its beginning, because the only motive for settling the town, for most of its inhabitants, was money. And Molly's only reason for staying, in the end, was vengeance. When religious values are ignored or upended, societies do not survive. Blue's account of the fall of Hard Times is a subjective historical record, but it is also a lesson and a warning, like the Bible itself.

Notes

1. Speaking of the Hollywood scripts, Doctorow says, "An awful lot of them at the time—the late 1950's—were westerns, and I found them oppressive. They made me ill. So I thought to myself, I know more about the true West than these people do, even though at the time I hadn't been west of Ohio." See the Catherine O'Neill interview with Doctorow titled "The Music in Doctorow's Head" in the Books and Arts section of The Chronicle of Higher Education, September 28, 1979, p. 6.

2. See my discussion of this aspect of the novel in "History as Fate in E. L. Doctorow's Tale of a Western Town," South Dakota Review, 18 (Spring 1980), 53–63.

3. E. L. Doctorow, Welcome to Hard Times (New York: Bantam Books, 1976; first publ. 1960), p. 124. Subsequent page references will be cited parenthetically.

The Burden of the Past:
Doctorow's *The Book of Daniel*

Eugénie L. Hamner

Because it deals with events, issues, and the tone of the period since World War II and emphasizes the McCarthy era and the Rosenberg case, E. L. Doctorow's *The Book of Daniel* (1971) has been interpreted as a "description of the hysteria of McCarthyism," as a modern version of the alienation of Jews, and as "the document more of voice than of a character," concentrating on "live social issues."[1] Although broader in scope, this book bears kinship with the plethora of recent documentaries—books such as Wambaugh's *The Onion Field* (1973), Bugliosi and Gentry's *Helter Skelter* (1974), Krause's *Guyana Massacre* (1978), Howard's *Zebra* (1979), and of course those on Watergate. It bears greater kinship with Capote's *In Cold Blood* (1965), which attempts to re-create the truth and make sense of seemingly senseless events, and with Mailer's documentary fiction, *The Executioner's Song* (1979). Yet *The Book of Daniel* does not simply exploit a current writing and reading vogue. Doctorow has done more than provide an anatomy of a period; he has done more than re-create the fullest possible truth about a particular case history.

The Book of Daniel is a work of serious fiction on the order of—and in fact similar to—Warren's *All the King's Men* (1946). Like Warren, Doctorow uses a sensational case as a touchstone to a particular era and to certain timeless facts of life. To be more precise, he uses the lives and times of the Rosenbergs (Paul and Rochelle Isaacson, Daniel's parents) as Warren uses the life and times of Huey Long (Willie Stark). Furthermore, these two authors have embedded these public stories in the personal stories of their narrators. Among the significant similarities of Daniel Isaacson Lewin and Jack Burden are these: each serves the technical function of arranging and telling, each is a minor character in the public story told, and the world-view of each is altered by that story. As Charles R. Anderson explains, "it was not Warren's purpose to write a fictional biography of the King Fish. By the device of the narrator he frames one story within another, so that the rise and fall of Willie Stark becomes merely illustrative matter. Though this master of violence is the one

Reprinted from *Research Studies* 49, no. 1 (1981): 55–61.

who comes to a tragic end, the reader's interest centers in Jack Burden, the rootless and alienated modern man."[2]

Holding the thematic center of his book and the means by which form and content fuse into meaningfulness, Daniel is Doctorow's rootless and alienated modern man. His is a story of an agonizingly difficult quest for the truth about his parents' imprisonment and execution, a story of "a young man trying to interpret and analyze the awful visions of his head."[3] Doctorow has magnified the public scene through its initiatory effects on Daniel and has placed it in perspective against the larger screen of history from the time of Nebuchadnezzar. In his retrospective account, Jack Burden details a political assignment which leads him unwittingly to a startling discovery about his parents. Unlike Jack, Daniel fails to establish truth earnestly sought and instead acquires insight in spite of ambiguity. His quest becomes an initiation into the inexplicability of some actions (even of his own family), the endlessly cruel ways of the world, and the centrality of the heart in meaningful experience.

Both Jack and Daniel reached the stage of writing a dissertation in history. Jack abandoned the editing of Cass Mastern's journal because he could not then understand its meaning. Daniel records his own story, present and past, to evade (and prepare himself for) writing his dissertation. His means of presentation provide the first clues to the faltering nature of his quest. Similar to his Biblical predecessor and to Jack on occasion, he alternates between first-person and third-person accounts of his experience, for he lacks the personal stability requisite to maintaining the objectivity of a historian. For example, frequently he suddenly shifts to first-person as his emotions become caught in re-living an event. Also, like Jack, he shifts from past tense and times to present tense and times, for times impinge on each other. Additionally, he interrupts those accounts, often abruptly, with references to contemporary and historical public events, because too many intense images crowd his mind for him to maintain a chronological sequence, because he sees connections between his story and information he has researched, and because at times a subject becomes too painful to be continued.

Two bodies of images which dominate Daniel's thoughts influence his erratic pattern of behavior and help account for his inconsistencies in presentation. At one point he says, "Images are what things mean . . . they are essentially instruments of torture" (pp. 83–84). Images of torture and death form the larger category. Some of these are literal; some are figurative. Some appear as juxtaposed examples from history, some are childhood and later memories, and a few characterize Daniel's language and behavior in the present.

The images from history include eating a defeated enemy's heart, smoking, knouting, drawing and quartering, burning at the stake, guillotining, and executing by firing squad. Daniel describes Molotov and Stalin as "the rulers . . . whose only plenitude is violent death" (p. 252). He refers to Nazi concentration camps and mockingly characterizes the free world in terms of its prison camps. These images of violence cover the period from Nebuchadnezzar's fiery furnace to the post–World War II hysteria, "like a fiery furnace at white heat" (p. 22) which kills his parents. And they reinforce his memories of his grandmother's curses as she ran crazily from the house "calling down cholera and Cossacks and typhoid and wholesale terrors of the burning fiery furnace" (p. 79).

Other remembered images of torture include his father's arm and head injuries after the Robeson concert and the "overwhelming burning smell" from the furnace in their cellar, presided over by the janitor William, who, in the boy's view, had a "voice of murder and menace" and "red, murderous eyes" (pp. 103, 104). When the FBI is closing in on Paul and Rochelle, Daniel thinks of the phone as strangled, and he expects "our house will smell and smoke and turn brown at the edges and flare up in a great, sucking floop of flame" (p. 122). He describes the FBI's increasing the number of his parents' criminal deeds as "FRYING, a play in ten overt acts" (p. 172). And several times in describing events in the turbulent year 1967 Daniel uses terms of torture.

These images repel Daniel, yet at times they serve as his model of behavior. His acts of cruelty and insensitivity greatly exceed Jack's. On Memorial Day, for instance, he deliberately offends the Lewins, his adoptive parents, and frightens his wife Phyllis with reckless driving before he burns her with a cigarette lighter. One summer day, with a "murderous feeling" (p. 146), he throws his son Paul higher and higher, terrifying both Paul and Phyllis. On a visit to his sister Susan at the sanitarium that fall, he goes on a rampage to kill (or at least frighten) Dr. Duberstein.

This extreme behavior accords with Daniel's conception of citizens as soldiers (p. 85) and existence as warfare. He uses the language of war repeatedly. Rochelle directs the family "like a military commander" (p. 54). The friendly crowd at the Robeson concert is "like an army" (p. 59), and after Paul is wounded, Rochelle is "like an army nurse in a field hospital" (p. 124). The FBI is an "army of madmen" that goes "marching" through their house in its search (pp. 123, 127). And Daniel thinks Disneyland's methods of handling crowds "would light admiration in the eyes of an SS transport officer" (p. 306). Daniel has concluded that life is war and, as Cass Mastern learned, to be human is to inflict and suffer pain. This concept of human existence goes back at least to his seventh year, when the buses leaving the Robeson concert used low gear, to Daniel "the gear of pain, the sound that makes an engine human" (p. 60).

In contrast to images of torture are images of protective seclusion; in contrast to cruel involvement is retreat. Retreat is a strategy of Jack Burden, Brass-bound Idealist, Great Sleeper, maker of the Great Twitch theory to eliminate personal responsibility. Daniel also practices the strategy of retreat. As a child, he sought places of safety. One was the back of his father's radio repair shop: "I loved it there. It was a place to feel safe" (p. 50). The idea of working in a change booth in the New York subway system provided another: "You're underground in a stronghold that has barred windows, and a heavy steel door that locks from the inside. It's a very safe, secure place to be" (p. 55). Others are rain, darkness, and the Fischers' basement where he and Susan hid as children. The present one is the library where he thumbs through books and writes.

Another form of retreat is his gradually cultivated attitude of detachment, in which he indulges to evade the past and the quest. He admits that "all my life I have been trying to escape from my relatives and I have been intricate in my run" (p. 41). This running from has come to include the continuing representative of his past, Susan. Through evasion, he has denied his past as well as his present responsibilities to decency. He is rootless and alienated even from himself.

Early in the novel Daniel identifies his plight in slightly modified Biblical words: "I Daniel, was grieved, and the visions of my head troubled me and I do not want to keep the matter in my heart" (p. 27). To come to terms with his jagged present, he must come to terms with his gnawing past. In addition, to bring his visions into focus, he must not rely on his head alone; his heart must accept his visions. The novel properly begins with his Memorial Day trip to see Susan, for her attempted suicide and her letter—accusing him of believing their parents are guilty and asserting that "You no longer exist" (p. 90)—precipitate his delayed, now desperate, quest for truth, for connections.

While the dark library cove remains available for retreat, Daniel begins his active search, first interviewing reporter Jack Fein, lawyer Ascher's widow, Robert Lewin, and Susan's associate Artie Sternlicht. He then participates in the march on the Pentagon in an attempt to understand and perhaps to help Susan. Ironically, after labeling his announcing the name Daniel Isaacson over the microphone as "a put-on" (p. 269), he makes his first significant connection with his parents: he drinks his own blood, swallows teeth, is imprisoned, and thinks, "INNOCENT, I'M INNOCENT I TELL YA" (p. 274), words from a re-run prison movie which in his childhood nightmares featured his parents. He knows how far such places are from home, yet this prison experience takes him home to this part of their experience. He marks the event by wearing prison clothes thereafter.

The culminating event in Daniel's quest is his Christmastime meeting with Dr. Mindish in Disneyland. Daniel wants to test his theory of the other couple. Instead of information, he receives a kiss on the top of his head. Daniel's quest ends here, for this spontaneous act of affection shocks him into recognizing that human beings are not simple entities and that the truth is not available to him.

At the same time, the kiss begins to activate his heart and thus signals the turning point in his initiation. Daniel has become a connoisseur of disconnection, as spectator and as actor. Imitating the Inertia Kid, for example, he had to manage "disconnected eyes, and unconnected tongue," and more to the point, "you had to disconnect your heart muscle, you had to give up your heart" (p. 187). As deliberate disconnection is a mistake, so the "failure to make connections is complicity" (p. 243)—as Jack too learns after the deaths of his father, Willie, and Adam Stanton. Furthermore, Daniel's places of retreat are more like prisons or graves, and in fact their prison cells become wombs for Paul and Rochelle. Immediately following Dr. Mindish's humanizing kiss, Daniel inserts an account of heart transplants—cases of heart rejection, ejection, and dejection. This, his only abrupt insertion in the final book, is thematically appropriate, for it declares not only the powerful effect of this meeting on him but also his recognition of the nature of the struggle in which he has been engaged.

Only then can Daniel describe his parents' electrocutions. The historical images of execution which he inserts in his book are evidence that torture has a long history. Variations on this theme have occurred of course in his personal experience as well. The earliest example is a car's smashing a pedestrian, her arms holding two grocery bags. The boy observed that "milk was mixed with her blood, and glass was in it" (p. 101). He recalled this event and expected its repetition when the FBI was closing in: "And our blood will hurt as if it had glass in it" (p. 122). Violent occurrences, epitomized for him by the smashed pedestrian on the one hand and his parents' executions on the other, can be either random or deliberate. They are a condition of life, the glass that becomes mixed with the milk and the blood. His parents' case is therefore not unique, albeit excruciatingly magnified for him. His being able to write about this appalling event signifies that, even without the certainties about his parents which Jack Burden acquires about his, Daniel can at last live with his past and with the paradoxical facts of life symbolized by the key word *electricity*. Concluding the execution scene, he quotes his mother's final statement: "'Let my son be bar mitzvahed today. Let our death be his bar mitzvah'" (p. 314). In describing these executions, Daniel concludes his initiation.

Following the execution scene, Daniel offers three endings which are basically repetitive in that each shows him as a novice learning to put away childish things and to account for his actions as Jack does at the end of *All the King's Men*. The final statement of the novel is an apocalyptic passage from the Book of Daniel which ends with the words, "*Go thy way Daniel: for the words are closed up and sealed till the time of the end*" (p. 319). The Biblical Daniel, in an alien land, suffered and begged forgiveness for his people's past sins and interpreted visions of the future. Daniel Isaacson Lewin in this book presents images which caused his alienation and suffering, visions which confirm the visions of his predecessor. With acceptance of his visions, together with renewed capacity to feel and perhaps even love his son, Daniel can close his book and keep the matter in his heart as he walks in the sun of his present time and place, even if his life will be, like his predecessor's, "a life of confrontations" (p. 21). As Anderson says of Jack Burden, so of Daniel: "He can now accept the responsibility of being human, face the evil in the world and his part in it. He can find the faith and courage to give up his role of narrator and go back 'into the convulsion of the world'" (p. 290).

Unlike Capote and Mailer, Doctorow concentrates on a non-participant who was nevertheless acutely affected by a sensational case. And Doctorow has not explored the case: Daniel has—not out of exploitation or self-indulgence but out of need and longing. Through coming to terms with his own past in this deeply personal, zigzagging story, Daniel, the student of history, comes to understand mankind's past. His milieu may be recent and raw, but the historical parallels are clear and the meaning is timeless. His story is thus any maturing person's. This rootless, alienated modern man becomes rooted in awareness and heartfelt acceptance.

Notes

1. Barbara L. Estrin, "Surviving McCarthyism: E. L. Doctorow's *The Book of Daniel*," *Massachusetts Review*, 16 (1975), 577; John Stark, "Alienation and Analysis in Doctorow's *The Book of Daniel*," *Critique*, 16, No. 3 (1975), 101–110; Cobett Steinberg, "History and the Novel: Doctorow's *Ragtime*," *Denver Quarterly*, 10, No. 4 (1976), 125.

2. "Violence and Order in the Novels of Robert Penn Warren," in A. Walton Litz, ed., *Modern American Fiction* (New York: Oxford University Press, 1963), p. 286.

3. *The Book of Daniel* (1971; rpt. New York: NAL, 1972), p. 221. Subsequent references are to this edition.

Ragtime and the Movies

ANGELA HAGUE

One of the most important structuring devices in E. L. Doctorow's *Ragtime* is the presence of references, both explicit and implicit, to still photography, motion pictures, and the burgeoning film industry. In a sense, *Ragtime* is *about* the movies, for one of its major characters, Tateh, becomes an early pioneer of the movie industry, and Tateh's metamorphosis into the "Baron Ashkenazy" represents film's potential for movement and transformation in both political and aesthetic terms. In addition, photography and motion pictures illustrate one of the most important philosophical themes of *Ragtime,* the human need to preserve and replicate experience so that it can be analyzed and understood; film becomes a means for characters bewildered by the seeming mutability and formlessness of reality to subject time to rational control. This discussion will explore both the political and aesthetic implications of photography in the novel.

Doctorow's choice of the new film industry as a political analogue to the social background of *Ragtime* is apt, for the early history of the cinema illustrates in a variety of ways the situation of the working classes and the increasing industrialization of the United States at the turn of the century. In *A History of Narrative Film,* David Cook notes that the age of the robber barons coincided with the wrecking of the equipment of rival production companies by Thomas Edison's "goon squads" during the same years that witnessed "bloody strikebreaking by police, National Guardsmen, and Pinkertons all over the country as well as race riots and lynchings"—events which are essential elements in *Ragtime* and form an important backdrop to the political radicalization and growing aesthetic vision of Tateh.[1] Even more important, however, was the existence of a new art form which emerged in the ghettos of New York and Chicago and appealed to a mass audience for the first time, a phenomenon which blurred distinctions between "art" and "entertainment" and thrived, according to Robert Sklar, because it fused technology on the one hand and the urban working-class districts on the other."[2]

The growing popularity of nickelodeons in the United States—and the fact that in 1911 a Russell Sage survey revealed that 78 percent of the New York audience was working class[3]—testifies to the fact that the lower classes

Reprinted by permission from *North Dakota Quarterly* 50, no. 3 (Summer 1982): 101–12.

had indeed discovered a pastime which would eventually pose a threat, both social and aesthetic, to traditional culture. It is estimated that by 1907 between 8,000 and 10,000 storefront theatres existed across the country,[4] and that by 1908 daily attendance in New York City alone was between 300,000 and 400,000 persons.[5] By 1910 nickelodeons, called "democracy's theatre" by the popular press, were attracting 26 million Americans every week, or a little less than twenty percent of the country's entire population; in New York City more than 25 percent of the city's population went to the movies weekly, while in Chicago it is estimated that the figure was closer to 43 percent. The economic result of the 1910 attendance figures was that national gross receipts totaled $91 million.[6]

More significant, however, than the economic success of the cinema was the implied threat to traditional art and culture which it would soon pose. Walter Benjamin, in "The Work of Art in the Age of Mechanical Reproduction," would be one of the first theorists to acknowledge the power and potential of what Doctorow in *Ragtime* calls the "duplicated event." According to Benjamin, the end result of an art form which, because it lacks an "original" also lacks what he calls an "aura" or the concept of authenticity characteristic of non-reproducible art forms, was nothing less than "the liquidation of the traditional value of the cultural heritage," an outcome he saw as simultaneously destructive and cathartic.[7] Photography destroys the traditional elitist concept of art by replacing its "ritual" value with an exhibition value, substituting a plurality of copies for the single work of art's unique existence. And at the moment the concept of authenticity is destroyed and art is no longer based on ritual, says Benjamin, it "begins to be based on another practice—politics."[8]

Susan Sontag has also explored photography's political implications, noting that from its inception photography, unlike painting, "implied the capture of the largest number of subjects. . . . The subsequent industrialization of camera technology only carried out a promise inherent in photography from its very beginning: *to democratize all experiences by translating them into images*" (italics mine).[9] Sounding a great deal like Walter Benjamin, whose influence she acknowledges, Sontag says that the traditional fine arts, elitist because they are characterized by a single work produced by an individual, imply a hierarchy of subject matter; the media, on the other hand, weaken the role of the *auteur* by using easily-learned techniques based on chance and by making use of collaborative efforts. (The truth of Sontag's statement can be seen in the fact that in the early days of film-making credits did not exist, even for the film's "stars"; and film theorists, in their attempts to make cinema a more reputable art form, would have to "invent" *auteur* theory.) Unlike the traditional arts, which attempt to "rank" or "order" reality, the media regard the whole world as material; the photographer's approach, like that of the collector, is "antisystematic . . . an affirmation of the subject's thereness, its rightness."[10] When Tateh appears in *Ragtime* after his metamorphosis into the filmmaker Baron Ashkenazy, this concept of reality is a crucial aspect of his rejuvenation. His "simple delight" in his surroundings, the fact that "Life excited him. He dwelled on his own sensations and liked to talk about them: the taste of wine or the way the candle flames multiplied in the crystal chandeliers. . . .. it was enormously pleasurable to see the world as the Baron did, alive to every moment"—all this results from his new cinematic vision, symbolized by his constant use of the viewfinder.[11] As the narrator states, "He was a new man. He pointed a camera"; in his new role as a photographer he has discovered what Benjamin calls the "sense of the universal equality of things."[12]

The political ramifications of film would not become a major issue in Great Britain and Europe, where audiences were middle class from the very beginning; and middle-class America did not become concerned with the political and cultural implications of the cinema's popularity until well after it was firmly established as a mass entertainment for the working class. The political implications of the new art form were not, however, lost on Soviet Russia. Lenin's statement that "The cinema is for us the most important of the arts" was based on his realization that a country which spoke one hundred different languages would need a unifying force which could consolidate the nation and communicate effectively without necessitating a common language—or even literacy. The U.S.S.R. set up its state film school in 1919, and its young filmmakers would go on to make important filmic experiments and to articulate montage theory as a political and aesthetic doctrine for the first time. The kind of cultural diversity and need for cultural unity present in post-revolutionary Russia existed in the New York that Doctorow depicts in Ragtime; and what photojournalist Jacob Riis calls the "crazy quilt of humanity" in the novel, America's huge and diverse immigrant population, soon discovered that the entertainment offered by the storefront theatres required little money and even less knowledge of received culture. This phenomenon was soon perceived by many of the immigrant businessmen who, realizing the popularity of the nickelodeons in the ghettos, began to set themselves up as theatre managers.

As a result, Tateh's choice of film-making as a career allows him to remain philosophically entrenched in the working class—he still calls himself a "Jewish socialist from Latvia" at the novel's end—and provides him with the economic mobility to leave the ghetto. Tateh's Jewish immigrant background, frequently stressed in Ragtime, makes him accurately representative of the early entrepreneurs of the film industry, for many of the movies' early producers, as well as their audiences, emerged from the newly-arrived working-class immigrants. Although the film companies were controlled by American-born white Anglo-Saxon protestants before 1910, after the 1915 federal court break-up of the Motion Picture Patents Company, control of the industry shifted to the immigrant (and frequently Jewish) ethnic groups who had initially opened storefront theatres.[13] These men make an anonymous appearance in *Ragtime* as part of the audience at the trial of Harry K. Thaw and shrewdly watch cultural history being made.

Evelyn Nesbit's court appearance, described as creating "the first sex goddess in American history" and providing the "inspiration for the concept of the movie star system and the model for every sex goddess from Theda Bara to Marilyn Monroe," is especially important in terms of her supposed effect on the development of film history and its relationship to capitalism. The narrator mentions that two groups perceived the significance of her impact on the public, the business community and left-wing political agitators. The "business community" is characterized as "a group of accountants and cloak and suit manufacturers who also dabbled in the exhibition of moving pictures, or picture shows as they were called. Some of these men saw the way Evelyn's face on the front page of a newspaper sold out the edition. They realized that there was a process of magnification by which news events established certain individuals in the public consciousness as larger than life. These were the individuals who represented one desirable human characteristic to the exclusion of all others. The businessmen wondered if they could create such individuals not from the accidents of news events but from the deliberate manufactures of their own medium" (pp. 70–71). The "businessman" Doctorow actually has in mind is Carl Laemmle, the German-born Jewish immigrant who, like many other Eastern European Jews who had immigrated to the United States around the turn of the century, initially went into the clothing business and later opened and supplied the nickel theatres. (Hungarian Jewish immigrants William Fox and Adolph Zukor would later follow in Laemmle's footsteps, radically transforming the film industry and founding Twentieth Century-Fox and Paramount Studios, respectively.) Laemmle, a leader of the independent producers who helped defeat the monopoly created by the Motion Picture Patents Company, can also be credited with the creation of the star system which Doctorow suggests that Evelyn Nesbit may have inspired. Laemmle, who suspected the media's potential to create myths out of the individual personalities of film actors and actresses, decided to break with tradition and allow the public access to an actress's name. In 1910 he hired Florence Lawrence, known only up to that time as "The Biograph Girl," for his own international Motion Pictures Company and proceeded to stage one of the first media events. Laemmle planted reports of Lawrence's death in newspapers, in the process revealing her name to the public for the first time, and then angrily denounced the story as a lie spread by the Motion Picture Patents Company; later he had Lawrence appear publicly in St. Louis to prove his point, an appearance that created a near riot. As David Cook observers, "The star system was born," and the film industry would continue to exploit the economic benefits of Laemmle's discovery.

The second group who comprehends the importance of Nesbit's performance, the radical political leaders who "correctly prophesied that she would in the long run be a greater threat to the working man's interests than mine owners or steel manufacturers," realize from the beginning how the film industry in the United States, despite its proletarian origins, would become an active agent of capitalism. Emma Goldman, who frequently functions as a kind of Delphic Oracle in the novel, supplies the explanation for this paradox in her letter to Evelyn Nesbit: "I am often asked the question How can the masses permit themselves to be exploited by the few. The answer is By being persuaded to identify with them. Carrying his newspaper with your picture the laborer goes home to his wife, an exhausted workhorse with the veins standing out in her legs, and he dreams not of justice but of being rich" (p. 71). Walter Benjamin lamented what he called the "cult of the movie star," blaming the phenomenon on the fact that the studio must compensate for the disappearance of the film star's "aura" by promoting an artificial build-up of the star's personality outside the studio, a process which creates the "phony spell of a commodity." As long as the film industry's capital dictates the content of the cinema, says Benjamin, the only socially beneficial effect of the cinema is to promote a "revolutionary criticism of traditional concepts of art."[14]

Robert Sklar, who takes a more positive view of the political potential of film in his book, believes that the cinema from its beginning provided information that enabled the working classes to move outside the limitations of their social and cultural situation, facilitating social movement and gradually, at least in terms of the composition of film audiences, leveling social distinctions. The cinema has always, he believes, posed a threat to middle-class traditional culture, for many of the earliest films attempted to subvert authority and social control, and movies have continued to be a means of mirroring and criticizing the problems of society. Doctorow's position in *Ragtime,* particularly as it is reflected in his characterization of Tateh, combines these diverse political attitudes to cinema, and Tateh himself embodies the political dichotomy present in the early founders of the movie industry. As Sklar has observed, despite the feelings of distrust they engendered in the middle-class guardians of traditional culture, the early film-makers, although working-class immigrants, were men "deeply committed to the capitalist values, attitudes and ambitions that were part of the dominant social order."[15] Doctorow's rag ship filled with immigrants which inspires such "weird despair" in Father illustrates the same principle, for the narrator ironically observes that "aboard her were only more customers . . . the immigrant population set great store by the American flag" (p. 12). And although Tateh maintains his earlier political ideals, he finds it necessary to "conceive of his life as separate from the fate of the working class" before he can "point his life along the lines of flow of American energy"—a decision which culminates in the naming of his own film company after the most capitalistic of symbols, the buffalo nickel (pp. 108–111). In spite of all this, however, and the fact that in order to become the dynamic and extroverted Baron Ashkenazy Tateh must adopt a faked "nobility," his final filmic vision in the novel is an inclusive, democratic fusion of children of all races and creeds. Unlike Coalhouse Walker and Mother's Younger Brother, whose political radicalism ends in death and destruction, Tateh uses the aesthetic form most available to him, film, to overcome class consciousness by means of creative synthesis rather than destructive fragmentation.

Although clearly interested by the political and social ramifications of the new art form, Doctorow is equally intrigued by its philosophical and aesthetic dimension. The various still photographs taken in the novel, as well as the continual references to motion pictures, illustrate one of its major thematic concerns, the difficulty of comprehending and analyzing the world of ceaseless flux and mutability that perplexes many of the major characters. Theodore Dreiser's search for the "proper alignment" of a chair and Admiral Peary's effort to determine the exact location of the North Pole are equally unsuccessful because both men inhabit a world which is intrinsically unmeasurable, chaotic, and fluid; the narrator observes, while describing Peary's vain attempts to find a "center," that "On this watery planet the sliding sea refused to be fixed" (p. 68). Like the Little Boy, J. P. Morgan seeks a system which can reveal "universal patterns of order and repetition," a philosophy to palliate the ceaseless flux which surrounds him. Both the Little Boy's fascination with the duplicated event and Morgan's obsession with reincarnation are reactions to a world perceived as resisting rational analysis; the Little Boy desires a replication of reality in order to comprehend the mutability of his surroundings, while Morgan accepts a philosophy which combines the concepts of change and repetition—*and* insures a final victory over mortality.

In *Ragtime,* the duplicated event receives the most attention as a way of overcoming—and, paradoxically, exemplifying—the fluidity of reality. The Little Boy goes so far as to attempt a self-duplication which accomplishes the negation of his own distinct personality. Benjamin's essay may help explain the relationship between the Little Boy's experiment with self-duplication at the mirror in Chapter Fifteen and his interest in reproducible events such as photography and aural recording. Speaking of Pirandello's novel *Si Gira,* Benjamin quotes the playwright's observation that "The film actor . . . feels as if in exile—exiled not only from the stage but also from himself. With a vague sense of discomfort he feels inexplicable emptiness: his body loses its corporeality, it evaporates, it is deprived of reality, life, voice . . . in order to be changed into a mute image, flickering an instant on the screen, then vanishing into silence" and then observes that the "feeling of strangeness" is basically the same kind of estrangement that we feel before our image in the mirror.[16] The Little Boy's interest in duplication leads him to test the principle, finally, upon himself; he experiments with destroying his own aura by using the mirror as a camera and in the process, like the film actor, undergoes an almost mystical experience: "He would gaze at himself until there were two selves facing one another, neither of which could claim to be the real one. The sensation was of being disembodied. He was no longer anything exact as a person. He had the dizzying feeling of separating from himself endlessly" (p. 98). The Little Boy, who carries the principle of replication to its final extreme, discovers his own personality to be as mutable and reproducible as the other objects in the physical universe.

The duplicated event of photography provides one means to "fix" the flux of time, a way, in Sontag's words, "of imprisoning reality . . . of making it stand still."[17] Several of the still photographs taken in *Ragtime,* among them Riis' photograph of the poor, Peary's photograph at the Pole, and Morgan's photograph of the robber barons, are pseudo-scientific attempts to use the camera to verify and analyze reality by duplicating a fragment of it. The ability of still photography to "stop" time and subject it to analysis is also true of motion pictures, a characteristic which Tateh claims is one reason for their popularity: "People want to know what is happening to them. For a few pennies they sit and see their selves in movement, running, racing in motorcars. . . . This is most important today, in this country where everybody is so new. There is such a need to understand" (p. 215). However, although photography can furnish us with the sense of manipulating time in order to understand experience, it also, paradoxically, underscores our helplessness before the passage of time. According to Benjamin, the image seen by the "unarmed eye," that is, unmediated, unreproduced reality, has uniqueness and permanence, while still and moving pictures combine the fact of their reproducibility with the sense of their transitoriness. Chapter Fifteen of *Ragtime,* one of the novel's most puzzling chapters, becomes more understandable in light of this statement, in particular the narrator's discussion of the Little Boy's obsession with mutability and instability which is suddenly interrupted by what may at first appear to be a *non sequitur,* the statement that "He liked to go to the moving picture shows downtown at the New Rochelle Theatre on Main Street" (p. 97). The Little Boy's interest in motion pictures results from the fact that they both contradict and reinforce his belief that the universe is eternally evolving into new forms, that it "composed and recomposed itself constantly in an endless process of dissatisfaction," for film simultaneously captures the object in time, thereby preserving it from the mutations of time, while also testifying to time's passage (p. 99). André Bazin, who believes the plastic arts emerged from man's desire to triumph over the ultimate result of time, death, says that still photography gives us "the disturbing presence of lives halted in a set moment in their duration, freed from their destiny . . . it embalms time, rescuing it from its proper corruption."[18] However, this very process, according to Sontag, creates an awareness of the "mortality, vulnerability, mutability" of all things, for "All photographs are *memento mori.*"[19]

It is important to realize that both Sontag and Bazin are talking about still photography here; motion pictures differ from still photographs in that they both freeze time *and* actually show movement in time. In Bazin's words, the cinema is "objectivity in time," capable of capturing the very passage of time and the resulting physical changes. The movies' embodiment of the principles of movement and metamorphosis makes them a particularly appropriate medium for Tateh, who discovers that in order to survive he must transform himself physically and psychically. Significantly, Tateh's film career does not begin with an interest in still photography; rather, his early artworks, called "movie books" in his first contract, create the illusion of movement. In fact, Tateh's first moment of happiness in America comes about when he rides on a train whose ever-increasing speed causes him to smile and then laugh: "for the first time since coming to America he thought it might be possible to live here" (p. 79). After his metamorphosis, he is characterized by constant movement, and the important scene on the beach in which he, Mother, and the children are united culminates in an explosion of motion as he begins to run, somersault, cartwheel, and walk on his hands. In this he contrasts sharply with Father, whose static nature becomes more pronounced as the novel progresses; the fact that he sleeps through the scene on the beach testifies to his growing inability to adapt to—or even be aware of—circumstances. As Mother realizes, "more and more he only demonstrated his limits, that he had reached them, and that he would never move beyond them" (p. 210). Father, who is predictably ignorant and disapproving of Tateh's profession, evinces an almost Jamesian distaste for its economic details, while Tateh, unconstrained by psychological or social boundaries, chooses to work in an art form whose essence is movement and transformation. Tateh bears an interesting resemblance to another Jewish immigrant, Charlie Chaplin, whose portrayal of "The Tramp" embodied both the themes of poverty in the New World—one of his films is entitled *The Immigrant* (1917)—and the possibilities of gaining wealth through magical metamorphoses. Sklar, who describes Chaplin in terms which are equally applicable to Tateh, says that "The Tramp was a masquerader. He possessed mysterious pasts and unknown futures. He could pose as anyone: could he be, or become, that person too?" and believes that Chaplin's recognition of social extremes led him to "subvert the social order and put in its place . . . a powerful new imaginative order founded on the creative possibilities of magical transformations."[20] Like Chaplin, who also impersonates a baron in *Caught in a Cabaret,* Tateh uses the power of his imagination to transmute reality and to enlarge his personal boundaries. Tateh provides a sharp contrast with Houdini, who, as the narrator observes, "To the end . . . would be almost totally unaware of the design of his career, the great map of revolution laid out by his life" (p. 29). In one sense the statement is political, for although Houdini is another immigrant in the novel whose life illustrates the possibilities for acquiring fame and wealth in America, he remains awed and intimidated by those born into a higher social class. More important, however, is Houdini's failure to realize what his audiences pay to see: their fascination with his ability magically to transform—and escape from—a reality previously perceived as static and impervious to manipulation. In this sense Houdini appeals to the same need in the public that motion pictures would later satisfy; not coincidentally it was another professional magician, Georges Méliès, who from the earliest days of the cinema began to make films which violated the viewers' conception of the physical world by exploiting the illusionist potential of the medium.

Ragtime posits a world which is ultimately mysterious, beyond a final rational explanation which can bring together all the threads of the narrative. Of all the characters in the novel, Emma Goldman, who has accepted what she calls the "mystical rule of all experience," is least concerned with an insistence on rational analysis and causality. "Who can say," she says to Evelyn Nesbit, "who are the instrumentalities and who are the people? Which of us causes, and lives in others to cause, and which of us is meant thereby to live?" (p. 50). In this she illustrates what Susan Sontag believes is a typically American approach to reality; Sontag suggests that Americans have always felt their national experience to be "so stupendous, and mutable, that it would be the rankest presumption to approach it in a classifying, scientific way." As a result, reality, particularly in its American version, must be got at indirectly, by "subterfuge—breaking it off into strange fragments that could somehow, by synecdoche, be taken for the whole."[21] Photography becomes a uniquely American way of dealing with experience, for photographers abandon attempts to comprehend reality and instead begin to "collect" fragments of it. Significantly, the Little Boy's interest in the concept of duplication is combined with a passion for collecting discarded items whose worth are proved by their neglect (in this he resembles another collector, Walter Benjamin, who perceived an object's significance to be in inverse ratio to its size). Photography can be described as an unscientific effort to collect pieces of a world which is unclassifiable and incomprehensible; and photography, still or moving, becomes a statement about the fundamental mysteriousness of experience by providing a wealth of visual information while denying any kind of attitude or explanation; in Roland Barthes' words, the photograph is a "message without a code."[22] Diane Arbus has observed that "A photograph is a secret about a secret. The more it tells you the less you know," and photography, which gives us objective statements about our surroundings by preserving events in time, can also function to mystify further our conception of reality. Doctorow's prose style, with its almost hypnotic repetition of short, standard English sentences which rarely make use of metaphorical or figurative language, is an attempt to approximate the mysterious opacity of the photographed image. The novel's simplistic prose and plethora of "facts" create the very impenetrability of the narrative; it is as if the narrator presents the reader with an interminable series of photographs and challenges him to decipher them.

Doctorow also seeks other characteristics—and privileges—of photography and cinema for his novel. America's appropriation of European art forms, seen as "vulgar" by an appalled Sigmund Freud and dismissed as "picking the garbage pails of Europe" by a contemptuous Henry Ford, is accurately under-stood by immigrant Jacob Riis as "the birth of a *new aesthetic* in European art" (p. 36, italics mine). The cinema is an important dimension of this "new aes-thetic," a uniquely American art which unabashedly combines business, tech-nology, and aesthetics and subsumes the traditional arts—literature, music, painting, and history itself—while creating a new mass medium which shat-ters conventional distinctions between high art and popular culture. Doc-torow, who has stated that he wants *Ragtime* to be read by working-class peo-ple, desires the same audience which created the early film industry and tacitly claims one of the cinema's privileges for the novel form: the right, in the words of John Fowles' Daniel Martin, to "gut" other arts for its material, even if this may mean making use of the works of other novelists such as Dos Passos and Kleist. As a result, critics who believe *Ragtime* to be derivative have simply missed the point, for Doctorow attempts to make the novel, like film, part of a "new aesthetic" which irreverently appropriates all of art and experience for its material without compromising its artistic independence.

Notes

1. David Cook, *A History of Narrative Film* (New York: W. W. Norton and Co., 1981), p. 34.

2. Robert Sklar, *Movie-Made America: A Cultural History of American Movies* (New York: Random House, 1975), p. 123.

3. Russell Merritt, "Nickelodeon Theaters 1905–1914: Building an Audience for the Movies," in *The American Film Industry,* ed. Tino Balio (Madison: Univ. of Wisconsin Press, 1976), p. 63.

4. Cook, p. 28.

5. Sklar, p. 16.

6. Merritt, p. 63.

7. Walter Benjamin, "The Work of Art in the Age of Mechanical Reproduction," in *Illuminations,* trans. Harry Zohn and ed. Hannah Arendt (New York: Harcourt, Brace, and World, 1968), p. 223.

8. Benjamin, p. 226.

9. Susan Sontag, *On Photography* (New York: Farrar, Straus, and Giroux, 1977), p. 7.

10. Sontag, p. 77.

11. E. L. Doctorow, *Ragtime* (New York: Random House, 1974), p. 217. Subsequent page references to *Ragtime* will be given parenthetically.

12. Benjamin, p. 225.

13. Sklar, p. 14.

14. Benjamin, p. 233.

15. Sklar, pp. 90–91. Sklar describes the reaction of many Americans to the newly-acquired wealth and power of the theatre managers as a "mixture of awe and amusement" and mentions that the term "movie mogul" came into American English around 1915, "nicely describing the immigrant producers in the eyes of the public—part splendid emperors, part barbarian invaders" (p. 47).

16. Benjamin, pp. 231–232.

17. Sontag, p. 163.

18. André Bazin, "The Ontology of the Photographic Image," in *What Is Cinema?* Vol. 1, trans. Hugh Gray (Berkeley and Los Angeles: Univ. of California Press, 1967), p. 14.

19. Sontag, p. 15.

20. Sklar, pp. 110–111.

21. Sontag, p. 66.

22. Roland Barthes, "The Photographic Message," in *Image-Music-Text,* trans. Stephen Heath (London: Fontana, 1977), p. 17.

E. L. Doctorow's *Ragtime* and the Dialectics of Change

MARK BUSBY

The epigraph for E. L. Doctorow's *Ragtime* is, appropriately, a quotation from Scott Joplin: "Do not play this piece fast. It is never right to play Ragtime fast." This epigraph suggests the conflict that seems to hold together Doctorow's odd mixture of fictional and historical characters and events: the struggle between change and stability.[1] Like Joplin's caution for restraint in the face of an impulse for speed, most of the characters and events reflect the dialectical struggle between time's inexorable force toward change and the human desire for stability. Generally, the characters who recognize the nature of the conflict fare much better than those who resist change. Both the content and the form of *Ragtime* support this theme.

The time the book covers, roughly 1900–1917, the Ragtime Era, was a time of great social, political, scientific, and industrial change in America, reflected as well in the age's other name—the Progressive Era. The population of America rose significantly during the period, influenced greatly by the flood of immigrants who washed over Ellis Island onto America's shore. Most settled in the cities as America became an urban rather than a rural nation. Some languished in a poverty they did not expect to find; others found jobs in sweatshops; still others manned posts in Henry Ford's assembly line. Both the assembly line and the automobile greatly affected the course of American history. The growth of labor unions, begun in the late nineteenth century, continued. Political leaders resisted the unions, but most Americans were confident that humankind was moving toward perfection. Women, likewise, believed in and worked for positive change. The nature of leisure altered as well: the magic lantern turned into the motion picture; musical tastes turned toward ragtime music.

Doctorow uses ragtime music as a metaphor for the struggle between stability and change. The basis for ragtime music is the tension between a restrained, ordered rhythm played by the left hand and free-flowing syncopation by the right (Blesh and Janis 7). Doctorow acknowledges this dual aspect when Coalhouse Walker plays ragtime for the family: "The pianist sat stiffly

Reprinted from *Ball State University Forum* 26, no. 3 (Summer 1985): 39–44.

at the keyboard, his long dark hands with their pink nails seemingly with no effort producing the clusters of syncopating chords and the thumping octaves" (183). Yet even with these thumping regular octaves, the illusion ragtime music creates is of overwhelming change: "This was a most robust composition, a vigorous music that roused the senses and never stood still a moment" (Doctorow 183).

Illusions of stability in change or change in stability heighten the novel's use of the theme, as Doctorow's emphasis on Harry Houdini attests. Houdini creates illusions of escape, freedom, untethered change: "He went all over the world accepting all kinds of bondage and escaping" (Doctorow 7). In a wry aside, the narrator comments: "Today, nearly fifty years since his death, the audience for escapes is even larger" (8). Whereas in Houdini's public life he could exclaim freedom and escape, in his private life, as Doctorow sketches it, Houdini is bound to his mother, later to her memory, and finally to an obsessive desire to make contact with her spirit

Since the Freudian implications here are clear, it is not unusual to find Freud himself in the book. Moreover, Freud's ideas were another source of great change in the era. Previously reality seemed to exist on the surface of both personality and the physical world. As realistic novelists had indicated, one came to know the physical world by charting its externals. Einstein's relativity along with atomic theory turned this notion upside down, and Freud's theories of motivation buried in the subconscious mind did the same thing for human psychology—the appearance of freedom, the reality of control.

While humans in the Freudian model may exhibit almost changeless psychology, society, on the other hand, demonstrates great change in spite of human control. Doctorow has Freud visit America and see "in our careless commingling of great wealth and great poverty the chaos of an entropic European civilization" and conclude, "America is a mistake, a gigantic mistake" (44).

Entropy, according to the second law of thermodynamics, is the tendency of the universe to move from a state of order to disorder and "measure of the capacity of a system to undergo spontaneous change" (Morris 437).[2] The universe moves overwhelmingly toward change, toward chaos. The human impulse, however, is toward order, stability.

The little boy perceives this dialectic when his grandfather, a former classical scholar, tells stories from Ovid:

> They were stories of transformation. Women turned into sunflowers, spiders, bats, birds; men turned into snakes, pigs, stones and even thin air. . . . Grandfather's stories proposed to him that the forms of life were volatile and that everything in the world could as easily be something else. The old man's narrative would often drift from English to Latin without his being aware of it, as if he were reading to one of his classes of forty years before, so that it appeared nothing was immune to the principle of volatility, not even language. (Doctorow 132–33)

The little boy, possibly the narrator, seems to provide a center for the novel. Not only does he recognize the "principle of volatility," but he also understands the human desire for stability. He loves going to movies—stable images that give the illusion of change. He enjoys watching baseball games because the "same thing happens over and over" (Doctorow 266). He stands gazing at himself in the mirror "as a means of self-duplication" (134). He also "listened with fascination to the victrola and played the same record over and over, whatever it happened to be, as if to test the endurance of the duplicated event" (133).

In the midst of overwhelming change, the ability to create a sense of stability becomes a marketable item: "The value of the duplicable event was everywhere perceived" (Doctorow 153). Its value was especially recognized by Henry Ford, whose assembly line was based upon repetition:

> Instead of having one man learn the hundreds of tasks in the building of one motor car, walking him hither and yon to pick out the parts from a general inventory, why not stand him in his place, have him do one task over and over, and let the parts come past him on moving belts. . . . From these principles Ford established the final proposition of the theory of industrial manufacture—not only that the parts of the finished product be interchangeable, but that the men who build the products be themselves interchangeable parts. (154–55)

Ford, as Doctorow presents him, extends his belief in the value of duplication to include reincarnation, which he supposedly learned about from a twenty-five-cent pamphlet.

Reincarnation's emphasis on a stable world is also central to the portrait of J. P. Morgan in *Ragtime.* In the remarkable scene when Doctorow's Morgan invites Ford to lunch, Morgan wants to reveal to Ford his conclusion that "the universe is changeless and that death is followed by the resumption of life" (162). Morgan asks Ford: "Suppose I could prove to you that there are universal patterns of order and repetition that give meaning to the activity of this planet" (169).

Despite their great wealth and power, both Ford and Morgan are unsympathetic, almost pathetic figures as they embrace this theory of a changeless universe. Ford is a small-minded, anti-intellectual bigot. Morgan's actions become laughable first when he tries to discuss his theories with the redneck Ford and later when he spends the night in a pyramid, hoping to "learn the disposition by Osiris of his ka, or soul, and his ba, or physical vitality" (Doctorow 358). Instead, he awakens to find pinchered bedbugs crawling all over him.

Although many of the small episodes connect with the theme of change versus stability, Doctorow reserves its full treatment for the major actions that shape the novel: the stories of the three families—Coalhouse Walker's, the Little Boy's, and Tateh's—stories which move from the tragic to the hopeful.

Both Walker, the black piano player, and Will Conklin, the racist fire chief who causes Walker's Model T to be vandalized, are caught in changeless versions of reality. Conklin believes his racism to be a fundamental principle of the world; therefore, he is dumbfounded that some do not share his belief: "From the beginning Conklin had been unable to understand how anyone who was white could feel for him less than the most profound admiration" (Doctorow 275). Whereas Conklin's illusory, changeless world is a racist one, Walker lives in a volatile world where racism exists, but he refuses to recognize it: "It occurred to Father one day that Coalhouse Walker Jr. didn't know he was a Negro" (185). Symbolic of his desire for an unchanging world which reflects his own view of reality is his persistent demand that his Model T be restored to "just the condition it was" when Chief Conklin's men forced him to stop near the firehouse.

While Coalhouse Walker and Sarah's story is a tragic one, the narrative concerning Father, Mother, and the Little Boy bridges the tragic and the hopeful. For Father, change is bewildering. Caught in nineteenth-century attitudes toward family and sexuality, he seems to impose his Victorian values on Mother, who at first treats sex as a duty. Father is shocked when he discovers the Eskimos openly having intercourse on board ship: "The [Eskimo] woman was actually pushing back. It stunned him that she could react this way. . . . He thought of Mother's fastidiousness, her grooming and her intelligence, and found himself resenting this woman's claim to the gender" (Doctorow 84). On his return, he is further confused by finding that Mother was "not as vigorously modest as she'd been" (125). When he looks in the mirror, he sees "a man who lacked a home" (124). Later, after Father dies on the *Lusitania,* the narrator (the boy?) laments his death in an image suggesting Father's continuing search for a stable self:

> Poor Father, I see his final exploration. He arrives at the new place, his hair risen in astonishment, his mouth and eyes dumb. His toe scuffs a soft storm of sand, he kneels and his arms spread in pantomimic celebration, the immigrant, as in every moment of his life, arriving eternally on the shore of his Self. (368)

The image catches the sweet ironic sadness of Father's life: searching for an unchanging self, Father is caught in an unchanging pattern.

Mother, on the other hand, reacts positively to change. While Emma Goldman lectures about the need for women to become aware of their own potential, Mother begins to move in that direction. Not only do her attitudes toward sexuality change, but she also starts to understand Father's limitations:

> During his absence when she had made certain decisions regarding the business, all its mysterious potency was dissipated and she saw it for the dreary

unimaginative thing it was. No longer expecting to be beautiful and touched with grace till the end of her days, she was coming to the realization that whereas once, in his courtship, Father might have embodied the infinite possibilities of loving, he had aged and gone dull, made stupid, perhaps, by his travels and his work, so that more and more he only demonstrated his limits, that he had reached them, and that he would never move beyond them. (Doctorow 290)

Mother's changes estrange her from Father, but she moves so far beyond his limitations that she can find an almost ideal relationship with Tateh: "She adored him, she loved to be with him. They each relished the traits of character in the other" (368).

This seemingly perfect match based on mutual respect represents the most positive one in the novel. Tateh, in fact, reacts to change more positively than any of the other characters in the novel. Ironically in what is basically an anti-nostalgic novel that sighs with a deep pessimism, Tateh is almost an embodiment of the American dream: a Jewish socialist from Latvia, he overcomes the hardship and uncertainty of his immigration and the deep dishonor he felt at his wife's sexual favors to her employer to become a wealthy filmmaker, creator of what sounds like the *Our Gang* series.

Indeed, Tateh, like the Little Boy, represents the dialectics of change in the novel. The silhouettes that he cuts out offer a stable reflection of a volatile world. Later when he becomes a filmmaker, he carries "a rectangular glass frame in metal which he often held up to his face as if to compose for a mental photograph what it was that had captured his attention" (Doctorow 295). The frame, like art, gives shape to the flux of life, satisfying, Tateh explains, an innate human desire:

In the movie films, he said, we only look at what is there already. Life shines on the shadow screen, as from the darkness of one's mind. It is a big business. People want to know what is happening to them. For a few pennies they sit and see their selves in movement, running, racing in motorcars, fighting and, forgive me, embracing one another. . . . There is such a need to understand. (297)

Tateh, like the boy, stands between the poles of order and stability. He recognizes the human need for order and coherence in the midst of change; through his silhouettes, his frame, and his films, he gives order to the chaos and provides understanding.

By trying to accomplish a similar task in *Ragtime,* Doctorow seems to align himself with modernism, which according to Gerald Graff "expressed a faith in the constitutive power of the imagination, a confidence in the ability of literature to impose order, value, and meaning on the chaos and fragmentation of industrial society" (33). Modernists, Graff continues, defined art as "the imposition of human order upon inhuman chaos" (55).

But Doctorow seems to have found the position which Graff in his provocative book, *Literature Against Itself,* deems necessary for the contemporary writer:

> The writer's problem is to find a standpoint from which to represent the diffuse, intransigent material of contemporary experience without surrendering critical perspective to it. Since critical perspective depends on historical process, this task demands a difficult fusion of the sense of contemporaneity with the sense of the past that gives contemporaneity distinct definition. (238)

Doctorow's contemporaneity makes him aware of the postmodernists' contempt for the modernists' belief in art's transcendent ability to provide truth. Doctorow, therefore, uses a postmodernist convention—contaminating historical truth with his fiction—as he sets forth the ironic truth that human beings struggle for stability (through such means as art) in the face of overwhelming change.

Doctorow, therefore, has affinities with modernism, postmodernism, and finally with realism. Like the modernists, he believes that art gives shape to the world. Like the postmodernists, he recognizes that language infuses human experience. But he rejects the modernists' attempt to make a religion of art; art may provide a temporary stasis in the flux, but in *Ragtime* the ordering provides only temporary balm. Doctorow also rejects the postmodernists' contempt for the world "out there." The outside world (historical fact), although subject to appropriation by language in fiction, can still be used to test the basis for the work of art. (Did, for example, Sigmund Freud really make a trip to America? He did.) Art can give some fleeting sense of the world out there, but the world out there cannot be denied by art.

Change remains central to E. L. Doctorow's *Ragtime.* Just as he merges various elements in his fiction, Doctorow also merges the various major approaches to literature that have produced great change since the turn of the century.

Notes

1. For almost the opposite interpretation, see David Emblidge. Emblidge's thesis is that all of Doctorow's novels present "the idea of history as a repetitive process, almost a cyclical one, in which man is an unwilling, unknowing person, easily seduced into a belief in 'progress.'" He adds that "these surface details which smack of growth, change and differentiation are illusory. We find that beneath them certain patterns of belief and action prevail no matter how much the outer world may seem to change" (397).

2. For an excellent discussion of entropy as a theme in American literature, see Tony Tanner, 141–52.

Works Cited

Blesh, Rudi, and Harriet Janis. *They All Played Ragtime.* New York: Knopf, 1950.

Doctorow, E. L. *Ragtime.* New York: Bantam, 1975.

Emblidge, David. "Marching Backward into The Future: Progress as Illusion in Doctorow's Novels." *Southwest Review* 62 (1977) 397–409.

Graff, Gerald. *Literature Against Itself.* Chicago: Univ. of Chicago Press, 1979.

Morris, William, ed. *The American Heritage Dictionary.* Boston: Houghton Mifflin, 1976.

Tanner, Tony. *City of Words.* New York: Harper and Row, 1971.

Radical Jewish Humanism:
The Vision of E. L. Doctorow

JOHN CLAYTON

There is no generalization you can make about Jewish writers to which someone can't object, Do you think only Jews do that? So Peretz elaborates on the irony that human justice must *exceed* divine justice. Doesn't Camus? Aren't French writers, English writers, Swedish writers as expert in suffering? Did Chekhov need to be Jewish? And yet. There's something about the writing of even secular Jews that I am aware of as originating in Jewish culture, in a Jewish way of seeing. I'm thinking of Kafka when I say that—metaphysical quandaries seen through the suffering heart, the comedy of suffering as the contract we live by and try to evade. It is the heritage of Jewish writers to deal with suffering, especially suffering as a result of some essential injustice in the human or divine world, suffering to which they offer a response of compassion and yearning for a life modeled on human kindness. Identifying with the oppressed, the Jewish voice, in a passionate, non-modernist tone, argues in defense; humor or pathos or both come out of the ironic tension between human beings expressing kindness, dignity, hope, and a world expressing injustice. It is also the heritage of Jewish writers to insist on probing, often self-torturing examination of themselves, of institutions, of life itself. Partly, it's a habit of Diaspora perception. The Jew, as Thorstein Veblen saw, is, as outsider, the natural sociologist.

Qualities, then, of heart and of mind.

Is E. L. Doctorow part of this tradition? Is it useful to consider him a *Jewish* writer? "The truth is," Allen Guttman writes, "that there has been for Jews of the Diaspora a negative correlation between Judaism and political radicalism.... 'Jewish' radicals have actually been converts to the secular faith in revolution."[1] That Doctorow is a radical, humanist writer is clear. Why see him as Jewish at all?

In opposition to Guttman I would argue that radical, secular Jews are in fact *central* to the Jewish tradition. In *The Book of Daniel* Doctorow writes:

Reprinted from *E. L. Doctorow: Essays and Conversations*, ed. by Richard Trenner (Princeton, N.J.: Ontario Review Press, 1983), 109–19, with permission of Ontario Review Press.

Ascher [the lawyer defending the Isaacsons] understood how someone could forswear his Jewish heritage and take for his own the perfectionist dream of heaven on earth, and in spite of that, or perhaps because of it, still consider himself a Jew.

Here is the paradox I'm insisting on. In a sense, the code of being Jewish can put so much pressure on one to be universally responsive to human suffering that in the absence of strong pressure to accept the religious doctrine, the code takes one beyond parochialism.

And yet one is taken to a kind of faith.

In the brutal electrocution scene in *The Book of Daniel,* Rochelle Isaacson, like the old woman in Tillie Olsen's "Tell Me a Riddle," refuses the comfort of the rabbi: "Let my son be bar mitzvahed today. Let our death be his bar mitzvah." On one level, of course, her cry expresses her rejection of Judaism. But beyond that rejection, it asserts a counter-ritual to bring her son to manhood, an initiation into the community of the oppressed. At the funeral of his sister, when Daniel hires the flock of shamosim to pray over the grave, he is being bitterly ironic, but he is also calling upon his heritage as a way of releasing himself to weep. We are reading the book of Daniel, the Old Testament prophet who lives in an alien land and whose people, always threatened, frighten the rulers. *The Book of Daniel,* caught between irony and longing, is a Jewish book. Rochelle's bequest is suffering, paranoia, and bitterness, but it is also a kind of faith.

Regardless of the revision of history by conservatives like Louis Feuer,[2] immigrant Jewish culture *was* largely radical—anarchist, socialist, communist, zionist, or some amalgam of these with faith in the labor movement. (See Elazer, Howe, Ruchames, Chametzky, Rischin, et al.)[3] The *Forward,* the Yiddish newspaper which, under the editorship of Abraham Cahan, became such a powerful voice of immigrant Jews, was both a socialist *and* Jewish paper, always struggling to maintain its balance between the two. "Cahan felt ever more strongly," Chametzky writes, "that at its core socialism was essentially the acting out of a spiritual ideal."[4]

In both *Ragtime* and *The Book of Daniel* Jewish socialist immigrant life provides a normative vision. In *Ragtime* it is not just the little girl whom Evelyn Nesbit loves—it is the life of the "Jewish slums." Nesbit begins to see through a film of salt tears—that is, begins to see *truly.* Tateh is working-class Jew, revolutionary Jew. That he becomes a self-made man and self-styled "Baron" is part of the irony of the novel, but it does not affect the truth of his original vision. Doctorow also uses Emma Goldman as a way of expressing the injustice, the oppression, in America at the turn of the century—that part of reality unacknowledged by the family of Father, Mother, and (until he is converted) Younger Brother. The real Emma Goldman, like the old revolutionary woman in "Tell Me a Riddle," very strongly rejected her Jewish roots. It was, nevertheless, these roots that nurtured her, and it was the people of the Lower East Side to whom she turned for refuge. It is interesting that Doctorow chose her to express so much unacknowledged reality.

Doctorow's own grandparents were themselves Russian Jews, his grandfather and father socialist, atheist, strugglers with ideas. Atheist—and yet Doctorow himself had traditional Jewish training and was bar mitzvahed. It is to the generation of immigrant Jews that Doctorow turns for his image of what Life is about. I'm thinking particularly of the figure of the grandmother in *The Book of Daniel*—Rochelle Isaacson's mother. Her job in the novel is to suffer, to express, through Daniel's words, that suffering, to go mad from suffering, like someone staring unprepared into the face of God. Doctorow has acknowledged this grandmother as biographically his own—a tie to Jewish immigrant suffering.[5] "Grandma goes mad," Rochelle tells Daniel as a child, "when she can no longer consider the torment of her life." Her curses express her "love for those whom I curse for existing at the mercy of life and God and for the dust they will allow themselves to become for having been born." The madness, then, is not from passive suffering but from fury at that suffering, from arguing against God. All of Doctorow's books deal with impotent revenge against injustice and oppression. The figure of Daniel's grandmother represents the *heart* of that revenge.

The *heart:* Daniel speaks of the "progress of madness inherited through the heart." From his grandmother to his mother, Rochelle, to his sister, Susan. Unable to bear the pain of loving those who suffer, they go mad.

In Daniel himself the pain of being unable to assuage suffering leads to torture and self-torture. He enacts the injustice he can't end—by burning his wife's skin with a cigarette lighter, by burning his reader: "Shall I continue? Do you want to know the effect of three concentric circles of heating element . . . upon the tender white girlflesh of my wife's ass? Who are you anyway? Who told you you could read this? Is nothing sacred?" Reader as voyeur, as accomplice. Finally, of course, it is Daniel whom Daniel is burning.

Unlike most modern characters, those of Doctorow act or agonize on behalf of a collective, a community.

"A NOTE TO THE READER," Daniel announces after describing a piece of the destruction, within the Soviet Union, of the Bolshevik dream—the show trials (both like and unlike the trial of the Isaacsons):

> Reader, this is a note to you. If it seems to you elementary. . . . If it *is* elementary and seems to you at this late date to be pathetically elementary, like picking up some torn bits of cloth and tearing them again. . . . If it is that elementary, then reader, I am reading you. And together we may rend our clothes in mourning.

During mourning, Jews symbolically rend their clothes (in fact, a piece of cloth pinned to their clothes). Mourning is transformed into an obligatory ritual so that it can be contained and be kept from becoming the private subjective province of an individual; it is collective, communal. Here, Daniel speaks to us as if we were part of his congregation or family, sitting *shiva* over the agonies of this century. It is, of course, Daniel, not Doctorow, in mourning, Daniel who swallows the suffering, tortures himself with it, Daniel who is clearly a product of Jewish culture. We are not meant to identify with Daniel's sadism, his acting-out of false revolutionary roles. At times, Daniel, splitting off a judging, observing ego, creates his imagined reader into an enemy: "I suppose you think I can't do the electrocution. I know there is a you. There has always been a you. YOU: I will show you that I can do the electrocution." But it seems clear to me that we are meant to *identify* with Daniel's pain and his ironic vision. We as readers are pulled into community with the suffering Daniel.

This relation between the reader and the narrator is intensified by the letter Daniel imagines his grandmother sending to the *Forward.* The letter-to-the-editor page, like Daniel's letter, was entitled *Bintel Brief* (Bundle of Letters), and like Daniel's letter, was a repository of pain or problems. "I am an unhappy lonely orphan," an actual letter begins, "and I appeal to you in my helplessness. . . . My story is a tragic one."[6] The story of Daniel's grandmother is not so unusual for the *Forward.* "My dear Mr. Editor, you who hear the trouble of so many, and share the common misery, permit me to say what I have to if my heart is not to burst." The letter is beautiful, very real and painful—and at the same time verges on pastiche. Daniel has it both ways—as true and as ironic. And behind Daniel, Doctorow gives us the letter as the agony not of the old woman alone but of the writer, Daniel, needing the forms of Jewish culture to enable him to express his pain.

At the same time Daniel—though not Doctorow—rejects the code of *mentschlekhkayt*—the ethical code requiring one to be a *mentsch,* to be fully human—caring and doing for others—which is at the heart of Jewish culture. He refuses to be thought of as a "good boy." He will be the executioner, not the victim. Yet his cruelty is, like his grandmother's curses, his rebellion against a world that makes victims. It is a perverted scream of compassion.

The compassion of the novel itself, its longing for justice, can be underneath the self-torture of the narrator. Not only is Jewish culture present specifically in the narrative but in the sensibility underlying the narrative—the sensibility not of Daniel but of Doctorow.

Jewish culture is not in evidence in *Welcome to Hard Times* or *Loon Lake,* but themes of justice and injustice, victimization and revenge, pervade these novels. In all these books we are looking at some of the essential *collective* experience of this century: exploitation, class struggle, and racial oppression. In all a futile compassion for others is central.

In *Welcome to Hard Times* Blue is an odd sort of hero for a "Western." He is a "Jewish" hero in a Clint Eastwood movie. "Probably," he tells Jimmy, "your Pa did only one shameful thing in his life and that was to rush in after Turner." Turner, the Bad Man from Bodie, is not to be fought Clint Eastwood style. Blue tries to fight by loving the survivors of Turner's destruction of the town, by re-creating the town—generating new life and new building—and by recording its history. He is a contemplative man of the Book. He certainly acts—does as much as a person can to turn Hard Times into a town whose spirit will dispel the Man from Bodie. Failing, he gives into the spirit of six-shooter justice, and nearly kills Turner. But then he carries the Bad Man, smashed and dying, off the barbed wire, brings him to the cabin, where Jimmy kills both Turner and—by accident—Molly. At the end Blue, guilt-ridden, dying, writes the history of the empty town.

Blue is motivated by compassion for the community and by a desire to prove—as if to God—that to build a community need not be futile. As Molly grows increasingly sure of coming destruction, Blue tries to prove to her that the law of the West breeds more destruction—that in a sense she is wed to the destroyer. And indeed she dies in am embrace by Turner, killed by Jimmy with the gun she herself bought him to use to protect her.

If the narrator of *The Book of Daniel* tortures himself, unable to stand the suffering and injustice he is helpless to prevent, so too does the narrator of *Welcome to Hard Times.* Unlike Daniel, Blue does not enact the injustice; he simply suffers it for Molly and the others—indeed, he seems to accept full responsibility for ending it at the same time that he understands his own powerlessness. At times he seems to love victim *as* victim, needs to take upon himself the role of victim.

A futile, agonized struggle against injustice is at the heart of *Ragtime* and *Loon Lake.* Coalhouse Walker, in *Ragtime,* stands up to injustice at the inevitable cost of martyrdom. Younger Brother becomes unable to keep see-ing with the eyes of the official culture of the turn of the century. He takes on Coalhouse's vision, becomes a revolutionary, and dies. The survivor is Tateh, who joins, as popular artist, the ranks of the powerful. In *Loon Lake,* when the retarded Fat Lady has literally been screwed to death by the rubes, Joe, in revolt, screws the wife of the carnival owner and tosses to the winds the money earned from the death of Fanny. The poet Warren Penfield originally goes to Loon Lake to assassinate the man of power, F. W. Bennett, who has murdered and dispossessed workers; Joe, it seems, returns to Loon Lake to take up Penfield's purpose. But the Fat Lady is dead, Penfield becomes Ben-nett's house pet, and Joe becomes his adopted son—following in his footsteps in industry and as master of Loon Lake, becoming an accomplice of power in the CIA.

An agonized but futile compassion, then. Is this the vocabulary of Jew-ish culture? Yes and no. The figures of Jewish culture suffer for others, often seem to embrace suffering for its own sake. And, in Josephine Knopp's metaphor, they put life "on trial."[7] On behalf of the powerless, they demand. But there is, finally, as Irving Howe insists, a "sweetness" about the Jewish writer. Peretz, in "Bontsha the Silent," a story about a victim who has *not* cried out and whose silence and the littleness of his demands shame heaven, is as ironic as Doctorow. But there is, I think, less bitterness in Peretz. Doctorow's vision has Jewish roots, but it is a terribly dark vision. It seems impossible to defeat the Bad Man from Bodie, J. P. Morgan, F. W. Bennett, or the powers that need to create the mythos of the Cold War—*and* impossible to live human life in the presence of those powers.

If Doctorow's work reveals a compassion for common suffering, a compassion whose roots lie deep in Jewish culture, it reveals also a critical detachment from ordinary institutions and culturally held truths. Jews, Doctorow has said, "take exception to prevailing mythologies."[8] As Thorstein Veblen argued in "The Intellectual Pre-eminence of Jews," it is "by loss of allegiance, or at best by force of a divided allegiance to the people of his origin that [the intellectual Jew] finds himself in the vanguard of modern inquiry. . . . The first requisite for . . . any work of inquiry . . . is a skeptical frame of mind." And the Jew in the Diaspora, the outsider working on the inside, has this frame of mind. "He is a skeptic by force of circumstances over which he has no control." It is the tension between traditional Judaism and modern life that gives the Jew his valuable critical ability.[9] But it is not only this tension; Judaism is *essentially* iconoclastic. "The acknowledgment of God is, fundamentally, the negation of idols," Erich Fromm writes.[10] And by "idols" Fromm means any fixed system of authority external to living experience. Fromm believes that the Old Testament itself is susceptible to a radical humanist interpretation. "Radical humanism," he writes, "considers the goal of man to be that of complete independence, and this implies penetrating through fictions and illusions to a full awareness of reality."[11]

Doctorow begins from myth, but his work is always an act of demythicizing. *Welcome to Hard Times,* for example, takes traditional figures and situations from "realistic" Westerns and enlarges them. The Bad Man from Bodie is the mythic outlaw, appearing, magically, when a town is ready for death. The town itself, Hard Times, is as super-real, as stark, and nearly as self-contained as a Beckett landscape. It is in the hands of an invisible power—the mining interests which determine its fate. The battle—between love, pity, and community and the spirit of destruction—is so absolute as to be metaphysical. And there is a terrifying, insistent, cyclical, inescapable pattern of destruction that seems larger than life.

But the realistic dialogue, the naturalistic voice of the narrator, Blue, and the explicable motivations demythicize the world of *Hard Times.* As hero, furthermore, Blue, while not Jewish, *is* radical humanist—and in harmony with the peaceable, compassionate, guilt-ridden, even masochistic figures of Jewish fiction. Standing outside the dominant ethos, he criticizes six-shooter heroism and the myth of the self-made man, the rugged individual.

Similarly, the job of *Ragtime* is to undercut the vision of an innocent, turn-of-the-century America, an America without economic, social, and racial problems.

Everyone wore white in summer. Tennis racquets were hefty and the racquet faces elliptical. There was a lot of sexual fainting. There were no Negroes. There were no immigrants.

In *Ragtime* history is flattened into myth only to demolish the myth. And *The Book of Daniel* is a work of brilliant cultural criticism, demolishing the American official myth of the Cold War, the sentimental counter-myth of heroic communist resistance, and even the myth of youth revolt of the sixties. Daniel is a brilliant invention; he is so passionately, bitterly involved that every word of his narrative is drenched in pain and yet he remains outside of all the paradigms of contemporary history.

But what of *Loon Lake*? Events are wrenched so far out of chronology as to seem to deny chronology. We get computer printouts of the vitae of Penfield, Clara, Crapo, F. W. Bennett, and his wife, but the life of Penfield fuses with Joe's, denying historical time, denying even individuated consciousness. At the end the narrative moves from Joe's awareness to Penfield's fantasies. In fantasy, Penfield enters the giantess in search of Godhead (as Joe in imagination entered the Fat Lady). Then the narrative voice says, "You are thinking it is a dream. It is no dream. It is the account in helpless linear translation of the unending love of our simultaneous but disynchronous lives." Joe *is* Warren Penfield. Like Penfield before him, Joe first rebels against, then accommodates himself to, power. But, of course, if Joe is one with Penfield, in other ways he is one with Bennett. Even the clubs and corporations of which Bennett was a member become Joe's as well. Like Bennett he is tough, shrewd, a winner (whereas Penfield is a loser). The novel projects, then, a closed system, a cyclical pattern, repeated over and over, from which there is no escape.

But then whose is the recording instrument, the ultimate voice, in *Loon Lake*? Who is it who knows Power so well, sees oppression so sensitively, sees the pattern so clearly, stands so far outside the cycle? Bennett and Penfield are dead at the novel's close. Joe is Master of Loon Lake. If the consciousness that has shaped this novel is his, then we see the evolution of a character from ignorance and poverty not only to power but to awareness.

But this is, perhaps, to read the novel too naturalistically. It is the artist who stands outside—Joe as artist, Penfield as artist, Daniel as artist, Blue as artist, in the middle of a dying town completing his record. It is the artist who demythicizes by expressing and exposing cultural myths.

There are a number of artists in *Ragtime*—especially Tateh, revolutionary become movie-maker, and Houdini. They are successful. They please audiences. Tateh pleases partly because his silhouettes that flip to create movement and, later, his motion pictures are like Henry Ford's infinitely reproducible cars—his art reflects his times. At the end of the novel he is to make comedies like the Our Gang series, of "mischievous little urchins . . . a society of ragamuffins, like all of us . . . getting into trouble and getting out again." It is a comforting art. One critic has seen this film series as an analogue to the historical futility implicit in Doctorow's vision.[12] But isn't it in fact a *critique* of an art which offers nothing but comfort—tension and release, like Houdini, in trouble and out again. Houdini feels frustrated with his—literally—escapist art, but when he comes too close to reality, audiences become nervous and flee.

"Rather than making the culture," Doctorow has said, "we seem these days to be in it. American culture suggests an infinitely expanding universe that [as his benefactor imprisons the poet in *Loon Lake*] generously accommodates, or imprisons, us all."[13] Doctorow is surely ambivalent about the possibilities of art in society, fearing that perhaps "the artist, no matter how critical or angry or politically dissenting his work may be, is inevitably a conservator of the regime."[14] And certainly he believes that art assists the work of exploitation: in *Ragtime* Emma Goldman is asked, "How can the masses permit themselves to be exploited by the few?" The answer—a Marcusian answer—"By being persuaded to identify with them." The newspapers carrying Evelyn Nesbit's picture help the laborer to dream "not of justice but of being rich." In *The Book of Daniel,* two images of art that seem utterly opposed turn out, on second reading, to be ironically similar: Disneyland, which offers a "sentimental compression of something that is already a lie"—the lie being the Disney animated film version of some original cultural artifacts—and Sternlicht's collage of cultural images, from Babe Ruth to F.D.R. to Mickey Mouse to Elvis to (had Susan brought the poster of her parents) a Save-the-Isaacsons poster. And the title of the collage: "EVERYTHING THAT CAME BEFORE IS ALL THE SAME." Both Disney and Sternlicht deny history, deny change, turn history into myth.

Does Doctorow? At least one critic believes so.[15] As I have shown, Doctorow struggles with the possibility. But he also sees the novel as "a major transforming act of the culture."[16] While refusing to place his art at the service of an ideology or party, fearing to destroy it, he also refuses the conception of "literature as an intellectual elitist activity, [denying] art any connection to life whatsoever."[17] In fact, Doctorow is tossed back and forth between the rock and the hard place of his dialectic. His art is committed yet unconvinced. He writes out of a Jewish view that history makes manifest the sacred, that history is redemptive—and also out of Modernist doubt. Blue, writing his record, feels that it will never be read. That sounds hopeless, and yet the record, in the form of the novel, *is being read.* And the voice of quiet courage conveys a vision of life's possibilities that stands as a critique of the bleak cycle contained in Blue's record. Blue's hope, at the very end, that "someone will come by sometime who will want to use the wood," is, literally, the last word.

In his Introduction to *A Treasury of Yiddish Stories,* Irving Howe speaks of the "moral seriousness" in Yiddish writers. "The sense of aesthetic distance, the aristocratic savoring of isolation, which make for an intense concern with formal literary problems, were not available to the Yiddish writer. From birth, so to speak, he was an 'engaged' writer. . . . Art for art's sake, whether as a serious commitment or a shallow slogan, finds little nourishment in the soil of Yiddish literature. . . . But then, how could any theory of pure aestheticism take hold in a culture beset by the primary questions of existence and survival?"[18]

E. L. Doctorow, both in those books dealing with Jewish material and those that ignore Jewish material, is in harmony with this tradition. Such an attitude towards art—an attitude of moral seriousness—is by no means the property of Jews, but it runs deep and strong in Jewish culture. Again, caring and doing for other people and a critical attitude to contemporary myths do not belong to Jews. But Jewish culture has always insisted on these qualities; Jewish culture is a deep channel through which such a spirit flows. It is one of the sources of the vision of E. L. Doctorow.

Notes

1. Allen Guttman, *The Jewish Writer in America* (New York: Oxford, 1971), p. 136.

2. Louis Feuer, "The Legend of the Socialist East Side," *Midstream,* XXIV (February, 1978), p. 35.

3. Daniel Elazer, "American Political Theory and the Political Notions of American Jews," and Louis Ruchames, "Jewish Radicalism in the United States," in *The Ghetto and Beyond;* Jules Chametzky, *From the Ghetto: The Fiction of Abraham Cahan* (Amherst: University of Massachusetts Press, 1977); Irving Howe, *World of Our Fathers* (New York: Simon & Schuster, 1976).

4. From the Ghetto, p. 14.

5. In conversation.

6. See the book of selected letters, *A Bintel Brief* (New York: Ballantine, 1971).

7. Josephine Knopp, The Trial of Judaism in Contemporary Jewish Writing (Urbana: University of Illinois Press, 1975).

8. In conversation.

9. In *Essays in Our Changing Order* (New York: Viking, 1954), pp. 226–27.

10. Erich Fromm, *You Shall Be As Gods* (New York: Holt, 1966), p. 42.

11. *Ibid.*, p. 11.

12. David Emblidge, "Progress As Illusion in Doctorow's Novels," *Southwest Review,* LXI (Autumn, 1977), pp. 397–409.

13. E. L. Doctorow, "Living in the House of Fiction," *The Nation,* CCXXVI (April 22, 1978), p. 459.

14. *Ibid.*

15. Emblidge, "Progress As Illusion."

16. "Living," p. 460.

17. *Ibid.*

18. Irving Howe, *A Treasury of Yiddish Stories* (New York: Schocken, 1973), p. 37.

Writing as Witnessing:
The Many Voices of E. L. Doctorow

Susan Brienza

The moment you have nouns and verbs and prepositions, the moment you have subject and objects, you have stories . . . nothing is as good at fiction as fiction. It is the most ancient way of knowing but also the most modern, managing when it's done right to burn all the functions of language back together into powerful fused revelation.

—Doctorow, in *Esquire,* August 1986

Father kept himself under control by writing in his journal. This was a system too, the system of language and conceptualization. It proposed that human beings, by the act of making witness, warranted times and places for their existence other than the time and place they were living through.

—Little Boy, in *Ragtime*

Because of his genius and versatility, E. L. Doctorow is equally and simultaneously comfortable in both the mainstream and the margins of American fiction, the realm of realism and the edges of experimentation. He creates recognizable characters and compelling plots with social import, yet he is boldly innovative with time, structure, point of view, syntax, and prose rhythms.[1] Even his most political comments on history, he says, must be conveyed through distinctly literary language, because factual speech cannot recreate or even depict the past: "My premise is that the language of politics can't accommodate the complexity of fiction, which as a mode of thought is intuitive, metaphysical, mythic."[2] A writer with many voices, many styles, Doctorow can be as minimalist as Joan Didion or as baroque as Nabokov. Often playful with forms, syntax, and punctuation, he is always deadly serious in his social treatises on America. But until recently, critics have focused on his themes of injustice, class, and democracy, his critique of American history and politics, and his blendings of fact and fiction, all to the relative neglect of his style.[3]

Reprinted with permission from *Traditions, Voices and Dreams: The American Novel Since the 1960s*, eds. Melvin J. Friedman and Ben Siegel (Newark: University of Delaware Press, 1995), 168–95.

In Doctorow's many interviews and articles, the motif of language and voice emerges as often as concerns with truth and moral character; he implies, while he does not state, the connections between style and ethics. In his appeal to Congress on support for the arts, "For the Artist's Sake," he applauds programs "that suggest to people that they have their own voices, that they can sing and write of their own past."[4] History is the supreme fiction, he argues, one that we must continuously recompose. Elsewhere Doctorow suggests a direct link between style and moral vision, especially in that the version of history of those in authority becomes the privileged rendition, and confines the individual imagination. "There is a regime language that derives its strength from what we are supposed to be and a language of freedom whose power consists in what we threaten to become," he states. "And I'm justified in giving a political character to the nonfictive and fictive uses of language because there is conflict between them."[5] Specifically, one of the bridges between linguistics and politics, as he sees it, is the metaphors one chooses (as Orwell has argued and our century has shown). In Doctorow's view, therefore, "the development of civilizations is essentially a progression of metaphors."[6] Those metaphors are often determined by the government, but they also may be supplanted or co-opted by writers, just as Daniel/Doctorow switches the metaphor of electricity and "connections" from negative to positive meanings in *The Book of Daniel*.

To begin with beginnings, language is an important impetus for Doctorow's work. An example was the word "ragtime" that kept suggesting new complexities of that novel, or the road sign "Loon Lake" that sparked his next fiction. The germ, he says, "can be a phrase, an image, a sense of rhythm, the most intangible thing," any verbal element that makes a book "yield" to the writer.[7] In the introduction to his one play, *Drinks Before Dinner* (a long essay-like preface that Shaw would have liked but judged too short), Doctorow affirms that language has been essential in his work. He states that the play started with his noticing the similar *sound* of two voices, that of Gertrude Stein and Mao Tse-tung (significantly, one of them literary and one political). He then explains his desire to explore their similar voices—that is, their speech patterns, syntax, and repetitions:

> This play originated not in an idea of a character or a story, but in a sense of heightened language, a way of talking. It was not until I had the sound of it in my ear that I thought about saying something. The language preceded the intention. . . . Writers live in language, and their seriousness of purpose is not compromised nor their convictions threatened if they acknowledge that the subject of any given work may be a contingency of the song.[8]

He goes on to argue that the style is the moral man, that in the play Edgar's opinions derive from and are in turn fostered by a particular way of speaking: "I must here confess to a disposition for a theatre of language [as opposed to character], in which the contemplation of this man's fate or that woman's is illuminated by poetry or philosophical paradox or rhetoric or wit."9 This is a corollary to Wittgenstein's famous generalization that the limits of one's language mark the limits of one's world. Susan, the daughter in *The Book of Daniel,* dies of "a failure of analysis," concludes her brother. Susan's political rhetoric is limited, her voices few. Over and again in Doctorow's characters, language creates a personal fiction, and that fiction determines a personality. This idea of a self constructed through style, blatantly illustrated in *Loon Lake,* clearly articulated in *The Book of Daniel* and *Lives of the Poets,* and subtly presented in *World's Fair,* operates in every novel. Moreover, and quite self-referentially, several of his novels—especially *The Book of Daniel* and *World's Fair*—are, at one of their many levels, *about* language. I will discuss each of his fictions in order to reveal Doctorow in his multi-talented variety. But I will concentrate on these two novels because they are the richest linguistically and because their two protagonists, Daniel and Edgar, are the most self-conscious writers.

Doctorow's first novel, *Welcome to Hard Times* (New York: Simon and Schuster, 1960), shows in part how either the speech or the silence of Eastern businessmen is just as lethal as an outlaw's gun in destroying a Western town. It explores the age-old theme of moral courage through an Old West story about the outlaw Bad Man from Bodie, who terrorizes towns and challenges men and who is recorded but not conquered by the "mayor," Blue. Doctorow narrates this familiar tale that plays with the genre of the Western in a manner reminiscent of Faulkner: Blue chronicles the town's history in three parts, as he writes in three huge ledger books he inherits from a lawyer. Not for the last time in Doctorow does writing confer power: "I kept the books and they called me Mayor." Blue wants to believe that justice, law, order, and goodness derive from accurate and orderly language:

> . . . it pleasured me to feel the legal cap or read the briefs all salted down with Latin. In all my traveling, whenever I came across a Warrant or a Notice of any kind I never failed to read it through. Some people have a weakness for cards, or whittling, my weakness has always been for documents and deed and such like. (p. 100)

The ledgers begin simply as lists of inhabitants and their property, but then they expand to become the very novel we are reading.10 Blue realizes that his story may be told in different ways, and that his writing has various purposes—legal, psychological, emotional, practical. The reader realizes that what starts as a list of transactions asserts the poverty of language itself:

> No, maybe I'm not telling it right. When I dipped my pen in the ink it was not just for celebration, it was as something that had to be done. . . . What other way was there to fix people's rights? (p. 132)

This word "fix" recurs in several contexts in *Welcome to Hard Times*. Nobody is fixed in place, and thus towns materialize and evaporate overnight: "Nothing fixes in this damned country, people blow around at the whiff of the wind." But marking names down does affix marital, family, and property rights; writing helps Blue to remember, to fix events in time. It allows him to fix the Bad Man in his mind, to fix events in space. But ultimately writing does not fix. It does not mend the town or Molly. Nor does it fix the situation, for the Bad Man "fixes" or "takes care of" or kills or terrorizes everyone. At the end the dead are fixed to the spot ("they're all as they are") because Blue has only one good hand left, so he writes instead of digging graves.[11] "I scorn myself for a fool for all the bookkeeping I've done; as if notations in a ledger can *fix* life, as if some marks in a book can control things" (pp. 184–85, my italics).

Bleeding into a cotton rag, and bleeding onto the page, Blue admits that writing brings suffering and never "fixes" anything accurately in prose, even as—*Tristram Shandy*–like—narrative time chases clock time:

> I'm trying to put down what happened but the closer I've come in time the less clear I am in my mind. I'm losing my blood to this rag [cf. journal or newspaper as "a rag"], but more, I have the cold feeling everything I've written doesn't tell how it was, no matter how careful I've been to get it all down it still escapes me. . . . [H]ave I showed the sand shifting under our feet, the terrible arrangement of our lives? (p. 199)

Paradoxically, in his final lament about the ineffectiveness of his expression, Blue expresses himself most beautifully, and the earlier pages in his ledger have a lyrical, almost biblical quality.[12] In fact, these passages show that early on Doctorow the novelist was part poet. Later in his work, poetry surfaces to capture the emotional climaxes in *The Book of Daniel,* and Warren Penfield's verse becomes one of the three main voices in Loon Lake.[13] In *Welcome to Hard Times,* Blue is especially moving when in down-home Western images he tries to describe the indescribable. He sounds here like Thornton Wilder at his best:

> "We've both suffered," she said, but words don't turn as the earth turns, they only have their season. When was the moment, I don't know when, with all my remembrances I can't find it; maybe it was during our dance, or it was some morning as a breeze of air shook the sun's light; maybe it was one of those nights of hugging when we reached our ripeness and the earth turned past it; maybe we were asleep. Really how life gets on is a secret, you only know your memory, and it makes its own time. (p. 138)

Yet, as an unrelenting optimist, Blue still writes for a purpose. He hopes that the ledgers will be recovered and read, as in fact they are—by us. He wants his writing to be an act of making witness, a warning.

At the end the novel circles around to its beginning; it suggests that young Jimmy Fee, earlier orphaned by the Man from Bodie, is transformed into another Bad Man himself. Doctorow implies this with one simple verbal echo: both outlaws vent their rage with the senseless and malicious destruction of the Indian's garden. So the series of disasters continues, not just the double leveling of the town of Hard Times, but evil multiplying evil. The conclusion is so disheartening that when Blue finishes his chronicle, he states that "it scares me more than death scares me that it may show the truth." While false language is inaccurate, true language can be terrifying. Yet even surrounded by death and burning buildings, Blue admits: "I have to allow, with great shame, I keep thinking someone will come by sometime who will want to use the wood." Although Blue is envisioning wood to rebuild a new town, the reader can imagine the pulp required to write a new history.

Another test of moral courage motivates the plot of the next novel, which offers a different twist on popular materials. Although the author himself has disowned his second fiction effort, *Big as Life* (New York: Simon and Schuster, 1966) demonstrates Doctorow's early experiments with modes and forms. He here creates a science-fiction scenario about two giants, a modern Adam and Eve, suddenly appearing in New York harbor next to the Statue of Liberty. Since the events are told cinematically through a splicing of three subplots from three different perspectives, the novel is able to satirize by turns government bureaucracy, scientific research, and media sensationalism. It also probes the mind of the historian, Wallace Creighton (a reincarnation of Blue), who sees the creatures as neither an alien invasion nor a huge welfare case. For all of Doctorow's author/historians (Blue, Wallace, Daniel, and Edgar) reinforce the idea that the writer remakes history. "The principle which interests me," says Doctorow in many different formulations, "is that reality isn't something outside. It's something we compose every moment."[14] That is why he speaks not of history versus fiction, but only of "narrations" of events.

The optimist/survivor side of Blue is here represented by a hippie jazz musician named Red, who uses the syntax of music to describe the giants. Each type of character—Wallace, Red, the scientists, the General and the army, and the agents of NYCRAD—has his own type of language that reveals not only his view of the two "monsters" but also his worldview. The style of the agency, in particular, operates with Orwellian logic—that corrupt policies cause and are caused by corrupt language: "There seemed to be growing numbers of public relations and mass media executives in halls. Their vocabulary depressed him [Wallace]. They spoke of morale control and the manipulation of public attitudes" (p. 88).

Kahn the sociologist, who usually speaks the pseudolanguage of statistics, makes Wallace see that the agency NYCRAD (New York Crap?), whose main purpose is its own promotion, has mutated into an inhuman monster itself (p. 89). Government rhetoric becomes even more bureaucratic than in noncrisis times, and individuals are transformed by the disaster; the terms for the creatures constantly change as public attitudes shift. Creighton is sympathetic to "the big fellow's" pain, but the scientist is cool, comic, and irreverent; he calls them "Tarzan and Jane," "these bozos," "these honeys." New Yorkers turn the creatures into something familiar, a game, in the "Name-the-Giants contest." And the tone of letters about the giants becomes more belligerent and sexually violent as the "siege" continues. In a top secret report from NYCRAD, English is reduced to governmental acronyms, PSDs or "practical systems for destroying" the creatures (p. 211). Thus the final solution is to "take care of them," with the officials using that perfect Mafia phrase that transmutes affection to annihilation. It is the same phrase that Daniel employs ironically in *The Book of Daniel* when he laments, after the death of his sister, that "They are still taking care of us, one by one." In modern America the language of love is distorted into the language of murder.

In the repressive, bureaucratic world of *Big as Life* even Creighton's "objective" historical language begins to lie and languish. The only mode, ultimately, that maintains its purity, integrity, and dignity is the language of music. Indeed, inspired by the creatures who have aroused his emotions, Red composes some of his best jazz pieces:

> Red's arrangement called for six variations which progressed in complication and length, and in the third variation the crowd began to understand what was happening and the air began to charge. . . . The emotion was tightly locked in the form and there was nothing random about the instrumentation. At its most intense polyphonic moment the full passionate voices were in perfect tension and almost antagonistic, like four entwined dancers struggling to get out of step with one another. (pp. 130–31)

Stylistically, the jazz descriptions are the best passages in the novel. Here, for example, Doctorow borrows a concrete image from dance to convey an abstract concept of harmony. (Of course in *Ragtime* he would use musical metaphors to structure an entire novel.) In *Big as Life,* however, even the salvation promised by art flounders: the last of Red's concerts, extended beyond the official curfew, deteriorates into a riot, which destroys his bass. Incorporating social satire and political commentary in *Big as Life,* Doctorow aspires to moral fable. Yet here he does not achieve the moral conclusion of a fable. Sadly enough, the novel does not really conclude at all. In fact, its nonending and stilted formulas are probably why Doctorow has dismissed *Big as Life* as his one mistake. It may satirize bureaucratic language, but it fails to create any new narrative voice. Thus, for the only time in Doctorow's career, a poverty of style produces a poor fiction.

Many critics have marveled that just a few years after this semifailed novel Doctorow published *The Book of Daniel* (1971). It has proved to be his masterpiece and has been honored by inclusion in the Modern Library Classics series. Concentrating his interest in politics and history, Doctorow here fictionalizes the story of the Rosenbergs' execution and its aftermath, as told from the son's perspective. His narrative technique is brilliantly conceived. He uses a self-conscious adult Daniel to relate the present through first- and second-person perspectives. But he also intersperses first- and third-person child Daniels to depict the family's tragic past. Several other distinct American voices (friends, lawyer, foster parents), each with his or her own version of the truth, tell parts of the social saga. In addition, Doctorow infuses the whole with allusions to the biblical Daniel, bits of family myth, and "objective" descriptions of religious and political imprisonment and torture. The skillful choreography of a fragmented, nonlinear chronology allows him to superimpose the political events of the 1940s and 1950s on the upheavals of the 1960s and 1970s. This temporal overlay also means that emotional cause and effect (Daniel and Susan's childhood trauma and adult disorders) become intertwined and thus indirectly explained. A stylistic *tour de force, The Book of Daniel* resembles Joyce's *Ulysses* in its wordplay while it transcends Dos Passos' *U.S.A.* in its brilliant comminglings of fact and fiction.

To appreciate fully the style and narrative techniques of *The Book of Daniel,* the reader must keep remembering that the Rosenbergs/Isaacsons are Jewish. In fact, one critic sees in the fictional last name the implication that Paul, Rochelle, Susan, and Daniel are all "Isaacs," sons of Abraham who become sacrificial victims of U.S. politics.[15] Indeed, Rochelle declares that their deaths will be their son's bar mitzvah, and Daniel has the old Jewish men sing Kaddish for his family at the end. Hence the sensitive reader is likely to hear echoes from Jewish rituals—in particular the Yom Kippur service—in the novel's texture: "Rachel is weeping for her children, refusing to be comforted for her children, for they are gone."[16] Daniel concludes after his intellectual quest that truth is ambiguous, justice and certainty are elusive, and even God is elusive. He also realizes at the end that he can feel emotion. His reactions are echoed in another prayer from the Yom Kippur service:

> This is the vision of a great and noble life:
> to endure ambiguity and to make light shine through it;
> to stand fast in uncertainty;
> to prove capable of unlimited love and hope. (p. 446)

The biblical "Book of Daniel" is an even richer source—for dual time frames and for shifts in point of view, as well as for other technical and stylistic devices. Of course Doctorow makes the correspondence clear through the very title of the novel, *The Book of Daniel* rather than *Daniel's Book.* But he also does so by alluding explicitly to Israel's Daniel as an interpreter of dreams, and by drawing a parallel between Daniel's three friends as religious dissenters in the fiery furnace and the American Daniel's parents as political dissenters in the electric chair. (Doctorow tells us that he views electricity as the metaphor for fire.) The associations, however, extend beyond these to the deepest levels of verbal mode and style. First, neither the events nor work are told in chronological order, as they have temporal gaps. In fact most biblical scholars consider chapters 7–12 as an abrupt departure, reasoning that they are, perhaps, authored by a different person than the writer of Books 1–6. Again, most scholars agree that a dual time frame operates: The "Book of Daniel," though set during the Babylonian exile, actually was written about four hundred years later, in the second century B.C.E.; this would be "shortly after the Maccabean rebellion against the Syrian king Antiochus IV." Thus Daniel's story is told as a moral lesson, as "a call to arms, to defiance, and to faith. What Daniel and his three friends did, the second-century Jews, many of them already Hellenized, are exhorted to do: resist and pray and hold fast."[17]

The king's dreams, then, figure not as prediction but as history: the various elements of the "great beast" dream were designed by the later writer to represent kingdoms that had already risen and perished. Similarly, Doctorow shifts time frames to overlay two different periods and thus to suggest what the New Left can learn from the Old Left. He also appears to argue that the repressions of the seventies replay the McCarthy era, that history repeats itself. To make this point he has the hippie Artie Sternlicht entitle his collage "EVERYTHING THAT CAME BEFORE IS ALL THE SAME." The biblical Belshazzar asks: "What was that? A hand, writing giant words on the stone? . . . What mean these words?" Only Israel's Daniel can read the writing on the wall. Hence Susan Isaacson says to her brother, Get the picture?

Point of view also swerves and shifts in the Bible's "Book of Daniel," as it does in Doctorow's. Mark Mirsky has written that the biblical "book is full of voices, the autobiographical 'I' of Daniel, Nebuchadnezzar, the Aramaic of the Chaldean necromancers, and moves from third to first person and back to first again."[18] It even includes sentences in the second person—"But you, go to the end!" (12:13)—that find their counterpart in the modern Daniel's several taunts or threats to the reader. Repeatedly, in virtually every interview, Doctorow recounts that he originally wrote *Daniel* as a straightforward third-person chronicle and was stymied until he decided to have Daniel tell his own story: "That moment when I threw out those pages and hit bottom as it were I became reckless enough to find the voice of the book which was Daniel's. I sat down and put a piece of paper in the typewriter and started to write with a certain freedom and irresponsibility and it turned out Daniel was talking . . . and then I had my book."[19]

Analogously, in the Bible's chapter 3 Nebuchadnezzar is being discussed as "he," when suddenly in chapter 4 he begins narrating his own story in the first person. Significantly enough, it is a conversion story. His movement to faith and wisdom requires, perhaps shapes, a new "I." Daniel in Doctorow undergoes an emotional conversion—from sadistic to sensitive, from "What is the matter with my heart?" to "I think I am going to be able to cry." Understandably, Daniel swerves abruptly from first person to third at moments of emotional crisis. At such times he needs distance and detachment. One example is when he recalls his mother leaving home, never to return. Another is when he feels remorse as he recounts his past survival mechanism in the orphanage, imitating and therefore becoming the Inertia Kid.

Here and elsewhere Doctorow's Daniel is reminiscent of the biblical writer in that he makes stories out of his suffering.[20] He also specifically resembles his biblical namesake not only because he and his family (like Daniel and his people) undergo tests and trials, but also because he analyzes his family's nightmares just as Daniel interprets the king's most difficult dreams. Doctorow transposes Nebuchadnezzar's dreams into his novel's riddles; these become puzzles that the narrator poses to the reader, riddles of doom comparable to the king's nightmares of destruction:

> om om om omm omm omm om om ommmmmm
> ohm ohmm ohm ohm ohm ohhmm ohm ohmmmmm
> what is it that you can't see but you can feel
> what is it that you can't taste and can't smell and can't
>   touch but can feel . . .
>
> What is it that you can't feel but you look as if you do ohm
> what is it that can't move unless you put something in its way (p. 242)

In meditating (om) on the unit of electrical resistance (ohm) Daniel would have us guess the answer—that the same General Electric that sponsors Disneyland, with its Nazi-like crowd control, helps to kill his parents, a death where the human body closes the electrical circuit. Daniel's interpretation brings him closer to the truth about the past and closer to his own separate peace: if "Susan dies of a failure of analysis," then Daniel, just as his predecessor did, survives through success in analysis.

But most important, both books of Daniel focus on the artist and the power of the word. Lynne Sharon Schwartz points out that when early in the biblical book Daniel and his three friends are given new names (like black slaves in America) their positions are subordinate ones. The namers are the ones in authority, since naming automatically confers power, starting with Adam naming the animals. In his turn, Israel's Daniel is quick to realize the rhetorical powers of language as he debates and reasons with the eunuchs and as he flatters and fawns over the king. Schwartz's conclusion is that Daniel is the Bible's first real artist; as rhetorician, as interpreter of dreams, as prophet, he says what will happen, and his "words are proved powerful."[21] The idea that naming grants authority (or "fixes" truth) is repeated in Doctorow's courtroom scene. There Rochelle keeps a running tally of all the times she and Paul are referred to as "traitors" and their alleged activities as "treason." She realizes that the logic of the government is guilt by association of nouns.

Her wisdom does not save her, and the grandmother's curses (speech acts, words again as power) neither damn the government nor transcend poverty and tragedy, yet the son inherits a similar kinship with words. His research into the past—his actual writing—saves, if not his soul, then his heart. At the end of the biblical book the pages are sealed, and at the end of *The Book of Daniel* Doctorow echoes these words and allows Daniel to "close the book" on the past: his writing has "liberated" him.

Daniel's authorship entailed self-consciously trying to make "connections," positive and productive connections rather than the deadly electrical ones that killed his parents. This is one reason why Doctorow constructed the novel from fragments, from disparate assaults on the reader's mind, thus echoing the fragmented biblical "Book of Daniel." The original Hebrew and Aramaic, as one critic describes it, "is a language in which every other word is a concealed metaphor. . . . There is no room in it for niceties of relation expressed by subordinate conjunctions. The thoughts are flung at you in succession and you are left to relate them for yourself."[22] Doctorow imitates this style, thus suggesting that "The Book of Daniel" may be the first postmodern work, and that Daniel as prophet is the prototype of the modern artist who exploits dramatic devices to hold his audience.

> At issue is the human mind, which has to be shocked, seduced, or otherwise provoked out of its habitual stupor. Even the Biblical prophets knew they had to make it new. They shouted and pointed their fingers to heaven, but they were poets too, and dramatists. Isaiah walked abroad naked and Jeremiah wore a yoke around his neck to prophesy deportation and slavery, respectively, to their soon to be deported and enslaved countrymen. Moral values are inescapably esthetic.[23]

By turning themselves into walking metaphors, the biblical prophets had hoped to awaken the Israelites from their lethargy. A few thousand years later, a new generation of prophets—the seventies radicals and protesters—created similar dramatic metaphors (Artie Sternlicht argues that the battle is fought in images) to compel their brethren to revolutionary action. The "connection" was not lost on Doctorow.

Experimentation with style in the service of political statement takes a new turn in *Ragtime* (New York: Random House, 1975). Here Doctorow invents narrative analogies to musical structures and artistic and cinematic techniques. These include syncopation from ragtime and cartoon silhouette in fast motion.[24] Initially, Little Boy's secretive fantasy life provides clues to Doctorow's narrative modulations. The Boy "was alert not only to discarded materials but to unexpected events and coincidences" (p. 131). Doctorow, too, is alert to unexpected turns of plot and coincidental meetings of his characters. For this is the way he intertwines the three ordinary (though allegorical) families of his novel and then has them intersect with the extraordinary figures of history. Besides the unexpected, the Boy is enchanted also by Ovid's stories of transformation. These teach him that all life is volatile and cause him to search for sudden change in himself (pp. 132–33). The same principles of volatility and transformation apply to most of the characters in the novel. For example, Tateh deteriorates into an old man with white hair and then is reincarnated as the middle-aged, black-haired Baron. Throughout all the transmutations, Little Boy grows into Boy, scrutinizing the mirror to see the change: instead, what he sees is a mirror image, a magical self-duplication. Doctorow then employs duplication as metaphor and motif. Characters feel a doubleness within themselves, and some characters are doubles of each other—white and black, rich and poor, powerful and helpless. They are the "haves" and "have nots" that have always divided America.

Even in Harry Houdini's sleights of hand and body (dramatizing and repeating his death and resurrection), we can see metaphors for Doctorow's stylistic maneuverings. But most of his techniques derive from the Boy's artistic imagination, from Tateh's artistic creations, and from the musical form of the time. Tateh constructs portraits through complicated paper silhouettes: "With his scissors he suggested not merely outlines but textures, moods, character, despair" (p. 51). With his words, Doctorow creates vignettes that capture the textures and moods of his characters, and of an entire era. Of the turn of the century, he writes: "Women were stouter then. They visited the fleet carrying white parasols. Everyone wore white in summer. Tennis racquets were hefty and the racquet face elliptical. There was a lot of sexual fainting. . . . On Sunday afternoon, after dinner, Father and Mother went upstairs and closed the bedroom door" (p. 4). Each sentence is a silhouette, and then the silhouettes move in sequence. Each vignette, each concept is framed by the surrounding ones. We see this process just as Mother sees the two children on the beach: "The idea of examining through a frame what was ordinarily seen by the eye intrigued her. She composed them by her attention, just as if she had been holding the preposterous frame" (p. 298). The word "compose" here applies to the reader as well as to Mother. We must formulate some of the narrative pictures ourselves, using as background what we already know of the age.

If we then take the silhouetted sentences and link them together, we move associatively from stout women to demure parasols to summer whites to summer sports to repressed sex to half-repressed sex. Similarly, Tateh takes his silhouettes and binds them together in a book to create the "moving pictures" of the girl on ice skates. After technical refinement and big business intervene, the Baron makes his moving pictures, his films, with quickly succeeding frames that show us Life in a new way (as Mother re-sees the children when she frames them). "In the movie films, he said, we only look at what is there already. Life shines on the shadow screen, as from the darkness of one's own mind" (p. 297). With this explanation we shift back to Little Boy looking at his changing image in the mirror. Yet we can also expand the metaphor outward from Tateh's string-bound silhouettes to Doctorow's images in the sentences, scenes, chapters, and sections, all bound into *Ragtime*. By transforming history into a novelistic narrative, Doctorow (like the big screen) is merely showing us what is "already there." In effect, he represents the period through a narrator who seems as distanced, as detached, as a camera eye.

The verb "compose" suggests musical as well as visual composition. Coalhouse Walker, Jr., plays a Scott Joplin piece while Doctorow plays with aural and visual images: "This was a most robust composition, a vigorous music that roused the senses and never stood still a moment. The boy perceived it as light touching various places in space, accumulating in intricate patterns until the entire room was made to glow with its own being" (pp. 183–84). *Ragtime* (which Doctorow says has a furious pace, never standing still) accumulates unexpected events in intricate patterns. It shows the robust changes of post-Victorian America, and it does with characters and plot structure what ragtime does with syncopation and polyrhythm. Syncopation is a shifting of accent so that the normally unaccented beats are stressed. Transposed to the novel form, narrative syncopation means that *Ragtime* will not be concerned with the great historical figures of the time, but rather that the average people will be stressed. Not just the "accented beat" or ordinary families take part, but also the marginal groups. In chapter 1 Doctorow suggests the mood of the era with just a few flat, simple sentences: "There were no Negroes. There were no immigrants" (p. 4). Arthur Saltzman shows that flat language is used in *Ragtime* both for "the sentimental misrepresentations of history"—the "nostalgic catalogues" of the era—and for their refutations. For example, Doctorow writes matter-of-factly: "One hundred Negroes a year were lynched. One hundred miners were buried alive. One hundred children were mutilated." Saltzman sees this interplay between "the charmingly nostalgic and bitterly ironic" as another representation of the complex rhythms of ragtime.[25] Soon the counterpoint rhythm asserts itself, and the upper-class white family of New Rochelle must share its narrative space with two other families, one black and one immigrant. Shifting the normal accent, Doctorow elevates these families to the major roles and puts the geniuses of the age in the chorus. In syncopated motion, Father helps explore the Arctic, while Freud and Jung share a carnival car through the tunnel of love.

Doctorow's transposing of ragtime's polyrhythm (simultaneous and sharply contrasting rhythms) means that the shifts of accent between the rich and the poor, the famous and the mundane, co-occur. This provides another reason for the large number of coincidences and intersections of plot, and the many repetitions of phrases like "at this same time in our history." The little people make themselves bigger, like the children enlarging and exaggerating every limb in their sand figures of each other. Simultaneously, the grand figures become diminished: Coalhouse Walker grows into a tragic hero, while Henry Ford shows up J. P. Morgan as just a two-bit Egyptologist. These syncopations and polyrhythms are played in numerous variations, thereby echoing yet another property of ragtime pieces—seemingly endless repetition. Little Boy perceives repetition all around him both in the natural and the artificial, and many repeated actions suggest futility. Thus the ice skaters decomposing their tracks as they make new ones is a metaphor for history repeating itself: "The boy's eyes saw only the tracks made by the skaters, traces quickly erased of moments past, journeys taken." By the end the boy has become a mature and imaginative author, our narrator. Since all time is the present, he can yell after Houdini "Warn the Duke"; this is long before Houdini meets Archduke Ferdinand, whose assassination later will spark World War I. The boy's roving imagination again becomes the parallel for Doctorow's skipping in time and juxtaposing asynchronous events, for his ragtime structure and language.

Finally, this tale of ragtime America resolves itself in a parody of the fairy-tale plot, as Doctorow continues his innovative toying with standard genres, forms, and formulas. It becomes a rags-to-riches story when the poor Tateh, like a cinema Cinderella, overnight becomes the wealthy Baron. In addition to the musical references of "ragtime," there is, Doctorow has said, "a sense of satire in the word 'rag.' Also an idea of impoverishment of something sewn together from bits and pieces of colored cloth."[26] Then we recall Blue bleeding onto his "rag" and Coalhouse pouring his suffering into his ragtime. Resonance from this one word provided ongoing and expanding creative inspiration for Doctorow as he composed a "true" story of turn-of-the-century America.

He continued to focus on the problem of class in the United States but shifted to the 1930s. In *Loon Lake* (New York: Random House, 1980), he also moves to other voices and an intertwining of three different styles. He interweaves a first-person saga of his hero Joe (poor boy turned CIA wizard), prose poetry by a failed writer, and a computer-printout terminology to imitate and reflect CIA thinking. Throughout the novel Doctorow builds a refracting series of character doubles, visual and verbal echoes, and allusions to Hollywood. His purpose is to depict Joe as he seeks wealth and power in Depression America by imitating and role-playing, and thereby becoming a wealthy, influential figure, F. W. Bennett, the industrialist Joe both hates and loves.[27] Joe's dissatisfaction with his original station in life begins the novel. His first sentence—about his real parents—is "They were hateful presences in me." By the second page we are reading of Joe as a child. "I knew my life and I made it work," he declares, and then "I only wanted to be famous" (p. 4). No huge leap seems necessary from these goals to the self-made WASP and CIA man who appears on the last page. En route he compromises his morals while adopting the appropriate style and language. As a street kid, Joe practiced stealing and running. He also "went after girls like prey," and his quick hand promises animal survival: it was "like a frog's tongue, like a cobra" (p. 5). Instinctively, he later identifies with the loon at Bennett's lake: "Up he popped, shaking and mauling a fat fish. And when the fish was polished off, I heard a weird maniac cry coming off the water, and echoing off the hills" (p. 76). This cry of power echoes and expands so that the boy grown older admires men who reach out quickly and grasp wealth. One who does precisely that is F. W. Bennett, who owns the entire lake—land, water, and fish. Even the mansion on the property exudes an "enormous will" (p. 75), and the servants metaphorically, as well as the linens literally, are embossed with, and possessed by, the initials FWB. Thus when Joe scans the Bennett guest book and intuits that it contains "some powerful knowledge I could use," albeit "in code" (p. 70), he reaches out suddenly and deceptively for a pen to add his newly composed persona to the list of royalty and industrial magnates. "Joe, I wrote. 'Of Paterson. Splendid dogs. Swell company.'" Joe learns that power resides in names, the company one keeps, and the language one uses. By imitating the form and format of the wealthy, he begins to join them. Joe-as-cobra strikes again. Ruthlessly, he tricks the maid, erases his immigrant past and begins his re-creation—all with a few adroitly written sentences.

This forging of a personality and philosophy takes place through shifting points of view and ambiguous personal pronouns within a temporally fragmented story. The resulting nonlinearity lends the novel a fantasy quality which makes Joe's description of a dream serve as an analysis of Doctorow's technique: "The account in helpless linear translation of the unending love of our simultaneous but disynchrous lives" (p. 254). Characters replay each other and break into each others' stories (as in *Ragtime*), because their lives are at once parallel, intersecting, and tangential. At three strategic places in the novel, Joe hears the tune "Exactly Like You." This is a hint to the reader that the women characters form two basically identical series and that Joe becomes the moral equivalent of Bennett while trying not to become exactly like the failed poet Warren Penfield. Doubles and mirror images govern not just characters and plot elements, but also the prose of the novel. For example, Penfield's poems and anecdotes, while initially appearing digressionary and whimsical in terms of the novel's structure, actually mirror ethical problems and esthetic issues surrounding the poet's younger alter ego, Joe. They also reinforce the motifs of role-playing and self-made man. Penfield's *Child Bride in a Zen Garden* contains a stanza on the emperor who was "A self-impersonator, a self impersonating a self in splendor" (p. 98).

Role playing (saying the right lines at the right place) fashions a persona and thereby becomes a means to power. Since Joe of Paterson seeks both a new identity and the power of wealth, it is logical that his play-acting gathers momentum as he grows in ambition and cleverness. Joe admires "pictures with high style," and he gleans from the movies that he, too, can play different roles for different audiences and purposes. That most of his later lines derive directly from the movies, Joe concedes with a perceptive analysis: "He fitted himself out in movie stars he discarded them. I was interested in the way I instantly knew who the situation called for and became him" (p. 8). His acting lessons intensify at the carnival, and, as he had learned on the street as a kid, good acting meant survival: "It was as if I had to acclimate myself to the worst there was. . . . I knew it was important not to *act* like a rube" (p. 20, my italics). Once at Loon Lake, in Act I Joe portrays a trespasser/interloper and later cannot decide whether to play rich boy or servant. As a compromise, he works for Bennett by day and dons argyle socks by night. Joe and Libby play millionaires by dressing the parts; they take possession of Loon Lake temporarily by appropriating the Bennett wardrobes. In his early scenes with the intimidating leading lady, Clara, he feels as if he needs a "script" for his lines (p. 83). He reasons astutely that he must feign supreme calmness to win Clara (p. 104). He must *pretend* that he has a right to her in order to claim that right. A quick study, he easily learns to repeat possessive pronouns to appear to possess objects. Like Jay Gatsby's talk of "his" house, "his" car, "his" river, Joe appropriates his own "personal ethyl" for his auto. To complete the drama, he must lie to Penfield and concoct a story about Clara to insure their escape. Again Doctorow links morality and language: Joe attains power by lying and then believing and acting out his own lies, and by performing his part well. As a fugitive his very subsistence depends on the right props, costumes, and lines. On the road, when it comes time to register for a hotel room, Joe finds the right words not from experience but from the movies (p. 143). Then trading in the Mercedes for a common station wagon necessitates a new script. He weaves an elaborate fiction about Bennett as his father, which by now acquires a measure of truth, as he has acted the part of son so well and has inherited Bennett's legacy of amorality.

Ironically, the runaway lands himself in a sticky legal predicament with the Jackson police because he has revamped a typical cinema revenge plot: he chooses a job at Bennett Autobody expressly to taunt and goad the owner. The interrogation scene at police headquarters comes straight out of Bogart movies. "You've got the wrong man," protests Joe. Then he becomes a self-conscious scriptwriter, director, and actor simultaneously, as he fabricates a personal biography and a union history. By manufacturing his story piece by piece, the way F. W. Bennett manufactures cars, he illustrates what many of Doctorow's protagonists show in different ways—that language confers power. By playing innocent he is declared innocent. Joe's routine (part James Cagney and part Red James, his fellow worker and exposed spy) demonstrates the power of words for pure survival. Words represent "survival at its secret source," he explains, working against that which "threatens my extinction," a murder charge. "I had found a voice to give authority to the claim I was making—without knowing what that claim would be, I had found the voice for it, I listened to myself to the performance as it went on" (pp. 226–27).

In similar fashion, Joe talks himself out of confining romantic relationships and into inheriting Loon Lake from Bennett (his spiritual father all along). He probably also talks his way into a job at the CIA. Of course Joe will excel there—though some reviewers found the ending of *Loon Lake* contrived and unrealistic. After all, this government agency is a domain of power where role-playing, pretense, and disguise on a grand scale create a new reality, and where moral issues are routinely bypassed. Greed and lust for power have made Joe as mechanical and unfeeling as one of Bennett's automobiles: "Calculating, heedless, and without gratitude, I accepted every circumstance that had put me there, only gunning my mind [cf. gunning the engine] to the future, wanting more, expecting more, too intent on what was ahead to sit back and give thanks or to laugh or to feel bad" (p. 120). A lust for power has reduced him to an "autobody" indeed, a machine—one of the central metaphors (since T. S. Eliot) for modern, mechanized man.

Yet Doctorow does "feel bad" about ethics and morals in America. It matters little whether the period be the ragtime era, the Depression, the repressive forties or the radical sixties. In *Ragtime* and *Loon Lake* especially, he uses his many voices and styles not for their own sake but to show that both victors and victims are the losers. Desire for wealth may indeed be the root of all evil, concludes Doctorow, and the serious writer must address this truth: "No system, whether it's religious or antireligious or economic or materialistic, seems to be invulnerable to human venery and greed and insanity. . . . In the largest, most philosophical sense, the writer has to be subversive, of course. If he exists simply to endorse the complacent vision or the lies of the society then there's no reason for him to exist."[28]

Doctorow's most recent works of fiction are less political, more personal explorations. Closer to the writer himself, they still ask a socially important question: What precisely is the role of the artist in America? *Lives of the Poets* (1984) demonstrates experimentation with shorter fictional forms. It consists of six short stories, each in a distinct voice, and climaxes in a novella, the title piece. Here the self-conscious, self-reflexive writer talks about his domestic situation (the life of the poet) and his difficult creative process. He deals also with the troubled marriages of his artist-friends (the lives of the poets) and (implicitly) about his stories, the lives that we have just read. The first story, "The Writer in the Family," shows how, quite literally, a voice can construct a world. Here a young boy gets his artistic initiation when he is called upon by his wealthy and therefore powerful aunt to write letters in the name and style of his dead father. The idea is to keep the father alive for the grandmother. From the beginning, then, his art is co-opted: he is used by the aunt just as his father was used by his mother and sister. The boy skillfully mimics his father's voice and succeeds too well in this fiction; he can call a halt to the ruse only by killing off his father verbally. But before this, he perceives his father clearly for the first time.[29] He sees and understands Jack by matching a picture of his father in a sailor outfit with a remembered image of a shelf of books his father had given him, all sea tales. Now he is ready to write his last letter. He does so in a voice blending his father's with his own, in a moment of genuine truth that demonstrates to us, if not to his aunt, his real power as an artist. In an act of imaginative reconstruction, he gives his father's life the conclusion it deserves by placing his remains at sea:

Dear Mama,
    This will be my final letter to you since I have been told by the doctors that I am dying. . . . I know that I am simply dying of the wrong life. I should never have come to the desert. It wasn't the place for me.
    I have asked Ruth and the boys to have my body cremated and the ashes scattered in the ocean. (p. 17)

This is the end of the first story, that of a life of a young poet. It suggests that the artist is controlled by society's powerful forces and questions whether the artist can write freely and in his own voice. But Doctorow also suggests that there may be positive ways of taking on other personas. The final and longest story, "Lives of the Poets," quotes the voices of Delmore Schwartz and Robert Lowell, and it also alludes to the voices of Shakespeare, Mailer, Oates, Vonnegut, and Updike. But the voice it begins with is that of Samuel Beckett, which here sounds like Molloy or Malone:

My left thumb is stiff, not particularly swollen although the veins at the base are prominent and I can't move it backward or pick up something without pain. Have I had this before? It's vaguely familiar to me and it may subside, but it feels, bulging veins and all, as if it won't, it is either gout or arthritis unless, of course, death to the writer, it is that monstrous Lou Gehrig thing, God save us all.
    . . . And then of course this subtle hearing impairment. Every once in a while I hear the voice but not the words. Is the cervical pinch constricting sound, pinching me into silence?[30]

The narrator's descriptions of the scrotum (p. 105) and the sex act (p. 127) borrow from Beckett's Irish humor, but the tone of the rest of the story is humorous in a uniquely American idiom. "Lives of the Poets" contains the lightest and yet some of the most scathing social satire on the absurdities of America in the 1980s. It mocks everything from do-it-yourself bookcases and middle-aged joggers to gourmet health food. In fact, every page of this story demonstrates a quality of Doctorow's language apparent since *Welcome to Hard Times*—he is a very funny writer.[31] Yet the subject of this fiction is a serious issue, that is, "the infinite task of the human heart," to quote Doctorow quoting Schwartz. We are traveling in the Updike country of American marriage, adultery, separation, and divorce. But in this particular Doctorow vehicle the question becomes how should one, how can one, express ideas about affairs, love, relationships, for couples who are "no longer entirely together"? This is especially puzzling if one is ambivalent about the desire for confessional writing: "But everyone talks too much. . . . They violate their own privacy and everything gets hung on the line as if we all live in some sort of marital tenement. Whatever happened to discretion? Where is pride? What has caused this decline in tact and duplicity?" (p. 84).

Of course, one way to write about a difficult subject, besides through self-mocking humor, is through metaphor and analogy. In his stories of crumbling marriages, Jonathan intersperses his observations of the wrecking and reconstruction of a nearby building with his analysis of the emotional scaffolding of a relationship and the threads of a union—all the while chronicling the destruction of the United Thread Mills.[32] For example, he muses about "the lapse into dereliction of men who have taken down their establishments" (p. 122). Metaphor, along with euphemism and humor, also becomes the method the narrator/protagonist adopts to describe his feelings to his wife. He argues that writing is actually a form of imprisonment, which is why he considers himself justified in joking about giving Angel "visitation rights." Yet the reader also knows (as Jonathan begins to suspect) that his writing and fantasizing are divorcing him from the real world—or is his imagined world just as real?

> Jesus Christ, after a while you know you just don't look up in New York when you hear the sirens. There was just a full-complement arrest right out the window nine stories down on Houston, three cop cars parked askew, couple of blue-and-white motor scooters, a dozen cops and plainclothesmen milling about at the Mobil gas station and one slender man, hands cuffed behind his back, being shoved into an unmarked car with a turning red light on the roof. And sitting with the last paragraph, I missed the whole thing. (p. 90)

Ironically, he hasn't missed the whole episode but has recreated it in great detail. Hence he gives Art supremacy over Life.

The lover he awaits, his Dark Lady, materializes only through words—that is, through the narrator's lyrical descriptions of their loving and lovemaking and the woman's own scant words on postcards. When "Lives of the Poets" was interpreted as autobiography, Doctorow stated quite directly in an interview that the Lady was not a former lover but the Muse. Again, inspiration means the right language: "To do your job properly, always let the language do it for you."[33] As Jonathan traces the letters of a sentence announcing her absence ("I have met some people and am going on with them"), he recalls one of her observations: "Language is something that almost isn't there." What is there is not art but existence, not poetry but lives. His wife and children are very much present, and also there, newly arrived in New York, is a family of Spanish immigrants, needing shelter. Now the narrator gets the opportunity to literalize the metaphor Doctorow has stated repeatedly in interviews: the role of the writer in America is to tell the truth, to witness. When Jonathan tries to avoid taking in the poor family ("I want to help out but I have to confess I had in mind a less fervent participation"), the priest replies, "This is what it means to bear witness" (p. 143). Yet he does participate, even though his displacement complicates his creative work and may force him to experience "reentry" shock on a return to his old home in

Connecticut.[34] By the end of the self-referential story, Jonathan combines witnessing with bearing witness, good writing and good deeds, by playing typewriter with the little boy of the immigrant family: "Little kid here want to type. OK, I hold his finger, we're typing now, I lightly press his tiny index finger, the key, striking, delights him, each letter suddenly struck vvv he likes the v, hey who's writing this?" Thus *The Lives of the Poets* ends with joyous, childlike pleasure in writing combined with a metaphorical scene of the truly engaged, witnessing writer.

We are tempted to read *World's Fair* (1985) as autobiography, since the protagonist happens to have the same first name, birthday, and childhood experiences as Edgar Doctorow. Still, it is more valuable to read it as a contemporary American portrait of the artist as a young boy, as well as a view of the young artist as "a little criminal of perception" (similar to Daniel, or to Huck Finn). Here again truthful language leads to moral vision. Doctorow says that he "wrote the book on the presumption—which I realized after I started—that a child's life is morally complex, and that a child is a perception machine. A child's job is to perceive."[35] Indeed, one critic argues that perception or artistic understanding is the only hope and "counter-force" Doctorow offers against the injustice and disillusionment that are the norm for his characters.[36] In its form, *World's Fair* presents what Doctorow calls "the solace of shared perceptions." It offers a series of numbered chapters by the first-person protagonist the young boy Edgar. These are interrupted at strategic junctures by chapters named either "Rose," "Donald," or "Aunt Frances," in which mother, brother, and aunt expand and correct the vision of the young son.

Doctorow here gives the child the same kind of cloudy understanding he gave to Daniel and Susan, so that Frederick Karl's analysis of *The Book of Daniel* applies equally to *World's Fair:* "Doctorow has located the material in a kind of limbo or stillness that recalls Kafka's searching narratives. For the world of the children, while full of personally observed details, never contains the totality of experience; it is always partial, a search for missing elements."[37] Thus style and structure mirror perfectly Edgar's growing awareness and his attempt to learn the past from the vantage point of the present. In this and many other ways, *World's Fair* abides in James Joyce's world of *Dubliners* and *Portrait.* It, too, unfolds in a place of missed or partial epiphanies, visions and revisions of family history, moments of terrible disillusionment, and childish confusions of cause and effect. The most disturbing discovery for Edgar—and the most effectively portrayed by Doctorow—is the child's "insufficient knowledge" of his parents' coupling: "My mother and father, rulers of the universe, were taken by something over which they had no control. . . . The devastating truth was that there were times when my parents were not my parents; and I was not on their minds" (p. 78).

For both young artists, Stephen Dedalus and Edgar, the world is a universe of words, and ultimately through language comes knowledge, control, and power. Edgar's vision focuses on particular words: "This was a place called Kensico, an Indian name" (p. 51). His mind moves from events to names. He shifts, for example, from "They were the ones, I knew, who chalked the strange marks on our garage doors" to "it's bad, Donald told me. . . . it's a swastika" (p. 53). To the young Edgar, the strange yet "American" language of Yiddish connotes persecution and funerals, "mostly Jewish death words. Jewish death was spreading" (p. 101). Here and elsewhere Edgar confuses denotation and connotation, literal and figurative. Even as he tries his first metaphors ("I was a dust mop of emotions"), he is fearful of figurative language when the literal level is too bizarre, as in some song lyrics and in the images in *Alice in Wonderland*. He analyzes his mother's confounding image, "'I'm going to knock the spots out of you,'" by concluding, "maybe it was a dust metaphor." But even when he cannot measure the meanings, his way of uncovering reality is by language, whether written or spoken. Later, from the radio Edgar learns that words can create a new fictional universe as well as peopling the real world: "Listening to programs, you saw them in your mind" (p. 130).

There are famous scenes in *Portrait* where Stephen Dedalus experiences moments of transcendent understanding. These include when he sees the word "fetus" and later when he hears and profoundly recognizes his own name. These scenes are echoed in *World's Fair* when the boy ponders the word "scumbag" and thereby sees the world anew:

> It seems to me now that in this elemental place, these packed public beaches in the brightest rawest light of day, I learned the enlightening fear of the planet. . . . Beyond any name's recognition, under the shouting and teeming life of the world's public on their tribal Sunday of half-nude ceremony, was some quiet revelation in me of unutterable life. I was inspired in this state of clarity to whisper the word *scumbag*. It was as if all the sound had stopped, the voices, the reedy cry of gulls, the sirens and the thunderous surf, for that one word to be articulated to illumination. . . . All of this astonishingly was; and I on my knees in my bodying perception, worldlessly primeval, and home, fearful, joyous. (p. 63)

Significantly, by the end of this passage he sounds much like the Stephen Dedalus of the "Proteus" chapter of *Ulysses* remaking the world in his own images.

Words bring not just fear and elation but also power and honor in the development of both *Portrait* and *World's Fair*. Just as Stephen earns praise and family attention with his prize-winning essays in school, Edgar wins the joy of bringing his parents to the World's Fair (the reversal of his earlier childish wish) by writing on the ironic subject, the all-American boy. A good performance, Edgar had intuited earlier (like Joe before him), can get you what you want. In his mother's linguistic universe, life is a series of warnings and lessons. Edgar incorporates her vocabulary yet individualizes it when he learns the "lesson" of art, of writing, from the circus clown's disguises:

I took profound instruction from this hoary circus routine. . . . There was art in the thing, the power of illusion, the mightier power of the reality behind it. What was first true was then false, a man was born from himself. . . . [That] there were ways to dramatize this to an unsuspecting world was the keenness of my understanding. You didn't have to broadcast everything you knew all at once, but could reveal it suspensefully, and make them first cry out in fear, and make them laugh, and, above all, make them applaud, when they finally saw what an achievement had been yours by taking on so well and accurately the comic being of a little kid. (p. 116)

The clown's achievement, of course, self-consciously and self-referentially explained, is Doctorow's achievement in this very novel. He reveals Edgar's revelations gradually; he gives us all the moods of childhood, thereby taking on the comic persona of the little-kid version of himself.[38]

The child voice moving toward adult perceptions is one of many "oppositions" in *World's Fair*. In general, a cluster of cumulative images surrounding and subsuming the World's Fair of 1939–40 illuminates, for Edgar and for Reader, the basic dichotomies of male and female (figured in the pointed needle and round hemisphere of the fair, pictured at the beginning of every chapter), youth and maturity, innocence and experience, grand scale and miniature scale, and especially fictional world and real world. The adult Edgar realizes that his child view was only one of many possible fictions; he knows now that he must merge the language of Donald, Rose, and Frances to construct a truer history.

Doctorow was asked by Bill Moyers in an interview if he had ever considered following Tolstoy's example—that is, to do something about the world rather than merely describe it, to quit fiction writing and become "a prophet for justice." He replied:

Well, I cannot imagine not writing. . . . I love language. I love to be in it. I love to have my mind, sort of, flowing its way through sentences and making discoveries that I hadn't anticipated. It's really very selfish. You want to make something that's good and true and something that didn't exist before and hope it will last, that's all. That's all, but it's everything.[39]

Indeed, Doctorow has demonstrated that he can simultaneously create fictions that are stylistically sound, socially true, and culturally lasting. Traditional in his enjoyment of storytelling, Doctorow nevertheless is innovative in his fragmentation of form. He often plays against some other genre, convention, or mode in each of his novels, yet matches the technique perfectly to the content. As Red says of his music, Doctorow could say of his fiction, "The emotion was tightly locked in the form and there was nothing random about the instrumentation." Orchestrating self-conscious narrators, metafictional devices, the collage technique, multiple perspectives, or whatever he adapts or invents, E. L. Doctorow displays a linguistic richness and structural versatility that make each succeeding fiction a new departure.[40] Each proves an unexpected, unpredictable—but fully realized—experiment. And with each novel, each fusion of language and moral vision, he bears witness to and recomposes America, for in his writings "moral values are inescapably esthetic."

Notes

1. For more on Doctorow's placement within this dichotomy, see Paul Levine, *E. L. Doctorow* (New York and London: Methuen, 1985), pp. 11–15; and Geoffrey Galt Harpham, "E. L. Doctorow and the Technology of Narrative," *A Writer in His Time: A Week with E. L. Doctorow* (Davenport, IA: Visiting Artist Series, 1985), p. 20.

2. Doctorow quoted in Victor S. Navasky, "E. L. Doctorow: 'I Saw a Sign,'" *New York Times Book Review,* 28 September 1980, p. 44.

3. One exception is Arthur Saltzman, "The Stylistic Energy of E. L. Doctorow," in Richard Trenner, ed. *E. L. Doctorow: Essays and Conversations* (Princeton, N.J.: Ontario Review Press, 1983), pp. 73–108. But Saltzman finds the merger of the "artistically venturesome and socially conscientious" coming only with *Loon Lake,* whereas I locate it from the beginning of Doctorow's work. Also, Saltzman is more interested in structure and theme than in language.

4. Reprinted in Trenner, *Essays and Conversations,* p. 14.

5. In Doctorow, "False Documents," an essay included in Trenner, *Essays and Conversations,* p. 17.

6. Ibid., p. 26.

7. Doctorow quoted in Bruce Weber, "The Myth Maker: The Creative Mind of Novelist E. L. Doctorow," *New York Times Magazine,* 20 October 1985, pp. 23ff.

8. E. L. Doctorow, *Drinks Before Dinner* (New York: Random House, 1979), p. xi.

9. Doctorow, *Drinks Before Dinner,* p. xiii.

10. That Blue uses ledgers tends to literalize life as an inhuman "system of debits and credits," with relationships based on "a series of transactions rather than on emotional ties." See Saltzman, in "Stylistic Energy," p. 77.

11. Ibid., p. 76. Saltzman notes that the bad man who consigns people to their graves has the perfectly morbid name of Clay Turner.

12. However, Saltzman disagrees; he describes the language as "sparse, severe" and "without embroidery."

13. See Daniel L. Guillory, "Doctorow as Poet," *A Writer in His Time: A Week with E. L. Doctorow* (Davenport, IA: Visiting Artist Series, 1985), pp. 13–19.

14. Doctorow, as recorded by Navasky, p. 44. Quoted in Levine, *E. L. Doctorow,* p. 11.

15. Frederick Karl, *American Fictions: 1970/1980* (New York: Harper & Row, 1983), p. 262.

16. *Gates of Repentance: The New Union Prayerbook for the Days of Awe* (New York: Central Conference of American Rabbis, 1978), p. 434. Other references are to this edition.

17. Lynne Sharon Schwartz, "Daniel," in David Rosenberg, ed. *Congregation: Contemporary Writers Read the Jewish Bible* (New York: Harcourt Brace Jovanovich, 1987), pp. 428–29.

18. Mark Mirsky, "Daniel," in *Congregation: Contemporary Writers Read the Jewish Bible,* p. 441.

19. Paul Levine, "The Writer as Independent Witness," in Trenner, *Essays and Conversations,* p. 62.

20. Schwartz, "Daniel," p. 419.

21. Ibid., p. 422.

22. Bernhard W. Anderson, *Understanding the Old Testament* (Englewood Cliffs, N.J.: Prentice-Hall, 1957), p. 12. Quoted in Schwartz, "Daniel," p. 434.

23. Doctorow, "False Documents," p. 25.

24. For a fuller analysis, see my earlier article, "Doctorow's *Ragtime:* Narrative as Silhouettes and Syncopation," *Dutch Quarterly Review of Anglo-American Letters* 11 (1981/2): 97–103.

25. Saltzman, "Stylistic Energy," pp. 90–91.

26. Interview with Charles Ruas, *Conversations with American Writers* (New York: Alfred A. Knopf, 1985), p. 200.

27. For a fuller discussion of the motifs, techniques, and doubles in *Loon Lake,* see my article "The Cry of Power Once Heard: Patterning in Doctorow's *Loon Lake,*" in *A Writer in His Time: A Week with E. L. Doctorow* (Davenport, IA: Visiting Artist Series, 1985), pp. 1–12.

28. Paul Levine, "Interview with E. L. Doctorow," *Ideas,* CBS Radio, Spring 1978.

29. Images of vision and perception pervade this book, especially in "The Water Works." Here a detective, as he performs his private-eye work, notices himself being watched.

30. E. L. Doctorow, *Lives of the Poets* (New York: Random House, 1984), p. 81. Other page citations of the book refer to this edition.

31. Someone, not I, should write an entire article on Doctorow's satiric humor. Just one example from "Lives of the Poets" should make this clear: "A call from my mother: I saw your friend Norman's name in the newspaper, I see him all the time on television, why don't I ever see you on television? I don't know, Mom, I value my privacy. Why, she says, what are you hiding?" (p. 136).

32. Trenner points out that throughout his fiction Doctorow exploits "the symbolic force of architecture." He uses the details of buildings "to symbolize—generally to ironic effect—moral conditions" (pp. 7–8).

33. Doctorow in Weber, "The Myth Maker," p. 76.

34. The narrator often uses science and space metaphors to illuminate contemporary problems.

35. Doctorow in Weber, "The Myth Maker," p. 78. The boy admits, that on some subjects, "I could only make do, like a detective with the barest of clues, inaudible words, an indefinable sound of panic, a dim light, going on and off" (pp. 78–79).

36. Richard Trenner, Introduction, *Essays and Conversations,* p. 6.

37. Karl, *American Fictions,* p. 261.

38. In another nonfiction context, Doctorow again terms the artist a clown: "As clowns in the circus imitate the aerialists and tightrope walkers, first for laughs and then so that it can be seen that they do it better, we have it in us to compose false documents more valid, more real, more truthful than the "true" documents of the politicians or the journalists or the psychologists" ("False Documents," Trenner, *Essays and Conversations,* p. 26). In his interview with Weber, Doctorow again returns to the circus metaphor for the writer. Ideally, he says, "you get rid of the lights, you get rid of the music, you forego the drum roll, and finally you do the high-wire act without the wire" (p. 78).

39. Doctorow was speaking on Bill Moyers's T.V. special "World of Ideas" that aired 11 October 1988.

40. As I complete this article, Doctorow's novel *Billy Bathgate* (1989) has just been published.

The Young Gangster As Mythic American Hero: E. L. Doctorow's *Billy Bathgate*

MINAKO BABA

Among the creative principles held by E. L. Doctorow are the notion that "history lives in people as imagery" (Ruas 200), and the idea of "using disreputable materials and doing something serious with them" (McCaffery 36). In *Billy Bathgate* (1989), he has turned to the image of gangsters as a usable past to compose a fantasized history of the 1930s. As critics have often remarked, lawlessness, especially when it is associated with rugged individualism, has always appealed to the American imagination, but the attraction of the gangsters in the early 1930s was phenomenal because of the distressed economic conditions of the time.

Doctorow's recent novelistic rendition of the lawless era can be placed in the line of Jewish-American fiction exemplified by such works as Daniel Fuchs's *Low Company* (1937) and Meyer Levin's *The Old Bunch* (1937), which has given expression to one aspect of immigrant life: "crime was one traditional route out of the ghetto" (Guttmann 41). What is remarkable about *Billy Bathgate,* however, is its basic scheme of blending fiction and historical fact. Doctorow has set the story in the year 1935—the year in which New York Attorney-General Thomas Dewey brought rigorous indictments against racketeers (Gordon 153)—and against this historical background, he has conjured up an adolescent apprentice to Arthur Flegenheimer, alias Dutch Schultz, making the boy the big-time gangster's spiritual son. The result is the gripping historical fantasy of a young American hero's perilous journey fabulously patterned after the mythic hero's archetypal journey discussed by Joseph Campbell in *The Hero with a Thousand Faces*. The following essay is an attempt to read Doctorow's gangster novel as *Bildungsroman* and, simultaneously, to illuminate his view of the streak of lawlessness in the American consciousness.

Reprinted from *The Journal of the Society for the Study of the Multi-Ethnic Literature of the United States (MELUS)* 18.2 (1993): 33–46. Copyright © 1993 Society for the Study of the Multi-Ethnic Literature of the United States (MELUS).

1

According to the author, the idea of *Billy Bathgate* has its origin in a peculiar image lurking in his imagination—"men in tuxedoes on a tugboat" (Freitag 46). The opening chapter, evidently evolving out of this original image, introduces an episode of a ritual murder in New York Harbor as epitome of the young hero's initiation journey into the dark unknown world. The rolling sea water in the dead of night, which gives the tenement boy from the Bronx an alienating sensation of riding on "a beast of another planet" (6), adds a mythic quality to the episode and turns it into a symbolic confrontation with a monstrous father-figure. Billy experiences the cruelty of Dutch Schultz, his idolized gangster role-model, and the exasperated despair of Bo Weinberg, a loyal gunman, who is unfairly condemned to death for double-crossing. Billy as narrator confesses, "My witness was my own personal *ordeal*" (9, emphasis added). Moreover, Drew Preston, Bo's lover, who has been abducted from a party along with him,[1] is also portrayed here as a mythic figure. The beautiful but depraved society woman, characterized by her blond hair and her white neck and shoulders, is brought up to the cabin "as if she was rising from the ocean" (15). This image prefigures her role in Billy's adventure: an Aphrodite, a goddess of love and fertility, as well as a siren, a dangerous temptress.

In the second chapter, the narrative shifts back to the very first stage of Billy's adventure and begins the story again in a comic mode. Billy's early history of abandonment by his Jewish immigrant father not only mirrors the life of the historical Dutch Schultz but also makes him a comic orphan figure, like Huck Finn or Augie March, who lights out for a lawless realm. Mark Twain's novel, narrated in a rustic boy's unpretentious voice, presumably soon after the great adventure, recaptures both the pastoral dream and harsh reality of the antebellum South. Saul Bellow's *Bildungsroman,* on the other hand, is told in highly intellectual, allusive language, years after the main events, and represents the realistic and the idealistic adventures of a modern urban hero over a long period of time. Doctorow's novel is also told from a mature man's perspective, but it is focused on the memory of an intense criminal adventure experienced in adolescence, and is written in a style that intermingles a street boy's gritty, vulgar language with a successful businessman's eloquent, but not obviously allusive, language. Despite these stylistic distinctions, however, the three novels share the motifs of fatherlessness, lowlife, and brushes with criminality. Fleeing from his father and his society with a fugitive slave, Huck becomes involved with two villainous con men, the King and the Duke. Similarly, Augie, an illegitimate son from a ghetto, is at times made accomplice in such criminal acts as shoplifting, burglarizing, and selling stolen books.

Billy's sense of special endowment and his inclination toward self-dramatization—even more than his sense of fatherlessness—are major motives for his adventurous journey. Fifteen-year-old Billy prides himself on his dexterity and keen vision to the point of likening himself to a comic-book superhero, "The Phantom" (23). It is, in fact, his extraordinary juggling performance that distinguishes him from the rank of street-gang kids and draws Dutch Schultz's attention. Billy depicts his first encounter with Schultz as if it were a fairy-tale ritual of being knighted: on a bright summer day in a vacant lot in front of one of Schultz's beer drops, his "king" offered him a ten-dollar bill as a prize, called him a "capable boy," and then his hand "came down like a scepter" and held the boy's cheek (26–27). Here Schultz's whimsical act is interpreted by Billy as a symbolic call to adventure. A few days later, Billy buys a gun as "a kind of investiture" (33) and maneuvers himself into the inner-office sanctum of Schultz's racket, crossing the threshold into the unknown world.

Billy's apprenticeship under Schultz may be compared to Augie March's education under the tutelage of William Einhorn, the most influential and eloquent of the Machiavellian figures in *The Adventures of Augie March*. Just as Augie's introduction to Einhorn's library, as well as to his real-estate office and his poolroom, gives Augie his bookish frame of mind, so Billy's induction into the system of the underworld will have a lasting impact on his later business career. The basic difference between the two relationships, however, is that Einhorn, who has a biological son and heir, does not quite play the part of surrogate father for Augie in the way Schultz and Berman finally do for Billy.

In its declining days, Schultz's syndicate is kept afloat by his "rage of power" on the one hand and Otto Berman's "calm administration of numbers" (58) on the other, and Billy sees a different type of father figure in each of the two men. Berman, the financial wizard, is a practical mentor who employs Billy for the "brazen genius" (55) of his ambition and teaches him to respect the statistical laws of mathematics as well as the rigorous codes of racketeering. At the same time, he is a sympathetic man who takes the boy under his wing and shows gestures of concern for Billy's mother. Schultz is a charismatic father figure with a booming voice and a furious but humorous manner of speech. When he adopts Billy as his young confidant and elaborates on the tribulations and challenges of managing an illicit business, Billy sympathizes with him almost completely and internalizes his point of view:

> How I admired the life of taking pains of living in defiance of a government that did not like you . . . and wanted to destroy you so that you had to build out protections for yourself with money and men, deploying armament . . . patrolling borders . . . by your will and wit and warrior spirit living smack in the eye of the monster, his very eye. (67)

Here Doctorow plays with conventional heroic roles to convey the gangster's inverted notion of just and unjust: the criminal racketeer is the embattled hero and the reformist government is seen as the evil monster.

Notwithstanding his fascinated identification with Schultz, Billy retains a double attitude of involvement and detachment that resembles Augie March's dual disposition of adaptability and opposition. Furthermore, Billy's ambivalence parallels the mythic hero's agony in transcending ordinary human life, which he must undergo in order to attain reconciliation with the father. Billy understands in theory his spiritual father's outraged sense of injustice, but he cannot acquire the "feeling" for the "first pure inverted premise" (74) of that peculiar code. Obviously, this is because he does not have what Peter Lupsha, in his essay on American values and organized crime, acerbically calls "a talent for violence," a talent that is supposed to reinforce "the individual decision" of a street-gang youth to become a real mobster (Lupsha 150).

The positive obverse side of Billy's lack of talent for violence is his enduring sense of humanity, which first manifests itself when he witnesses the murder of a fire inspector who has appeared unexpectedly at Schultz's night club, possibly looking for a petty bribe. The unpremeditated murder disturbs everybody, including Schultz, the impulsive murderer, but Billy is especially horrified to see that "it [life] can be so humiliated, so eternally humiliated" (82). The respect for human dignity he expresses here will motivate him to protect Drew for the humane purpose of keeping his promise to Bo Weinberg, the promise termed as "the first act of mercy in my life" (160). The heroic act of formulating his own values in opposition to gangland's tribal code can be compared to Huck Finn's famous decision to save Jim at the risk of transgressing the civic law and bringing damnation upon himself.[2]

In tandem with Billy's sense of humanity and justice is his self-image as redeemer, which he derives from his love for his neighborhood and his mother. The homecoming episode after the murder of the fire inspector is a symbolic withdrawal to ordinary human life as well as to his sociopsychological origins. The familiar ghetto street, crowded with pushcarts and open stalls and alive with hawking merchants and haggling women, has a sobering, pleasing effect on Billy. As he claims to be moved by the "sullen *idyll* of all this impoverishment" (34, emphasis added), his indigent but lively immigrant neighborhood, together with the sooty but warm ambience of his mother's kitchen, is a pastoral, nourishing space for him.

Like Augie March's gentle, vulnerable mother, Billy's mother suffers from the fate of a deserted wife and betrays signs of half-crazed sorrow in her appearance and behavior. Nevertheless, she is a reliable parent who has struggled to raise her son without the benefit of a domineering but supportive presence like that of a Grandma Lausch. The most sustaining image surrounding Billy's mother is her memorial candles, kept burning in glass tumblers even while she is away at work. This ritual observed by the beleaguered Irish immigrant woman who has adopted her Jewish husband's religion, is freighted with graver significance than Grandma Lausch's "kitchen religion" (Bellow 17). It may be her own way of transforming her absconding husband into a dead one, thus giving order to her disrupted life. The candle glasses, which give Billy an uplifting illusion as if he were looking up into "a chandelier" or "a grand imperial firmament," are poignant reminders of the immigrant mother's unfulfilled material and spiritual dreams, as well as of her tall stature and "majestic" (90) air. Not only does Billy appreciate the spiritual significance of his mother's personal rituals, but he also respects her humble, honest work as laundress, as opposed to his unduly lucrative criminal job.

Another image pertaining to his loving mother is an old wicker baby carriage with a rag doll in it, which she has acquired during his absence and installed in his room. It is a pathetic token of the out-grown image of his innocent childhood, which his mother wishes to retrieve. Symbolically, the carriage will figure as his mother's protective amulet in the last stage of his journey, when he uses it as camouflage prop during his criminal mission.[3]

Succored by his impoverished but empowering neighborhood, Billy sports a reversible jacket with the team name, "The Shadows,"—a name suggestive of the mysterious comic book superhero of the 1930s—stitched on it. This symbolizes his secret wish to become "one of the possibilities of *redemption*" (94, emphasis added) in the middle of the Depression. In other words, Billy sees himself as a candidate for hero, who embodies for his neighbors a sense of "hope . . . that as bad as things were, America was a big juggling act and that we could all be kept up in the air somehow . . . in the universe of God after all" (95). Here Billy's vague sense of God may be another instance of Doctorow's application of one of Schultz's legendary character traits, "a respect for religion as such" (Thompson 307). However, while the real-life Schultz's religious sense appears to have been rather prosaic and opportunistic, the fictional Billy's metaphysical sense may be said to be more in line with the idea of America as God's republic and the American tradition of mystic desire for a union with the higher sphere—what Robert C. Fuller calls "aesthetic spirituality" (11). Billy, a self-conscious juggler who feels that his life is "charmed" (53) and who draws a self-congratulatory anthropomorphic picture of God as the juggler of human conditions, is a roguish version of the romantic American hero. Cherishing his mystic sense of redeemership, Billy responds to a summons back to the underworld, whereupon the plot of the novel comes full circle and returns to the opening scene of the murder in New York Harbor.

2

The major episodes of Billy's initiation take place during his journey to upstate New York, a journey that comes on the heels of the episode in the harbor. This part of the journey, basically grounded on the historical fact of Dutch Schultz's trial in the remote town of Malone, New York (see Thompson 332–34), represents both the young hero's geographical and social initiation into the heart of an America hitherto unknown to him, and his psychological initiation into the depths of the underworld.

Billy's initial encounter with rural America is in the mock-pastoral tradition of Jewish-American fiction, reminiscent of works like Bernard Malamud's *A New Life* and Saul Bellow's *The Adventures of Augie March*. Seymour Levin seeks a new life in an idyllic western town, only to become involved in encumbering love affairs and demoralizing college politics; Augie March prances off with rich, athletic Thea Fenchel to the exotic Mexican desert, where Augie is injured and shocked into recognizing the ferocity of nature and the falsity of his own love. Like his literary brothers, Billy first marvels at the peace and beauty of the country, only to be disillusioned later. Onondaga, ironically named after an Indian tribe and flaunting a statue of an Indian and a token museum of Indian culture, is a frontier ghost town, where the conflict between nature and civilization is either past history or absurd mockery. During a pleasant, solitary walk along the outskirts of the town, Billy is disconcerted to hear "an uncountrylike sound with an alarming breadth to it" (132) and to observe a group of destitute farmers scrambling to pick up potatoes missed by harvest machines. This is a distressing picture of the machine in the wasteland, as it were. Ironically, Billy himself will soon be guilty of adding to the jarring sound of the machine as he takes part in practice shooting, with a sense of excitement and satisfaction.

Indeed, the arrival of the gangsters turns what is already a material wasteland into a moral wasteland in which everybody is susceptible to corruption. The local banker is eager for Schultz's patronage; the police chief is paid off to let the gangsters use the police shooting range; the Catholic priest, willing to add a wealthy member to his flock, skirts around ecclesiastical rules to perform a hasty baptismal rite for Schultz; and finally, the local jury will be inveigled by the mobster's philanthropic gestures into handing down a verdict of not guilty.

Another phase of Billy's social education in an unfamiliar rural town is a public-relations masquerade he is obliged to participate in with the gangsters and the captive woman, who is now the boss's lover. Rigged up in fine clothes under the guidance of Drew Preston as his temporary "governess" (126) and passed off as his boss's "protege" (128), Billy receives a crash course in respectability, learning table manners and horseback riding, and attending Bible study classes. Here he is a mischievous Huck Finn figure, especially in regard to the disrespectful language he uses in reference to Biblical Hebrews: "the desert gangs" (129), a phrase which may remind the reader of Huck's cursory expression for Moses and his fellows: "dead people" (Twain 2). At the same time, he is—in his mocking self-description—like "Little Lord Fauntleroy" (138).

Billy's uneasy, ironic reaction to Drew's "project" (135) of gentrifying him reflects the general dissonance between the tenement-bred Jewish gang member and the upper-crust WASP woman, manifest, for instance, in the dining room scene, where Drew eats her dinner in an ostentatiously genteel manner that antagonizes Schultz's men, including Billy. The question of ethnicity is most strikingly foregrounded through Schultz's strategic conversion to Catholicism for the purpose of aligning himself with the Italian Mafia. By declaring his preference for the "dignity" of "everybody singing something together" in church over the Judaic tradition of "the old men davening . . . everyone mumbling to himself" (175), Schultz betrays his ignorance of the spiritual significance of his ethnic tradition and exasperates Irving, one of his men.

To turn from the sociological aspects of Billy's education in Onondaga to its psychological aspects, the most symbolic episode is a clandestine picnic in the hills with Drew. Here the visual images of the deep forest as "cave" and as "great sunlit gorge" (151) evoke the mythic motif of descent into the earth. In this prenatal locus ("cave" as womb) within a picturesque early-American natural landscape, Billy witnesses Drew's silent mourning, and then relates the story of Bo Weinberg's last moments, making a verbal descent into the underworld and discovering himself as a storyteller.

In recounting Bo's final testament, Billy recreates the brief moment of the gunman's "paradise of recollection," which in itself had the effect of carrying both the narrator (Bo) and the auditor (Billy) off the tugboat into downtown New York, as if "the story is a span of light across space" (159). Moreover, as Billy finishes transmitting Bo's pathetically euphoric reminiscence of his homicidal exploits, he compares the ecstatic, ephemeral quality of storytelling to that of juggling:

> The story was clearly over, as in juggling when the ball you throw up finds the moment to come down, hesitates as if it might not, and then drops at the same speed of that celestial light. And life is no longer good but just what you happen to be holding. (160)

This is a self-conscious metafictional remark, for when Billy concludes his own narrative of Bo's life and death with the haunting image of him disappearing into the sea, Drew silently climbs down the gorge and submerges herself in the water as if she wished to experience Bo's death vicariously or to escape from a reality that is "no longer good." Surfacing, she returns to life, establishing "an alliance of sorts" (166) with Billy. In this way, the pastoral episode of the picnic marks the self discovery of a self-conscious verbal juggler, at the same time as it inaugurates him in the role of Drew's protector and redeemer.

Another important episode in Billy's psychological education is the trauma of being made accessory after the fact to yet one more case of unpremeditated murder. For the greater part of his stay in Onondaga, Billy has been impressed to see Schultz continue to manage "a working tyranny" (186) in New York. He has expected it to ensure his own survival. However, when he is made accomplice to the disposal of the body and then is suddenly whacked on the nose to draw his blood to cover up the telltale blood stains at the scene of the crime, he is shocked into recognition of the essentially sinister, destructive nature of the criminal organization, and he feels a frightening sense of estrangement as well as a strong sense of injustice. Following as it does the reconfirmation of his secret pact with Bo to protect Drew, this episode underlines Billy's psychological independence from his surrogate fathers.

Fortified with an insightful, individuated mindset, Billy is now ready to be initiated into manhood. On his way to Saratoga Springs, presumably keeping Drew in custody, he is again led into the deep woods by her, whose initial image as Aphrodite is evoked again by the green landscape and the green car she drives. During the love scene that follows, Drew's characteristic green eyes are described as going dim "as if time had turned in her and she had passed back into infancy and reverted through birth into nothingness" (217–18). Here she is an Aphrodite figure who obliterates the past, grants "absolution" (219), and promises a renewed life. Unpredictable as Drew Preston is, she plays the role of initiator into both culture and nature, leading Billy to positive self-discovery, and is, therefore, a more benign version, as it were, of Thea Fenchel in the Mexican episode in *Augie March*.

Reinvigorated and redeemed by Drew, Billy arrives in Saratoga Springs, her annual summer resort, equipped with the wisdom and prowess to act as her redeemer. In this luxurious resort town, the social-cultural difference between Billy and Drew becomes most pronounced, making him feel a scornful sense of alienation from Drew and her aristocratic racetrack crowd. Nevertheless, the episode of her rescue takes place at a horse race, where people of different classes gather for "democratic ceremonies of gain and loss" (236). The motif of a racecourse as a theoretically democratic place is similar to that in the climactic episode of Daniel Fuchs's *Low Company*, but the situations in the two episodes clearly contrast. The callow young man in Fuchs's novel is coerced by a gambling hoodlum into stealing his boss's money and is taken to a race track where he loses all the money and becomes embroiled in a homicidal incident. Doctorow's ingenious young hero succeeds in blocking the planned murder of Drew by finding a way to call for her husband's rescue party. Waiting anxiously for its arrival, he fills her private box with flowers, thereby attracting a crowd of wealthy spectators who construct "a moving shield around her" (238), screening her from the plebeian Jewish gangsters standing at the rail. Billy's ability to act as a redeemer, though concluded in an obviously Hollywoodian fairy-tale scene where the fair lady takes off in a private plane, is supposedly a logical sequel to the pastoral scene of rebirth in the woods.

3

The apparent completion of Billy's initiation notwithstanding, the crossing of the return threshold is problematic. Billy comes home from the country to his urban neighborhood, feeling like "an absolute foreigner" (247), almost unrecognizable to his own mother. He, too, seems reluctant to go back to the realities of ordinary human life. His mixed emotions are best illustrated in the following scene: while he is having lunch with his mother in a restaurant, he suddenly sees Drew's image in his mother's face across the table, and is struck with horror at the illusory resemblance between the two women. In spite of his love and concern for his mother, his mind is still drifting in the extraordinary dream/nightmare world of adventure.

Accordingly, the last stage of Billy's initiatory adventure is a temporary reversion to the underworld. Reunited with Schultz after the gangster's upstate acquittal and entrusted with the critical assignments of delivering bribes and spying on the state attorney-general, Billy now moves around autumnal New York on behalf of his surrogate fathers, who have gone into hiding. Here he is not so much a classic orphan-hero on a mythic journey as a modern existential hero struggling for survival and at the same time celebrating the urban landscape: New York, seen from a double-decker bus during his business trips, looks to him as if "it was all for me, my triumphal procession" (283).

On the night Schultz and his henchmen are killed, Billy's "conviction of invisible empowerments" (256) and his identification with Schultz have reached their apex. As he reports on his mission (spying on Attorney-General Dewey to abet Schultz's outrageous assassination plot), he enjoys a sense of craftsmanship and feels "the malign pleasure of conspiracy" (298). Furthermore, the occasion turns out to be a symbolic moment of atonement with his spiritual father as Schultz puts his hand on Billy's shoulders, Billy feels "the warmth of the hand, and the weight of it, like a father's hand, familiar . . ." (299). Ironically, only a few minutes later, Billy is violently thrust back to the helpless state of fatherlessness and a sense of disorientation.

Billy's "extraordinary peripheral vision" (26) and his keen sense of hearing makes his own survival possible:

> It is the peculiar power of mirrors to show you what is not otherwise there. I see the blue neon cast of the clock tube above the bar as it encroaches on the floor of the passageway to the dark tavern. It is like a kind of moonlight on black water. And then the water seems to ripple. At the same time I hear the bartender's rag suspended in its swipe over the zinc bar beneath the draft beer taps. I hear now that I heard the front doors to the street open and close with unnatural tact. (300)

By shifting to the present tense and adopting a descriptive impressionistic style, Billy as narrator presents a suspenseful reproduction of the brief second of young Billy's almost preternatural awareness of the killers' presence and thus creates an exquisitely tense scene that simultaneously conveys of his own struggle for survival and the tragic, abrupt termination of the lives of the big-time gangsters who have figured as vivid characters until this point in the narrative.

In the anticlimax of the novel, the modern absurd hero is apparently clothed in the accoutrements of the nineteenth-century popular orphan-hero again by coming into a legacy and ascending to respectability. Here Doctorow capitalizes on the rumored existence of a man who may have had partial custody of the historical Dutch Schultz's hidden money (Thompson 345), as well as on the police record of Schultz's delirious last statement.

After mourning the death of his spiritual fathers "like a wretched orphan"(306) and enduring one final ordeal (he is blackmailed by a rival gangster),[4] Billy reawakens to the underworld's ongoing struggle for spoils and searches the record of Schultz's last words for clues to stashes of money. Subsequently, he brings his quasi-mythic journey through "the fateful region of both treasure and danger" (Campbell 58) to a successful completion, literally carrying away the "treasure" with him, in Tom Sawyer fashion, to the world of ordinary human life. To beguile the rival gangsters, he temporarily keeps a low profile, assuming the mask of a moneyless immigrant son. He moves himself up to a better high school and a better neighborhood by dint of his own intelligence and diligence. In this context, Billy fulfills his self-image as his mother's redeemer by taking her out of the ghetto and restoring her confidence, authority and beauty. At the same time, he effects a symbolic redemption for his Jewish neighborhood by setting an example of the American dream.

Moreover, the unexpected arrival of his own baby at his door the following spring somehow redeems his criminal past and, hopefully, brings about his atonement with the heavenly Father: "the event that doesn't exonerate the boy I was but may delay for a moment reading him out of heaven" (321). Handed over to him by Drew Preston and welcomed by him in such pious terms, the baby not only signals the unequivocal end of his boyhood and his miraculous ascension from fatherlessness to fatherhood, but also symbolizes his spiritual rebirth through his offspring. Thus, unlike the open-ended narrative of Augie March or Huck Finn, Billy's *Bildungsroman* is apparently wrapped up in fulfillment and stasis.

Nevertheless, Billy's spiritual redemption and rebirth are not unambiguous. In fact, Billy as narrator makes the following confession about his failed attempts at self-renewal:

> I have many times since my investiture sought to toss all the *numbers* up in the air and let them fall back into *letters,* so that a new *book* would emerge, in a new *language of being....* But ... always it falls into the same Billy Bathgate I made of myself and must seemingly always be. ... (321, emphasis added)

He has never been successful in creating a new self ("a new language of being") or a new life ("a new book"), but has always been left with his old self. The concept of "numbers" is a memento of Otto Berman's world view, and likewise, "Billy Bathgate" is the moniker by which he, as an apprentice gangster, named himself after his neighborhood street. Presumably, not only has he retained his precious immigrant origin but also has inherited both the material and spiritual legacies of his criminal surrogate fathers. As Billy the narrator says, he has made his way through an Ivy League college and the U.S. Army to a certain fame and responsibility in corporate America; and so, he adds, he prefers not to tell whether or not he is still in the criminal trades. The implied figure of a shady businessman may remind the reader of Dave Plotkin, one of the "boys" in Meyer Levin's *The Old Bunch,* who keeps his association with the underworld even after he becomes a lawyer. Also, the reader may recall the conclusion of *Augie March,* in which Augie, an avowed quester after truth and harmony, seeks profits in the black market in postwar Europe in collusion with Mintouchian, a New York lawyer.

It seems that Billy's deliberate obfuscation at the conclusion of his *Bildungsroman* is meant not only to make the nature of his own business suspect but also to hint at the general streak of lawlessness in American capitalism that Peter Lupsha has pointed out: "The line between sharp practice and criminal act has always been a blurred one" (145). Obviously, it is not Doctorow's intention to pass final judgment on such ambiguity. Moreover, in the scheme of the Jewish American hero's adventure, this ambiguity may serve to add a finishing touch to the mythic quality of his journey: after traveling from a ghetto to the mainstream American society via the Jewish underground and gentile rural America, Billy is finally the master of two worlds, mainstream and ethnic, "normal" and criminal, and is free to go across the border in a manner curiously reminiscent of the way the mythic hero bridges his two worlds, divine and human.

Furthermore, the above quotation from the novel, with its references to life as "letters," "book," and "language," inevitably poses another question of metafictional ambiguity—it expresses a degree of skepticism regarding the possibility of recollecting and redeeming human lives through verbal means. However, Billy, a verbal juggler with a fundamental respect for human life, is not wholly skeptical. Besides observing that his account differs from the public record, he makes the following comment on the nature of his memoir: "I have told the truth of what I have told in the words and the truth of what I have not told which resides in the words" (321). This cryptic remark is a deconstructive statement of a reconstructive way of reading/writing, which invites the reader to participate in deciphering the written words and reading between and behind the lines in order to give life to a young American hero and to resuscitate the gangsters who were once idolized by poor tenement boys but whose lives were so violently eradicated. This statement, together with the earlier comparison of storytelling to juggling and to "a span of light across space" (159), is Billy/Doctorow's proclamation of the role of literary art in straddling two worlds, real and imagined, in order to compose an alternative history and to keep the reader enthralled in a brief fictional time and space.

By creating an imaginative, adventurous street-gang boy with a mystic sense of being a redeemer and placing him at the end of gang rule in New York, thus keeping him just short of total commitment to the lawless realm, Doctorow has successfully played out the game of "doing something serious" with disreputable genres (McCaffery 36). Doctorow's gangster novel, rendered in a parodic style full of mythic and literary motifs and images as well as historical facts, is not only a violent but also a lyric-comic myth of the 1930s. At the same time, it is a *Bildungsroman* of a roguish but innocent hero with a variety of recognizable faces from the gallery of American heroes: Huck Finn, Tom Sawyer, Little Lord Fauntleroy, Augie March, Seymour Levin, Dave Plotkin, The Shadow, and The Phantom. In his review of *Billy Bathgate,* Terrence Rafferty argued, somewhat unfairly, that Doctorow clings to the notion of the Old World as the only true culture and that he "won't assimilate" (114). On the contrary, *Billy Bathgate* is not only in the mythic tradition but also in the American grain, with a certain Jewish-American texture. It is a fascinating performance of verbal juggling, a brilliant story, a bright "span of light across space" and time.

Notes

1.   The relationship between Bo (a gangster) and Drew (a society woman) is emblematic of the general atmosphere of 1930s café society. For the characterization of Drew, Doctorow may have taken a hint from the historical Dutch Schultz's short-lived association with Park Avenue people. See Thompson 336.

2.   The suggestion that Billy's protection of Drew is reminiscent of Huck protecting Jim has been made by Gary Wills (3).

3.   In the latter part of the novel, the baby carriage image is temporarily tainted by Schultz's account of a tragic shoot-out that had aroused public wrath because an innocent child had been killed while Dutch Schultz had survived unscathed. For biographical fact, see Thompson 315–17.

4.   To infer from Alfred Kazin's remark about the circumstances leading to Schultz's death (41), the blackmailer is a Lucky Luciano character.

Works Cited

Bellow, Saul. *The Adventures of Augie March.* 1953. Harmondsworth: Penguin, 1971.

Campbell, Joseph. *The Hero with a Thousand Faces.* 2nd ed. Princeton, N. J.: Princeton U P, 1989.

Doctorow, E. L. *Billy Bathgate.* New York: Random House, 1989.

Freitag, Michael. "The Attraction of the Disreputable." *The New York Times Book Review* 26 February 1989: 46.

Fuller, Robert C. *The Americans and the Unconscious.* New York: Oxford U P, 1986.

Gordon, Lois, and Alan Gordon. *American Chronicle: Six Decades in American Life 1920–1980.* New York: Atheneum, 1987.

Guttmann, Allen. *The Jewish Writer in America: Assimilation and the Crisis of Identity.* New York: Oxford U P, 1971.

Kazin, Alfred. "Huck In The Bronx." *The New Republic* 20 March 1989: 40–42.

Lupsha, Peter A. "American Values and Organized Crime: Suckers and Wiseguys." *The American Self: Myth, Ideology and Popular Culture.* Ed. Sam B. Girgus. Albuquerque: U of New Mexico P, 1981. 144–54.

McCaffery, Larry. "A Spirit of Transgression." *E. L. Doctorow: Essays and Conversations.* Ed. Richard Trenner. Princeton, New Jersey: Ontario Review P, 1983. 31–47.

Rafferty, Terrence. "Worlds Apart." *The New Yorker* 27 March 1989: 112–14.

Ruas, Charles. *Conversations with American Writers.* New York: Alfred A. Knopf, 1985.

Thompson, Craig, and Allen Raymond. *Gang Rule in New York: The Story of a Lawless Era.* New York: Dial P, 1940.

Twain, Mark. *The Adventures of Huckleberry Finn.* 1884. New York: Harper Brothers, 1912.

Wills, Garry. "Juggler's Code." *The New York Review of Books* 2 March 1989: 3–4.

Necropolis News
[Essay-Review of *The Waterworks* and *Jack London, Hemingway, and the Constitution: Selected Essays, 1977–1992*]

Andrew Delbanco

Everybody's favorite stage set this year has been old New York. It first turned up in Martin Scorsese's movie of *The Age of Innocence,* which made viewers feel as if they were inside a meticulously accurate diorama of Edith Wharton's fashionable Manhattan in the 1870s. Then Caleb Carr enlarged the set for his murder mystery of the 1890s, *The Alienist,* to include the wharves and the dark alleys where Wharton's grandees would never venture. Now E. L. Doctorow has returned to the immediate post–Civil War period for his own New York tale.

If the setting of *The Waterworks* is similar, Doctorow's way of representing it is entirely different. This is a writer who—ever since the first chapter of his first book, *Welcome to Hard Times* (1960), in which we meet a character known simply as "the Bad Man"—has been committed less to realism than to a kind of allegorical romance. Descended from the line of American fabulists that runs from Hawthorne to Malamud, Doctorow has always disavowed what Hawthorne (referring to the conventional fiction of his day) dismissed as "minute fidelity . . . to the probable and ordinary course of man's experience," in favor of a more imaginative "latitude . . . to mingle the Marvellous" with the real. Late in *The Waterworks,* Doctorow sums up the dream effect he is after:

> There are moments of our life that are something like breaks or tears in moral consciousness, as caesuras break the chanted line, and the eye sees through the breach to a companion life, a life in all its aspects the same, running along par-allel in time, but within a universe even more confounding than our own. It is this other disordered existence . . . that our ministers warn us against . . . that our dreams perceive.

From *The New Republic,* July 18, 1994, 44–48. Reprinted by permission of THE NEW REPUBLIC, © 1994, The New Republic, Inc.

To catch this "disordered existence" in fiction, the logic of the work must be more associative than sequential. Accordingly, the speech of the narrator is continually interrupted by ellipses that give his sentences a fractured quality and seem to represent a habitual pause—a hesitancy to deliver consecutive thoughts. "There is a difference," he remarks, "between living in some kind of day-to-day crawl through chaos, where there is no hierarchy to your thoughts, but a raucous equality of them, and knowing in advance the whole conclusive order . . . which makes narration . . . suspect." Yet, at the same time, a fiction that takes seriously this suspicion must commit itself to achieving something like the fluent exfoliation of images that one expects from poetry.

In the case of Doctorow's new novel, the images are those of a city closer to one of Red Grooms's cartoonish ensembles than to any actual New York. Doctorow calls this city a "necropolis." Its "paving stones pound . . . with horse-droppings," while carrion birds swoop in between the carts and carriages, "picking out their meals" from the dung. Wooden remnants of the antebellum town are being literally burned away ("we had fire all the time, we burned as a matter of habit") and replaced by the city of iron and stone that survives today in patches of cast-iron buildings, mainly below Houston Street. This New York was already the "huge jagged city" that Henry James would describe at the turn of the century as ". . . looking at the sky in the manner of some colossal haircomb turned upward and so deprived of half its teeth that the others, at their uneven intervals, count doubly as sharp spikes."

Thus is the gothic setting for a story that, briefly told, sounds outlandish. It begins with a tycoon named Augustus Pemberton, who grew rich during the War of Secession by abetting death itself—by "supplying the Army of the North with boots that fell apart, blankets that dissolved in rain, tents that tore at the grommets and uniform cloth that bled dye." Under sentence of death from pernicious anemia, he tells his family that he is going to an Adirondack spa to seek a cure. There he—apparently—dies. With due Episcopal ceremony, he is seemingly buried. But his estranged son, a freelance journalist—one "of that postwar generation for whom the materials of the war were ironic objects of art or fashion," who "walk[s] down Broadway with his Union greatcoat open, flowing behind him like a cape"—thinks he sees his father alive.

The startled young man, Martin Pemberton, is one of those whom Whitman had in mind when he wrote, in 1870, that "the aim of all the littérateurs is to find something to make fun of." A believer turned ironist, he produces caustic book reviews and half-fawning, half-mocking articles for the society page in which he enumerates the carats in the ladies' diamonds. Now, suddenly, he becomes the credulous object of scorn, surrounded by doubters. One stormy morning, while on his way up Broadway to deliver a review, he encounters a city omnibus carrying a group of pale old men who sit eerily still, oblivious to the lurches of the carriage and the bursts of lightning and the pedestrian shouts and traffic gongs. Peering in the carriage windows at its ghostly passengers, he sees that one of them has "the familiar hunch of his father's shoulders . . . and the wizened Augustan neck with its familiar wen, the smooth white egglike structure that from Martin's infancy had always alarmed him."

Most people dismiss Martin's report as fantasy or hoax, though a few take him seriously and even grope toward an explanatory idea of the Oedipal unconscious (everyone knows he loathed his father) to account for his delusion. When Martin himself disappears, his soft-boiled editor, McIlvaine—whose "newsman's cilia [are] up and waving" at the smell of a good story—joins the chase to find out what, if anything, his young free-lance has really seen.

After some further twists and turns the road of detection leads to a Mephistophelian character named Doctor Sartorius, who is a cross between one of Hawthorne's mad scientists and one of Poe's reclusive aesthetes. Ahead of Pasteur and Koch, he has intuited the germ basis of disease. He has trans-fused blood and is preparing to perform organ transplants. We discover him deep within the massive stone structure of the waterworks at a suburban reservoir, where, in a sort of futuristic bunker, he tests untried technologies on patients (including Augustus Pemberton) so rich and desperate that they are willing to try anything, pay anything, to forestall death. The medicines that Sartorius administers are derived from fluids extracted from children. "Shrunken, unnaturally darkened and sunk in on themselves, like vegetable husks," these old men have literally become vampires, feeding on the blood of the young.

No symbolic fiction can be fairly described by summarizing its plot (*Moby Dick,* in paraphrase, becomes a ridiculous story about a ship captain chasing the whale that ate his leg); and so it is difficult to convey the "sul-phurous" atmosphere of Doctorow's book. The seed of his strange fable had been growing in his mind since he published a short story in *Lives of the Poets* in 1984, in which two men find a toy boat capsized in a reservoir, and dis-cover the body of a drowned child in the adjacent waterworks. Now, in the novel that emerged from this image ten years later, the figure of the lost child is kaleidoscopically multiplied into clusters of "undersized beings on whose faces were etched the lines and shadows of serfdom." One of them turns up in what is supposed to be Augustus Pemberton's coffin (which Martin, in a half-parodic graveyard scene, digs up and pries open in the dark of night), laid out within on a "padded white silk couch," its "tiny leathered face with its eyes closed and lips pursed." These doomed children function in the novel as sym-bols of the age when, for the first time, American civilization began to pro-duce more human refuse than it could dispose of or hide away:

Vagrant children slept in the alleys. Ragpicking was a profession. . . . Out on the edges of town, along the North River or in Washington Heights or on the East River islands, behind stone walls and high hedges, were our institutions of charity, our orphanages, insane asylums, poorhouses, schools for the deaf and dumb and mission homes for magdalens. They made a sort of Ringstrasse for our venerable civilization.

As for those who stay within the ring, they scratch out a living as messengers, peddlers, shopsweepers, hawkers, newsboys and involuntary whores:

> More than one brothel specialized in them. They often turned up in hospital wards and church hospices so stunned by the abuses to which they'd been subjected that they couldn't speak sensibly but could only cower in their rags and gaze upon the kindest nurses or ministrants of charity with abject fear.

In imagining this world of brutalized children, Doctorow wants to drive home—sometimes relentlessly—its affinity with our own age. A purposeful war has just ended ("I am a man," says McIlvaine, who narrates the story in the first-person voice, "who will never be able to think of anyone but Abe Lincoln as president"), and has given way to "a conspicuously self-satisfied class of new wealth and weak intellect . . . all aglitter in a setting of mass misery."

The men who have taken over this postwar America have, like the arbitrageurs of a century later, no "loyalty . . . to any one business, but to the art of buying and selling them." Pallid and glazed-eyed, the old men whose dying is retarded by Dr. Sartorius have a zombie inertness that seems the final stage in the natural course of their lives—lives that have been spent in a moral obtuseness that, when they were young, might have taken the form of insouciance or arrogance or blinding greed. The parasitism of their dying is not fundamentally different from how they lived: as bloodsuckers indifferent to the human cost of their getting and spending. Augustus Pemberton, for example, is rumored to have been financially involved, even during the war, in the slave trade.

That Doctorow conceived this fantastic novel as a sort of moral prehistory of our own age becomes clear when one dips into the essays that he collected under the centerless title *Jack London, Hemingway and the Constitution,* while *The Waterworks* was taking form. In the introduction to this rather haphazard collection he likens the impact of Reaganism on American society—deregulation, the politicization of the courts and the distribution of "the enormous costs of the cold war democratically among all classes of society except the wealthiest"—to "the effect . . . [of] a vampire's arterial suck." Another essay, a meditation on nineteenth-century New York written for *Architectural Digest* in 1992, contains blocks of descriptive writing that are reiterated, verbatim, in McIlvaine's voice.

Doctorow's implicit subject in these pieces seems to be the end of our "fifty-year nuclear alert" and its replacement by a restless waiting for some yet-to-be-defined menace that might revive a sense of common purpose. We live, he believes, in a "stillness between tides, neither going out nor coming in," bewildered to the point of paralysis about how to deal, for instance, with the thousands of people in our midst "sleeping in doorways, begging with Styrofoam cups." One suspects that he also had in mind for *The Waterworks* the increasingly evident possibility that—for those able to pay—medical technology may someday sustain almost indefinitely a grotesque simulacrum of life.

Many of Doctorow's points border on cant. He is not an essayist. The most arresting piece in this collection is the least discursive. It is the one that was not commissioned—a brief rumination called "Standards," about the "self-referential power" of songs. A charming imaginative frolic, it moves among associated topics that include the origins of lullabies in mothers' crooning, the mixture of irony and militancy in wartime songs like "Goober Peas," the "compensatory" function of ballads about lost love. But when, in the other essays, he turns away from the associative mode and becomes resolutely expository in the service of an argument, he tends to sound callow and even pontifical. Here is a piece written before the 1992 election out of disgust at George Bush and with high hopes for Bill Clinton:

> The true president would have the strength to widen the range of current political discourse, and would love and revere language as the best means we have to close on reality. That implies a sensitivity attuned to the immense moral consequence of every human life. Perhaps even a sense of tragedy that would not let him sleep the night through.

Weakened by this mixture of outrage and sentimentality, the essays are more an expression of an offended sensibility than a serious effort at political analysis or understanding. They have a thin sloganeering quality—and, finally, a columnist's transience. But when, in *The Waterworks,* the same sentiments are realized as images and put to use within the context of a story of loss and rescue, they work to greater effect. "I have dreamt sometimes," says McIlvaine,

> . . . that if it were possible to lift this littered, paved Manhattan from the earth . . . and all its torn and dripping pipes and conduits and tunnels and tracks and cables—all of it, like a scab from new skin underneath—how seedlings would sprout, and freshets bubble up, and brush and grasses would grow over the rolling hills. . . . A season or two of this and the mute, protesting culture buried for so many industrial years under the tenements and factories . . . would rise again . . . of the lean, religious Indians of the bounteous earth. . . . Such love I have for those savage polytheists of my mind . . . such envy for the inadequate stories they told each other, their taxonomies, cosmologies . . . their lovely dreams of the world they stood on and who was holding it up. . . .

In earlier works, like *Loon Lake* (1980) and *World's Fair* (1985), Doctorow indulged in this kind of reverie at the expense of narrative momentum.

But in *The Waterworks,* he has pulled off the difficult literary trick of combining the grit and pith of a precisely located fiction with the reach of a moral exemplum independent of time and place. When, in the essays, Doctorow asks us to "pray for the dead and for the maligned and destitute," it feels as if we are being dunned for the annual charitable appeal. But when, in *The Waterworks,* he concentrates his pity and horror into images rather than arguments, the result is a persuasive portrait of an era akin to our own, when Americans found themselves living in cities of unprecedented scale, in which, for the first time, human beings had become indistinguishable from litter.

Index

◆

The Volume Editor

◆

D_{r.} Ben Siegel is professor of English at California State Polytechnic University, Pomona. He has chaired the Department of English and directed the Annual Conferences in Modern American Writing held at the university's Kellogg West Center for Continuing Education. He is a specialist in literature and religion (especially the Bible as literature), literary criticism, the contemporary American novel, the American Jewish novel, biography, and American humor. (He is second vice president of the American Humor Studies Association.) Dr. Siegel has been awarded 2 Meritorious Performance Awards (State of California) and 10 Golden Leaf Awards by the Library Association for his writing and teaching. His 14 books, alone or in collaboration, include *The Puritan Heritage: America's Roots in the Bible; Biography Past and Present; Isaac Bashevis Singer; The Controversial Sholem Asch; The American Writer and the University; Critical Essays on Nathanael West; Conversations with Saul Bellow; Traditions, Voice, and Dreams: The American Novel Since the 1960s; Daughters of Valor: Contemporary Jewish American Women Writers;* and *American Literary Dimensions: Poems and Essays in Honor of Melvin J. Friedman.* His critical essays deal with such writers as Saul Bellow, Daniel Fuchs, Bernard Malamud, Philip Roth, Isaac Bashevis Singer, and Nathanael West. He is now on the editorial boards of *Studies in American Fiction, Studies in American-Jewish Literature,* and the *Saul Bellow Journal.* He is president of the International Saul Bellow Society and has lectured in Japan, Australia, England, and Canada, as well as throughout the United States.

The General Editor

◆

Dr. James Nagel, J. O. Eidson Distinguished Professor of American Literature at the University of Georgia, founded the scholarly journal *Studies in American Fiction* and edited it for 20 years. He is the general editor of the Critical Essays on American Literature series published by Macmillan, a program that now contains more than 130 volumes. He was one of the founders of the American Literature Association and serves as its executive coordinator. He is also a past president of the Ernest Hemingway Society. Among his 17 books are *Stephen Crane and Literary Impressionism, Critical Essays on* The Sun Also Rises, *Ernest Hemingway: The Writer in Context, Ernest Hemingway: The Oak Park Legacy,* and *Hemingway in Love and War,* which was selected by the *New York Times* as one of the outstanding books of 1989 and which has been made into a major motion picture. Dr. Nagel has published more than 50 articles in scholarly journals and has lectured on American literature in 15 countries. His current project is a book on the contemporary short story cycle.